Praise for *The Last Days of Roger Federer*

"Dyer, having set out to write a book about endings, is drawn to endlessness, to the way that one thing leads to another . . . There are some gorgeous passages in *The Last Days of Roger Federer*, some marvelous bits of criticism, some enthralling descriptions of psychedelics."　　　　—Jennifer Szalai, *The New York Times*

"A masterful, beautiful, reluctantly moving book—that is, moving despite its subject being naturally moving, courting no pathos, shrewd and frank—and Dyer's best in some time. Indeed, one of his best, period . . . [*The Last Days of Roger Federer*], if it heralds a late style, promises [this]: a powerful and funny mind, ranging across the canons of both art and experience, cutting closer toward deep truths, telling us what things are like when time is shortening."　　　　—Charles Finch, *Los Angeles Times*

"Calling a book a 'tour de force' almost certainly means it isn't, but this book . . . is a tour de force."

　　　　—Tyler Cowen, *Marginal Revolution*

"[Dyer is] a writer who loves to frolic in the field of ideas as freely as Federer deploys his unsurpassed array of shots . . . Reading this book is a joyful experience . . . Dyer's exploration into mortality is often propelled into the sunlight."

　　　　—Joel Drucker, *Racquet*

"Dyer's mix of sparkling prose, rich insight, and mordant wit suggests that a well-lived life is worth even the bitterest of endings. It makes for a smart, memorable take."

　　　　—*Publishers Weekly*

"Tennis, jazz, Dylan, movies, drugs, Nietzsche, Beethoven. So why am I laughing? Because Geoff Dyer once again melds commentary and observation with intellect and wit. Bouncing between criticism and memoir, Dyer is one of the few writers whose paragraphs I can immediately reread and get more from. The twists, turns, and delights abound, and when you finally put the book down you think, 'Oh, yes, I've always been this smart, haven't I?'"

—Steve Martin

"Geoff Dyer the stylist is at the top of his game here, serving up conundrums, paradoxes, logical binds, and other cerebral delights. Even his syntax is witty. This generous offering of Dyer's insightful, often hilarious take on art, life, and sports is a feast for his readers."

—Billy Collins, former United States poet laureate

"Just like Roger Federer's backhand, Geoff Dyer's swing is a thing of beauty, complete with his signature follow-through. He captures so much, touches so much, and amuses all the while. This form-blending book is extremely smart, wise, and simply plain fun. I am smarter for having read it. This is a great book."

—Percival Everett, author of *The Trees*

"Who can make the world new again like Geoff Dyer? *The Last Days of Roger Federer* is an inspired cultural and personal meditation as well as an unsurprising delight. To read it is to feel relief that, despite Dyer's contention that his life's theme is 'giving up,' he hasn't."

—Sloane Crosley, author of *Cult Classic*

"Sumptuous, wide-ranging, streetwise, and precise, *The Last Days of Roger Federer* is a glorious ode to tennis, the arts, late style, and life itself. Full of surprises, hard truths, and deep feeling, this is a work like no other. Time remains undefeated, and yet Geoff

Dyer's beautiful, unsparing book feels like it can go toe to toe with it—from the baseline or the net. An essential read."

—Rowan Ricardo Phillips, author of
The Circuit: A Tennis Odyssey and *Living Weapon*

"*The Last Days of Roger Federer* showcases Geoff Dyer's gifts as one of the most distinctive writers of our times. Whether he's writing about tennis, Nietzsche, Burning Man, or growing old, Dyer brings such impeccable observation, original intelligence, and laugh-out-loud wit to the page that you want to keep on reading more—the perfect quality for a book about endings."

—Maya Jasanoff, professor at Harvard University
and author of *The Dawn Watch*

"Most authors use language to write about things. Geoff Dyer uses things to write about language. He's a clever clogs but he's one of us at the same time. Genius."

—Simon Armitage, poet laureate of the United Kingdom

Geoff Dyer
The Last Days of Roger Federer

Geoff Dyer is the award-winning author of many books, including *But Beautiful, Out of Sheer Rage, Yoga for People Who Can't Be Bothered to Do It, Zona,* and the essay collection *Otherwise Known as the Human Condition* (winner of a National Book Critics Circle Award for criticism). A fellow of the Royal Society of Literature and a member of the American Academy of Arts and Sciences, Dyer lives in Los Angeles, where he is a writer in residence at the University of Southern California. His books have been translated into twenty-four languages.

The Last Days of Roger Federer

The Last Days of Days of Roger Federer

And Other Endings

Geoff Dyer

PICADOR

FARRAR, STRAUS AND GIROUX

NEW YORK

Picador
120 Broadway, New York 10271

Excerpt from *Hotel Du Lac* by Anita Brookner © the Estate of Anita Brookner.

Parts of this book first appeared, in different form, in *The Guardian*,
The Observer, *The Spectator*, and *Freeman's*, and on *The New York Review
of Books'* website.

The Library of Congress has cataloged the Farrar, Straus and Giroux
hardcover edition as follows:
Names: Dyer, Geoff, author.
Title: The last days of Roger Federer : and other endings / Geoff Dyer.
Description: First edition. | New York : Farrar, Straus and Giroux, 2022. | Includes
bibliographical references.
Identifiers: LCCN 2021057145 | ISBN 9780374605568 (hardcover)
Subjects: LCSH: Older artists. | Older athletes. | Artists—Retirement. | Athletes—
Retirement.
Classification: LCC N8356.A43 D94 2022 | DDC 700.92/2—dc23/eng/20220118
LC record available at https://lccn.loc.gov/2021057145

Paperback ISBN: 978-1-250-86719-3

Designed by Gretchen Achilles

1 3 5 7 9 10 8 6 4 2

The names and identifying characteristics of some persons
described in this book have been changed.

For Rebecca

When she straightened up and stood with her hands on the rail, she saw that it was already dusk, or rather an afternoon twilight that would deepen imperceptibly into night.

—ANITA BROOKNER

The Last Days of Roger Federer

If it is so difficult to begin, imagine
what it will be to end—
                              —Louise Glück

01.

'The End' is the last track on the Doors' *first* album, released in January 1967, having been recorded the previous August, when the band had been together for just over a year. It grew out of multiple live performances at the Whisky a Go-Go in Hollywood, though no recordings of these evolving versions of the song have survived. From the get-go at the Go-Go, then, Jim Morrison was busy obsessing about the end—and not just in 'The End.' 'When the Music's Over' ends with repeated assurances that music is your only friend 'until the End.' It's a safe bet, contemplating or proclaiming the end like this; eventually you will be proved right.

'The End' was the last song the quartet performed live, at the Warehouse in New Orleans, on 12 December 1970. In March the following year the twenty-seven-year-old Morrison moved to Paris, where he was found dead, in the bathtub of his apartment, on July 3.

02.

In a version of 'Tangled Up in Blue' the unnamed lover tells Bob Dylan (or whoever the narrator of the song is supposed to be): 'This ain't the end, / We'll meet again someday on the avenue . . .'

She's right, it's nowhere near the end when she says this. It's the second verse of the long opening track of *Blood on the Tracks*. Dylan continued to tinker with the song in numerous ways after a test pressing of the album had been made, prepared for release, and, at the last minute, rejected in favour of a more rhythmically insistent version of

'Tangled Up in Blue,' rerecorded with different musicians, in Minneapolis. (The changes were made so late in the day that the record went on sale with the old sleeve, crediting only the original musicians.) He's since performed it live, sometimes with major overhauls to words and music, on more than sixteen hundred occasions.

03.

On the wall of the barbershop where I have my hair cut on Main Street in Venice Beach—where the Doors started out—is a mural of Jim Morrison with his bare shoulders and luxuriant black hair that always looked like it never needed cutting. Recently another similar mural appeared, right on my street. All over Venice, in fact, there are traces of the Lizard King, tributes to the rock-god Dionysus. On the boardwalk at least one busker is always playing 'Break on Through' or one of the Doors' other big hits.

04.

I was dilly-dallying, unsure how to start this book about how things end, on Thursday 10 January 2019, when, at the press conference ahead of his first-round match at the Australian Open, Andy Murray announced what amounted to his retirement. More than moving, it was devastating to watch. The first, fairly innocuous question proved too much for him. Unable to answer, he left the stage for several minutes to compose himself. It was the end, he said when he came back out. He hoped to bow out at Wimbledon in July but was not sure he would make it even that far. When another journalist asked if this meant the Australian Open might be his last tournament, Murray said that was quite likely. Which meant that his match on Monday—my Sunday in Los Angeles—against Roberto Bautista Agut might be his last. Murray sat there describing how the pain, not just of playing top-level tennis but of pulling on his socks and putting on his shoes at home, was too much. As often happens in these press conferences his common-sense answers made the questions a little superfluous. Had he seen a sports psychologist? Yes, but that didn't help because the pain was still there. If it had made the pain go away then he'd be feeling great. The whole thing made for harrowing and, of course, absolutely absorbing viewing. It was the end, Murray said, partly because there was no end in sight—to the training, the rehab, the pain; no sign when he might begin to get back to his best. A line from 'The End' floated through my head as I watched this gladiatorial athlete 'lost in a Roman wilderness of pain.'

One of the questions that had got me interested in this subject— things coming to an end, artists' last works, time running out—was the long-running one of Roger Federer's eventual retirement. The imminent departure of the first of the 'big four' male players brought an unexpected if indirect urgency into play. With a rival six years his junior on the way out Roger's time seemed also to be shrinking around him.

Writers often have an end in sight for completing a book. For some this can take the form of a proposal that leads to a contract in which a deadline for delivery of the manuscript is agreed upon in advance; I'm not one of them but Murray's going out of the Australian Open, as expected, in a blaze of beaten glory to Bautista Agut after five typically gruelling sets (the first two of which he had lost) concentrated the mind. It seemed important that a book underwritten by my own experience of the changes wrought by ageing should be completed before Roger's retirement, in the long twilight of his career.* Even with no idea of where, when, or how things might end up it was time to start work—on a book that ended up being written while life as we know it came to an end.

---

* Yes, 'Roger,' not 'Federer'; even though I've never met him it's Roger, always and only Roger.

05.

In 1972, during a Duke of Edinburgh's Award Expedition (Bronze), we were camping somewhere in Gloucestershire, about eight of us from grammar school, when the news came over the radio. George Best had quit football. He would have been twenty-six; I was fourteen. We had not started drinking then—just being out in the countryside rather than at home with our parents was enough to make our camping trip thrilling, but it was the news about Best that made it memorable. He actually returned after quitting, and it was not until 1 January 1974 that he played his last match for Manchester United before the long and wandering years of boozy decline. This was not the first time I had heard of someone's career coming to an end but it was the first time I knew of anyone stopping doing something they loved, the thing that gave their life meaning. It was also the first time I heard of a retirement that was not, of someone quitting and then resuming the thing they had retired from. In Best's case it established a pattern for giving up booze and then giving up on trying to quit drinking.

06.

Retirement in the world I grew up in—the world of poorly paid, often unpleasant and unrewarding work—was something my relatives began to look forward to from a surprisingly early age. It was a form of promotion, practically an ambition. In the world I've become part of, retirement is almost unheard of or at least seldom admitted to. If you have retired—are no longer able to write or are finding it impossible to publish what you have written—you keep it to yourself; you keep the manuscript to yourself because nobody wants it. And in any case, if part of the job is sitting in a chair at home with your feet up, reading, then the difference between work and retirement is imperceptible, even if you start reading—though it's something I advise against, whatever the weather—with a blanket over your knees.

07.

The Duke of Edinburgh's Award scheme was a big deal at my school. Probably it was one of many little attempts at importing something of the character-forming ethos of the public school to a grammar school where rugby, not football, was the official sport. I gave up ahead of the more rigorous demands and gruelling expeditions of Silver and Gold just as, at junior school, I'd given up on the personal survival swimming badges after Bronze, which I'd wriggled through by doing almost all of the required lengths in the chokingly chlorinated water of Pittville baths on my back. (*On* my back, not doing back-*stroke* as such. It barely even counted as swimming but by kicking my legs wildly and sort of waggling my hands by my sides I was able to cover distances far in excess of any that might have been achieved by conventionally recognised methods of propulsion.) My mum duly stitched the Bronze survival patch onto my trunks and that was the end of it. Neither of my parents could swim; both regarded the ability to do so as one of many things that were beyond their reach, and were content with this third-level endorsement of their child's aquatic survival skills as sufficient evidence of generational advance.

As a perpetually grumbling anti-royalist my dad had never been able to muster up much enthusiasm for the Duke of Edinburgh scheme, which, he suspected, must in some undisclosed way be lining the pockets of the dim-witted duke (whose physical resemblance to my dad was quite uncanny), and so was not at all displeased when I quit. Bronze, in my family, was always enough.

Many years later I contributed an essay to a series of radio broadcasts on a word associated with the Olympics. I can't remember what my word was but Gillian Slovo cleverly chose 'fourth,' focusing on competitors who narrowly miss out on a medal and are, as a result, completely forgotten and go away without recognition—become indistinguishable, in fact, from the anonymous mass who come trailing in their wake. So spare a special thought for members of this group of near-miss losers who, after the Olympic flame has been extinguished, having returned home to resume the acclaim-denied grind of training or the uncertainties of retirement, are subsequently and unceremoniously upgraded to bronze because of a drugs disqualification among the trio who basked in podium glory.*

08.

'I've always been a quitter,' announces the narrator of *Budding Prospects*, the second novel by T. C. Boyle, who's turned out to be the opposite of a quitter, who's gone on to set such a pace that his publishers have their work cut out trying to keep up with his productivity, but who no longer teaches at the University of Southern California, where I occupy the office and chair (not Chair) that used to be his. The first paragraph of the novel is a list of all the things the narrator has given up on: 'I quit the Boy Scouts, the glee club, the marching band. Gave up my paper route, turned my back on the church, stuffed the basketball team. I dropped out of college, sidestepped the army with a 4-F on the grounds of mental instability, went back to school, made a go of it, entered a Ph.D. program in nineteenth-century British literature, sat in the front row, took notes assiduously, bought a pair of horn-rims, and quit on the eve of my comprehensive exams.' This epic résumé of curtailed achievement culminates with

---

* The absolute difference between third and fourth—between bronze and nothing—in the Olympics does not apply to the World Cup. Although there is a third-place play-off for the beaten semi-finalists both teams are so consumed by shared disappointment that neither really wants to play—and no one really wants to watch them play. The competition is effectively over; there is no consolation in coming third rather than fourth.

the declaration that 'the only thing I didn't give up on was the summer camp.' The next paragraph is just six words: 'Let me tell you about it.'

Put like that it all sounds so easy.

09.

I gave up playing football gradually, the intervals between games increasing because of injuries until the games became intervals between injuries. The ongoing passage of time was still broken up in multiple ways but less frequently—and then not at all—by what became an obsolete and eventually forgotten marker called football. I can't remember when I played for the last time but at least twice a year I still *dream* that I am playing. My wife says that during these dreams my legs start kicking in the bed. She never wakes me up—as she does if I'm moaning in the grips of a nightmare—because she knows how happy I am. Those are my best dreams of the year. I *say* that, but, increasingly, these dreams do not involve scoring goals or even making long, powerful passes. Instead the ball seems to get stuck between my feet or somehow lodged in the leggy grass so that I'm stranded in a kind of stagnant dribble. Maybe my legs twitch in the bed because I am trying to free myself from whatever entanglements have taken root in the unconscious.

On nights after I've played tennis I often have trouble sleeping. Partly this is because I always collapse into a long nap or a brief coma after getting home so that by bedtime, although I'm exhausted and achey (lower back, both knees, left shoulder and elbow), I'm not sleepy. Plus it's fun lying there, replaying crucial sequences and points—up to a point. But then I become powerless to select or stop which bits are replayed and am stranded in a tormenting swirl of yellow balls that gradually becomes a Slazenger-sponsored meteor shower in the tramlines of space.

10.

'Seen a shooting star tonight . . .'

Even though Martin Scorsese's film about Dylan's 1975 Rolling Thunder tour had begun streaming on Netflix a day or two earlier, the Prince Charles Cinema in London, on 13 July 2019, was packed—with an audience of the widest possible age range, from teenagers to Dylan's contemporaries and beyond. Who else could pull in a comparable demographic, for something that wasn't even the streaming of a live show? There was periodic applause, starting at the climax of 'Isis,' which comes not at the end of the song but in the middle, after the shouted 'Yes' that completes the amazing quatrain of dialogue:

> *She said, 'Where ya been?' I said, 'No place special.'*
> *She said, 'You look different.' I said, 'Well, I guess.'*
> *She said, 'You been gone.' I said, 'That's only natural.'*
> *She said, 'You gonna stay?' I said, 'If you want me to, yes.'*

Everyone in the Prince Charles's notoriously lumpy seats was gripped throughout the 140 minutes of the film's duration. In the communal intoxication of the occasion I had the distinct sense that all around me people were asking themselves the same question that I was: how can someone be *so* great? I had no answer but the question played its part in ushering in another of the Dylan revivals that have punctuated my adult life. I'll go for six months without listening to him until something prompts me to play 'I'll Keep It with Mine,' 'Boots of Spanish Leather,' or whatever, and there I am again, instantly and completely enthralled.

With so much music from one's youth, curiosity about a given track—'Hmm, I wonder what "Keep Yourself Alive" or "Spanish Bombs" sounds like today . . .'—evaporates midway through the song, often earlier. With Dylan you're on the edge of your lumpy seat, even when you know the song off by heart (as long as you stay clear of the anthemic tedium of 'Blowin' in the Wind,' which I would happily never hear again—which is how I felt from practically the first time I heard it, which was probably sometime before I had even listened to it). It's not that his music never ages; it keeps step with our own ageing in a way that Freddie Mercury or even Joe Strummer never do. This is not because they died young; it's because we've grown old and out of the music they made. *London Calling* is a great album; seeing the Clash in Lewisham in February 1980 was one of the best gig-going experiences I've ever had, but these days, even when driving, I scarcely have the patience to get to the end of one of their songs.* There's nothing left to hear. But I'll be listening to Dylan, to new and old versions of songs I've been listening to for more than forty years, with undiminished wonder, till the end of my days, hopefully after Dylan himself is no longer around, when the incredible fact that he exists, that we could probably go to see him play somewhere tonight, no longer holds true.

Not that I'd bother going to see him tonight, tomorrow, or any other night, even if he were playing for free at a venue down the road—as he was, in Hyde Park, as it turns out, a month after I saw the Scorsese film at the Prince Charles.

11.

The film ends with a year-by-year list of all the gigs Dylan has played from the Rolling Thunder tour onwards, like names on a memorial: non-stop (almost) and never-ending (until Covid brought everything to an end). I've been to four of them, the first at Earls Court in 1978, the last in Austin, Texas, on 6 May 2015, in a smallish venue conveniently located only a fifteen-minute cycle ride from where I was

---

* I also saw Queen, at Cheltenham Town Hall on 14 March 1974, where I was able to get the cover of their second album signed by all four of them. This presumably valuable artefact has since been lost. (And I exempt the Doors, absolutely, from any strictures about growing out of once-loved music.)

living. The band was great, the sound was superb, and the seats were excellent (row twelve of the stalls). It was OK, I suppose, but I kept thinking of something a friend had said about the last time she'd seen him, also in Texas: 'He was *so* done.' Except he wasn't and isn't. Covid permitting, there's plenty more doing to be done.

So: why does he do it and why does anyone go to see him do it? The second is the easier question to answer: people go not to see Bob Dylan but to *have* seen him. I can understand that urge, though for me it has never been strong enough to render the quality of a musical experience irrelevant. There is little satisfaction to be derived from having seen any artist way past his or her best. I can say, truthfully, that I have seen Van Morrison (in Hay about twenty years ago) and Miles Davis, looking deeply amphibious, at the Royal Festival Hall in June 1987. Neither occasion was memorable but it is still possible, friends insist, to catch Morrison in top form (before he was reduced to complaining about his rights being trampled on by Covid fascism). I believe them in a way that I don't believe it when people claim that Dylan was recently fantastic on whichever stop it was on his ceaseless tour. I did believe another friend I bumped into the time before last that I saw Dylan, at Brixton Academy in 2003. He had been playing keyboards, mainly, it seemed, so that he could have something to lean on. I was familiar with the way Dylan changed his songs around, but his singing, combined with the murky sound at the Academy, made it difficult to tell which song from the back catalogue he was in the process of mauling at any given time.

'That was really dreadful,' I said as we milled around on Stockwell Road afterwards.

'You thought that was bad?' she said. 'You should have seen him last time.' So yes, some nights have been worse than others, but Michael Gray, in *The Bob Dylan Encyclopedia*, sums up a not untypical experience under what is surely the best entry heading to be found in any reference book—'frying an egg onstage, the prospect of: In Japan in 1986 Dylan reportedly said this: "Somebody comes to see you for two hours or one and a half hours, whatever it is . . . I mean they've come to see *you*. You could be doing anything up on that stage. You could be frying an egg or hammering a nail into a piece of wood." Instead of blitzing truculently through his 700th "Tangled Up in Blue" or his 1,500th "All Along the Watchtower," how infinitely more magical it would be if he *did* come on stage and proceed to fry an egg.'

We'll have more to say later about another unusual reference book, but for now and for whatever reasons, yes, people will flock to see Dylan. Why does *he* do it? You've got to serve somebody, he once sang. That claim might have been specific to his born-again period but certainly you've got to *do* something. This becomes problematic when you can do anything and the whole world wants nothing more than to serve and see you.

It's possible he enjoys it but if the stage is, as he claimed in 1997, 'the only place where I'm happy,' why then doesn't he show it? At the end of the Austin show, when other artists might have taken a bow, Dylan treated the audience to an extended *glare*. Not of aggression or hostility, just of indifference or obliviousness even. All writers like to get out of the house but is Dylan's home life so unhappy that he never wants to be in any of the properties in his impressive portfolio?* Maybe the money helps even if, at some level and in the most fabulous quantities, it doesn't help at all. Could it be that the way to get out of 'going through all these things twice' is to go through them two *thousand* times? The strange thing is that a life like Dylan's is so beyond comprehension as to seem almost meaningless: the result of some tangled extrapolation of the way his songs have brought so much meaning to the lives of people who have spent so much time trying to work out what they might mean.

---

* The mere notion of Dylan's home life exercises an inordinate fascination, partly because we have so few glimpses to go alongside the one of him alone at home in L.A. watching the seven o'clock news, on *Desire*. With nothing much happening except an earthquake in Black Diamond Bay, he turns off the TV and goes to grab another beer. Might a future archaeological technology be able to unearth, from this sliver of textual evidence, the brand of beer he was drinking, what else was in the fridge, whether he was wearing slippers . . . ?

12.

The relentless grind of touring has taken its toll on Dylan's voice, though witnesses report that on odd nights it's been magically restored. The rest of the time the voice David Bowie had famously described as sounding 'like sand and glue' has seemed, for a decade or more, to emanate from glands permanently afflicted by an incurable yet oddly sustaining strain of flu. The biographer Ian Bell rightly considers Dylan's voice his greatest instrument and powerfully evokes the 'eroded rock formation' of this 'magnificent ruin.' Combine that with the history-soaked imagery and deliberately archaic musical style of the later albums and an already legendary figure is elevated to a mythic realm in which he is lauded both as elder statesman of the 1960s and as sprightly survivor of the 1860s. To suggest that he rasps like a lizard with a frog in its throat, that the music consists of rock 'n' roll plods and retirement boogies, serves only to prove that one's sense of cultural heritage extends no further back than Donny Osmond. The flip side is that a terminal phase can easily become interminable.

But that voice—I'm listening to it again now, as I type . . . How could it not be shot to hell given what he's put it through, the unbelievable demands he makes on it in the course of the Rolling Thunder concerts alone when he's belting out every song, night after night? Specifically I'm listening to the opening line of 'Going, Going, Gone' from a bootleg featuring material omitted from the live *Hard Rain* album, recorded during the second part of the Rolling Thunder tour (not covered by the Scorsese film). When Dylan sings, 'I've just reached a place,' we believe that he has, at that very moment, *just reached a place*. We are there with him, at that place and in that moment. Or how about the line from *Oh Mercy*, when he sings, 'Seen a shooting star tonight, / and I thought of you.' That is nothing if not believable, even though the song goes on tacitly to undermine this claim. If he'd omitted the verse about 'listen to the engines, listen to the bells,' etc., and allowed the song to pass as quickly and insignificantly as a shooting star so that it was over almost as soon as it began—too fleetingly even to get to the required duration of a three-minute single—then the brevity of the whole would have been in sync with the transience of its opening claim. These days he rarely sounds like he's in either the place or the moment, wherever they may be. Even when he slows down a song he still sounds like he's in a hurry to get it over with. It doesn't matter that he can no longer reach certain notes—it's not like he ever thought he was Pavarotti—but it no longer sounds as if the truth of a given moment is able to achieve unprecedented fidelity of expression through him.

This is hard to accept precisely because people have always *believed* in Dylan—as the voice of the protest movement, of a generation, or whatever. More privately, we believe him when he comes out and confesses, in 'Sara,' that he'd been 'staying up for days in the Chelsea Hotel / Writing "Sad-Eyed Lady of the Lowlands" for you,' even if, as Clinton Heylin pointed out, 'it is fairly well documented that he wrote it in Nashville.' We believe him when he says, at the end of 'Up to Me,' that 'no one else could play that tune, you know it was up to me.' That is indisputable. No court in the world could overturn that claim.

We've believed him even though as a witness he's repeatedly testified, under the songwriter's oath, that nothing he says can be relied on: 'No, no, no, it ain't me, babe.' (Outside the sanctuary of the songs, in interviews and so on, it's best to assume that little he says is true.) It's not just that there's a discrepancy between the songs and what may or may not have happened in real life (inadmissible as evidence in the court of artistic appeal); the songs themselves are unusually vulnerable to cross-examination. Where was he employed—and in what capacity—in 'Tangled Up in Blue'? According to one account he was 'loading cargo onto a truck' at 'an airplane plant' in L.A. and, to another, he was working on 'a fishing boat right outside of Delacroix.' Even a destination that seems fixed—Tangier in the opening lines of 'If You See Her, Say Hello'—on one occasion shifts without warning to 'north Saigon.' This is admirably precise—i.e., neither west nor south Saigon—but it's possibly so far north that he actually means

Hanoi. (In a heavy rewrite of 'Tangled Up in Blue' from 1984 on *Real Live* he announces that 'all of the beds are unmade'; in this version of 'If You See Her,' from a concert in Florida, in April 1976, *everything* is unmade. The most striking line is surely, 'If you're making love to her watch it from the rear,' advice that, in the era of internet porn, has come to seem somewhat superfluous.) The whereabouts of the truth articulated by Dylan changes, as does its quality, but we used to be left with a choice not as to *whether* we believe him but which version—which location (of performance and incident)—of multiple truths we preferred. It beggars belief that anyone could prefer a recent version of an old song or indeed a new song over an old one. When I listen to a new Dylan album my reaction is to quote back his response to the Albert Hall heckler in 1966: 'I don't believe you.'*

13.

Scorsese's film includes a sequence—originally featured in *Renaldo and Clara*, which, in the late 1970s, I saw *twice*, undeterred by a running time of 235 minutes, at least half of which did not merit filming, let alone watching—of Dylan and Allen Ginsberg visiting Jack Kerouac's grave in Lowell, Massachusetts. They look down at the words written on the grave, 'He Honored Life.' In the longer sequence in *Renaldo and Clara*, they get into a slight pissing contest about writers' graves. When Dylan asks if he's been to Chekhov's Ginsberg says no, but he has been to Mayakovsky's, in Moscow. Dylan has visited Victor Hugo's grave in Paris but Ginsberg has visited Apollinaire's, laid a copy of *Howl* on Baudelaire's (naturally), *and* is able to tell Dylan what is written on Keats's grave in Rome: 'Here lies one whose fame

---

* Since history has been altered—or corrected (the 'Albert Hall' gig was actually at the Manchester Free Trade Hall, ten days earlier)—it's a shame that a further change to this apocryphal but true event couldn't be made. I've always wished that Dylan's spirited defiance could have been a literal announcement of the title of the next song—which, unfortunately, had already been played—rather than a prelude to playing 'Like a Rolling Stone,' 'fuckin' loud.'

is writ in water.' (Ginsberg gets this wrong; it's 'name' not 'fame,' but it's contrary to the spirit of Romantics and Beats to be pedantic.) When Ginsberg points at Kerouac's grave and asks Dylan if that's what's going to happen to him Dylan says he wants to be buried in an unmarked grave.

There's a wonderful moment in *Walk Me Home* (1993), a film written by and starring John Berger, when Berger's character says that he wants to be buried in land that no one owns. In Scorsese's film, meanwhile, we cut from the scene of Dylan and Ginsberg at the grave to a studio interview with the now aged and grizzled Dylan who says of Kerouac's great novel, 'He was talking about the road of life.'

14.

In 1959, three years before he took his well-known pictures of the young Dylan in the East Village, and less than two years after the publication of *On the Road*, John Cohen took this photograph of Kerouac. Kerouac was thirty-six or thirty-seven. His conviction that *On the Road* was 'a great novel' had been consolidated rather than threatened by its having been rejected by publishers for six years before Viking relented in September 1957. As early as 1952, in response to an editor who had called it a 'thoroughly incoherent mess,' he predicted what would happen: 'On the Road will be published by someone else, with a few changes and omissions and additions, and it will gain its due recognition, in time, as the first or one of the first modern prose books in America.' What he failed to anticipate was the sodden collapse of writer and man that would come in the wake of this prophecy's being fulfilled.

The hard-won struggle to master 'spontaneous prose' both enabled Kerouac to write a great book and condemned him, for the rest of his creative life, to banging out pretty terrible ones. By 1961 he was conscious of the paradoxical and hidden costs of his style of composition. 'What happened was, as soon as I had made a formal discovery of spontaneous prose, it wasn't spontaneous any more!' 'In fact,' he went on, 'I think I've forgotten how to write by now.' As the liberating idea of 'wild spontaneous yowks' hardened into an inflexible method, Kerouac became a prisoner of the 'fuckyou freedom' he had helped unleash. Conscious of how spontaneity could become stale, he announced his intention of 'going back to the careful writing of Town & City,' his first book. Had he followed through with this, he might have accessed a deeper seam of creativity than the one depleted by habitual reliance on 'enormous overdoses of benzedrine to write my novels' and 'phenobarbital tablets to offset the benny depression 8 hours after ingestion (after 8 hours of writing).'

He also experimented with acid but, while his old pals Allen Ginsberg and Neal Cassady played their merry parts in fomenting a psychedelic revolution, Kerouac became increasingly hostile to the narco-ideological claims of the emergent hippie movement. That hippies were the progeny of the Beats, that his passionate immersion in Buddhism anticipated their own fascination with all matters Eastern, served only to strengthen his befuddled reactionary resolve. As Timothy Leary recalled, Kerouac 'remained unmovably the Catholic carouser, an old-style Bohemian without a hippie bone in his body.'

Angered that his ideas were 'being lifted by Jews,' Kerouac sank into a swamp of paranoia and buffoonish alcoholism.

'Free to do anything I want,' he wrote in 1962, 'I've deliberately imprisoned myself, like a hair shirt, I dunno why.' Pining for a cabin in the woods, Kerouac settled for the suburbs of Florida or Massachusetts, where he lived with his mother amid 'endless rows of perfect new houses but all of them without exception full of flat housewives looking out of the window when someone dares to try to walk to the stores which are too far away anyway under broiling sun in flat treeless waste, ugh.' Even at this distance from the limelight, word always got out that the king of the Beats was in the vicinity, and Kerouac would be lured off on week-long swill-outs, 'drinking and talking with hundreds and hundreds of my acquaintances day and night, in shifts.'

Looking at a snapshot of himself one day, he saw what 'all this lionized manure has done to me; it's killing me rapidly.' His situation was made doubly intolerable by the fact that the lionisation didn't stop him getting critically mauled. Seen in retrospect hostile reviews tend to vindicate the writer and incriminate the critic; in Kerouac's case, the passage of time has served to prove the accuracy of Dorothy Parker's reaction to 'the appalling monotony' of *The Subterraneans*.

The best-known criticism of all—Truman Capote's that *On the Road* was not writing, but typing—was echoed poignantly by Kerouac himself when, in 1967, he confessed, 'I cant type like I used to, I'm afraid I cant write like I used to neither.' This was during the 'most dreadful part of [his] life,' when his mother was paralysed after a stroke and Kerouac—who, in February 1959, felt he was 'rapidly going to pot and on the verge of becoming a blob'—had become 'a big glooby blob of sad blufush.' Broke and drinking 'more than ever,' he had been 'thrown out of all poolhalls except the Negro poolhall where I'm bound to have me head bashed in someday.' An earlier beating had, he suspected, given him brain damage—'maybe once I was kind drunk, but now am brain-clogged drunk with the kindness valve clogged by injury'—and there were more beatings to come before his death in 1969.

But to view Kerouac's life as a tragedy of squandered talent is to think in clichés. From the time that Kerouac completed *On the Road*, he was indemnified against ever making—or ever having made—a serious mistake in his life. The value of a life cannot be assessed chronologically. He had waged everything on becoming a great writer and he had won. Nothing can offset the achievement and *victory* of *On the Road*. Kerouac was in Manhattan with Joyce Glassman when Gilbert Millstein's review appeared in *The New York Times* on 5 September 1957, lauding it as 'an authentic work of art' whose publication was 'an historic occasion.' According to Ann Charters, Kerouac's biographer and editor of his letters, they 'bought a copy of the paper at a newsstand on Broadway just before midnight and read the review together at Donnelly's Irish Bar on Columbus Avenue before returning to her apartment to go back to sleep. Joyce remembered that "Jack lay down obscure for the last time in his life. The ringing phone woke him the next morning, and he was famous."'

Everything else—not just everything that had come before but everything in the sloshy aftermath that was still to come—is insignificant in the face of that moment, when the long wait for vindication came to an end. Even if his 'kindness valve' did become clogged, the vivid generosity of spirit embodied in his conception of Dean Moriarty courses through every line of his masterpiece.

15.

The one time I set eyes on Boris Becker, at Wimbledon in 2018, he was struggling to open the door of a Centre Court toilet. The poor guy could hardly walk. It looked like he had knee trouble and hip trouble to go alongside hair trouble, bankruptcy trouble, and what, for a German, was the highly unusual loss-of-diplomatic-immunity-as-attaché-to-the-Central-African-Republic trouble. A photograph from the Covid summer of 2020 showed he had now acquired (big) pink belly trouble to go with his tennis-elbow trouble. Not tennis elbow in the traditionally painful but invisible sense; this looked like he had a tennis ball implanted in each sagging elbow: a hitherto unseen condition called testicular elbow. He appeared in especially bad physical shape because he was photographed on a yacht next to his girlfriend showing off what the tabloids justifiably called her bikini body. So, more power to his elbow, as they say. And leaving the girlfriend and everything else aside, even if he had not been on a yacht (with Björn Borg and his partner) near Ibiza, even if, Larkin-like, he was reduced to holidaying with his mum in King's Lynn, even if his dodgy legs and elbows were giving him twice the grief, if his hair were even more recalcitrant and his punditry for the BBC still more banal—all of that would count for nothing beside the simple fact that he won Wimbledon three times. By the time he was twenty-one. That is already a magnificent life whatever nonsense comes in its wake.

16.

'And I, the last, go forth companionless,
And the days darken round me . . .'

The blaze of youthful glory can sometimes be historic as well as personal. In *First Light* Geoffrey Wellum tells the story of how, a few months before the outbreak of the Second World War, he takes the first steps towards fulfilling his dream of becoming a fighter pilot. At eighteen he is an RAF pilot, flying Spitfires in the Battle of Britain. Unlike many of his friends, Wellum survives both the battle and multiple sorties over France. On returning from a mission in September 1941, he is met by the squadron's commanding officer, who tells him that he is 'off ops.' Because he's fallen short in some way? On the contrary, he's done too much: 'You've come to the end of the line, over the hill, you're finished.' As he makes his way to the mess, Wellum bumps into the adjutant, 'Mac' MacGowan. Seeing that Wellum is choked with emotion, Mac tells him, in the laconically starched register of the time, 'That's quite enough of that sort of balls.' In any case, he continues, 'The bar is due to open very soon and if it's not open then we'll bloody well open it and have the most enormous Scotch each that you have ever seen in your life.' Later, when Wellum drives 'out of the gates for the last time,' he reflects on his expulsion from the nerve-shredding, life-threatening paradise of aerial combat during the nation's finest hour:

> A has-been. No further use to anybody. Merely a survivor, my name no longer on the Order of Battle in the dispersal hut. A worn-out bloody fighter pilot at twenty years of age, merely left to live, or rather exist, on memories, reduced to watching from the wings.
>
> Will I ever know quite the feeling of truth and comradeship as experienced in a front line Spitfire squadron, and in such a period of our country's history, ever again? . . . Ask yourself, what's the use of anything any more? Far better to be with Peter, Nick, Laurie, Roy, Butch, Bill, John and the rest. [All dead.] There is just no purpose left now. How can anything replace or even approach the last eighteen months?

Written mainly when Wellum was middle-aged, *First Light* was published in 2002, when he was eighty.

17.

Cohen's picture of Kerouac tuning in to listen to himself on the radio captures not just *a moment* but the whole of the life; not just the man but the legend—and vice versa. He's listening to himself, to a *record* of his own achievement, but you also feel he's trying to locate what has been lost, partly by success, partly by age, partly because it could be powered only by the hunger brought on by rejection. His voice is there but, unable to actively create it, he can only replay and rewind it. Condemned to living out his life in the wake of his legend, he is trying to find again the voice that is fading even as it is remembered, as it echoes in memory. Gesturally, visually, the echoes are of his younger self hunched over the typewriter banging out his bop prosody, or of the pianist Bill Evans over the keyboard. It's poignant and beautiful, because while for Kerouac the echoes are from the past, they were in the process of being transmitted to the future via the radio, to the bedrooms of lonesome teenagers, filling them with the thought of adventure—not just the kicks of being on the road but of becoming a writer. You can hear it in the lines of a song that was played a lot on the radio—not one of Dylan's, but Bruce Springsteen's 'Dancing in the Dark.' 'I'm sick of sitting 'round here,' he sings, 'trying to write this book.' Not just any book but—implicitly—this *great* book. Kerouac's ambition, hope, and hunger live on. The romance—and doom—of that will never die. You can see it still. You can hear it.

Things change as you get older. Right now I don't want to do anything *except* sit around writing—more accurately, revising—this book.

18.

I saw Cohen's photograph in Paris as part of an exhibition devoted to the Beats. The centrepiece—a true secular relic—was the scroll version of *On the Road* on which Kerouac banged out a draft of the novel in a Benzedrine-driven binge of unfettered creativity. Kerouac's commitment to spontaneous prose did not stop him being sedulous, revising this draft in order to make it more spontaneous. For almost all authors the labour of revision leads to improvements—until, after a point, the improvements become self-stifling, which is exactly what Kerouac feared.

In Dylan's case, it would be impossible to say one way or another. For every loss incurred by revision there is a gain—and vice versa. Take some lines in 'Idiot Wind.' For the first several recorded versions that wind was 'blowing like a circle 'round your jaw / From the Grand

Coulee Dam to the Mardi Gras.' It was only on version five that it started blowing 'like a circle around my skull / From the Grand Coulee Dam to the Capitol.' There is no better example of the way that Dylan's words both imprint themselves on our consciousness and continue—even after he's stopped changing them—to adapt themselves to changing times, to wrap themselves around history. Ginsberg had deemed this the 'great disillusioned national rhyme' in the liner notes of *Desire*, but it was not until 6 January 2021—a very windy day as it happened—that the cumulative force of idiocy made itself felt at the Capitol in Washington. While that change to the lyric was an undoubted and monumental gain, another rhyme from the earlier version disappeared from subsequent takes: 'Figured I'd lost you anyway, why go on, what's the use? / In order to get in a word with you I'd have had to come up with some excuse.' Those lines are gone, like towns or villages flooded and submerged as a result of the construction of a dam. And that is a terrible loss.

19.

'There is nothing to save, now all is lost,' writes D. H. Lawrence in one of the late, dashed-off poems he called 'Pansies' (his poetic and irritably English take on Pascal's *Pensées*).

In J. C. Chandor's film *All Is Lost* (2013) Robert Redford plays a lone sailor, asleep on his boat one night in the Indian Ocean when a stray container punctures the hull. The remainder of the film painstakingly documents Redford's struggle to save his ship and himself. Like Chuck Yeager confronted with a suddenly catastrophic failure at the end of *The Right Stuff*—'I've tried A! I've tried B! I've tried C!'—he works his way through a checklist of options and procedures. Knowledgeable sailors might notice some errors in Redford's decisions or mistakes that no experienced solo yachtsman would make but to me it seemed—and had to seem—convincing. It's not just that the step-by-step, carefully itemised sequence of mishaps and recoveries make this almost wordless movie so compelling—that's *all* there is. There's no back story, no explanation as to why this man, whose name we never learn, undertook his solo voyage in the first place. Until the final moments the film focuses so tightly on practicalities as to avoid any undertow of symbolic, religious, or allegorical meaning—and is, as a result, unusually vulnerable to them. (Hamlet didn't call it a sea of troubles for nothing.) The more strictly stories of life on the ocean wave are stripped to their essentials the more susceptible they are to shipping larger resonances. Hemingway understood this—and milked it to death in *The Old Man and the Sea*. Redford is constantly trying to mend his boat. Unable to repair it, he concentrates on slowing the rate of its deterioration. Even at night, with only the undimmed whiteness of his teeth to see by, he's still toiling away. So, in his struggle to stay afloat, Redford is like Sisyphus, who, Albert Camus insisted, we must imagine 'happy.' At a certain point, as one bit of ill-fortune is followed swiftly by another, Redford starts to shout 'Fuck.' It never becomes a word, just a long howl of anguish: 'Fffwwuuuh . . .' That howl is the nearest he comes to prayer, after which he resumes the doomed chores of patching, pumping, fixing, plotting. He is in his element. This, surely, is what he went to sea for. And it would be wrong, as he reads the fateful words, 'All is lost,' from a letter he stuffs timelessly into a bottle, to take this as an admission of regret. It would be as accurate to say that he has achieved his destination and destiny.

You plan carefully, do everything correctly and then, at some point, something unpredictable, random, and entirely unforeseeable happens. You fix it. You continue on until the next setback. Acknowledging that it sounds like a 'dick thing to say,' Andy Murray in the documentary *Resurfacing* (2019) says that after dutifully going through all the rehab following his first hip operation, he felt he 'deserved a better outcome.' You make all this effort, go to all these lengths, and then at some point, whatever you have done, you run out of options. You run out of life or, as Al Pacino says in *The Insider*, you are 'about out of moves.' Those moves are all you have and while it becomes clear that they're getting fewer, with a lower chance of accomplishing anything except postponing the inevitable, for a shorter and shorter time, it's hard to believe that there's not something that can be done. 'I can,' writes Gerard Manley Hopkins in one of the so-called 'terrible sonnets': 'Can something, hope, wish day come, not choose not to be.'

Yeager, when he's out of moves, after he's tried B and C, still has one final option: to eject. It's a drastic and undesirable option but it's on the list, is one of the safety features built into the aircraft. The equivalent, for Redford, is to abandon ship and take to his life raft. But even after this there's a further, still more drastic option (or so I misremembered): not to abandon the life raft but to destroy it, to set it on fire in the hope that the light will be seen by the ship that has just passed him by. In fact he accidentally sets the life raft on fire while trying to attract the attention of the passing ship but the result is the same. So there is nothing left but to prepare to die, to prepare for oblivion.

20.

'The Ship of Death,' the longest of the poems in his posthumously published *Last Poems*, begins with Lawrence contemplating 'the long journey towards oblivion.' The imaginative frankness with which he faces this prospect contrasts sharply with the policy of his daily life as, right up till the end, Lawrence found it almost impossible to admit to anyone or to himself that he might be dying. One might quibble with the prognosis suggested by 'long'—the poem was completed in November 1929 when Lawrence had only three months left to live—but bear in mind that he had, by his own estimation, been 'born bronchial.' He fell ill with pneumonia aged sixteen and again, with double pneumonia, almost ten years later. Travelling with Frieda, his wife, setting up home, sometimes only briefly, in various parts of the world, Lawrence's life settled into a pattern of healthy optimism and contentment, rumbles of dissatisfaction, more or less severe sickness, convalescence, rejuvenation, and illness. The decision to leave a given place was often closely associated with the need to put an illness behind him, to head somewhere with a climate or altitude and air—New Mexico was perfect, on all counts, for a while—more conducive to well-being. From Ceylon (where he had 'never felt so sick in my life') Lawrence set out his options in a globally expanded version of Yeager's A-B-C checklist: 'If I don't like W. Australia, shall go on to Sydney. If I don't like that, then California. If I don't like America, then England.' In the last years of his life, as the options for a radical change of setting and circumstance diminished, he seized on any chance to deny he was sick ('Yet I'm not *ill*') or at least refused to acknowledge what he might be ill *with*. Even after suffering the first of a number of haemorrhages, in 1927, it was essential to his core idea of well-being to generalise his poor health as either a condition or a bad habit he had accidentally fallen into.

Anything that ails him is invariably downgraded. Rather than say he has been ill he prefers to tell friends that he has been 'seedy' so that it seems as if he had been temporarily under the weather. If he admits to being unwell he simultaneously dismisses it as something along the lines of an irritating travelling companion of whom he has grown weary: 'my health is very tiresome, and I'm sick of it altogether.' This tendency of seeing his illness as somehow external to or distinct from himself was maintained even as it was internalised. 'Somewhere I am not ill, but my bronchials and asthma *get me down*,' he wrote. 'I feel so strongly as if my illness weren't really me—I feel perfectly well and all right, *in myself*. Yet there is this beastly torturing chest super-imposed on me, and it's as if there was a demon lived there, triumph-ing, and extraneous to me.' If he has the flu or a cold he is at pains to emphasise that everyone else has gone down with it too, that far from there being anything unusual about his having succumbed, he has simply joined the massed ranks of the indisposed. So anxious is he to avoid confronting the reality of his plight that a recurring bout of the malaria that had laid him low in Mexico becomes a cause almost for merriment. Back in 'the malarial tremble-zone,' he explains to Rhys Davies how his 'teeth chattered like castanets—and that's the only truly Spanish thing I've done.' To his sister Emily King he prefers the more homely simile of his 'teeth chattering like a sewing-machine.'

Whatever he is suffering from it is always something—asthma, those troublesome 'bronchials'—brought on, invariably by nerves, or by the male change of life or chagrin. 'But I do believe the root of all my sickness is a sort of rage,' he writes from France in November 1929. 'I realise now, Europe gets me into an inward rage, that keeps my bronchials hellish inflamed.' Invariably it is the place—wherever he happens to be at the time he gets sick—that is to blame. Oaxaca and the Ad Astra in Vence, where he ended up are both 'beastly'; less specifically, as he repeatedly insists, 'it's Europe that has made me so ill.'

So there it is—a direct and unambiguous admission that he is ill but, as his friend Earl Brewster pointed out, 'Never did he give me the impression that he thought his recovery doubtful.' It had been a question, always, of moving on and, if that was impossible, of pulling through. Even the phase of becoming sicker and weaker could be got through, recovered from, left behind. The reality was that his capacity for doing anything was gradually leaving him. There would, he said, be no more novels after *Lady Chatterley's Lover*. But the cascade of shorter writings would continue: poems, essays, letters, an introduction to a book on the Book of Revelation by Frederick Carter that became a slim book in its own right: *Apocalypse*, his last. The world of a man who had spent much of the previous twelve years restlessly traversing it, always looking forward to the next place (which in turn became a place to leave), shrank inexorably, though he still cherished the idea of going back to New Mexico and even wished he 'could go to the moon.' He couldn't walk far without becoming tired, breathless, exhausted. He had prided himself on doing housework, making improvements to wherever it was that he and Frieda had set up home, but all of that became too much for him. His last novel had been a hymn in praise of sexual rapture and renewal but that was part of the process by which he had reconciled himself to living without desire: 'desire has died in me, silence has grown.' He lost more and more weight. 'Neither writing nor painting,' he was reduced to 'letting the clock go round.' There's nothing exceptional about this. It happens to everyone eventually—but it happened to Lawrence when he was in his early forties.

Lawrence recorded and wrote about everything he saw and smelled and touched, with delicacy and deliberate abandon. He became notorious for writing things about bodies that, it was believed, should never be written about, in language that should never appear in print. But there was one word he could not bring himself to use with regard to himself and his own body: 'tuberculosis.' That was unsayable, unspeakable.

At some level, a level of contradiction he had always found easy to access, he believed that one of the things he thought caused his illness—rage—also kept it at bay. The intensity of his rage, especially against England, was inseparable from his vitality. For 'the last two years he was like a flame burning on in miraculous disregard of the fact that there was no more fuel to justify its existence,' wrote his friend Aldous Huxley. That's true but life had a way of adding fuel to Lawrence's fire.

In 1929 the Warren Gallery on Maddox Street in London held an exhibition of his paintings. The show opened on 14 June, attracting both a lot of visitors and hostile press reaction to its pornographic contents before being raided by police who seized thirteen of the twenty-five paintings. For Lawrence this was the latest installment in his experience of repression and censorship that had begun in 1915 when *The Rainbow* had not simply been banned. At Bow Street Court on 13 November it was ordered that all copies be confiscated and destroyed, an offence for which he vowed in 1919 he would 'never forgive England.' Always in the face of rejection, humiliation, injustice—of anything life could throw at him—Lawrence insisted on being the overriding force in his life. It can still be felt flickeringly: 'But I do want to do something about my health, for I feel my life leaving me, and I believe it's this old moribund Europe just killing one.' But then comes the acceptance of passivity. 'They want to put me in a sanatorium,' he writes on 23 January 1930. Shortly before going to the Ad Astra he was 'in bed allowed to do *nothing*.' He submitted to this enforced idleness only because that would enable him to get well—to get up and about again—more quickly.

On 14 February, by which time he weighed only 'something over six stones,' he admits: 'There is a very slight tubercular trouble.' It appears on page 648 of volume 7 of his *Letters*. He has a fortnight left to live.

21.

Lawrence had already imagined the end in 'The Ship of Death,' about a little vessel setting off on its final voyage. As the ship sails on, all the signs and points that make navigation possible gradually disappear. It is as near as we can get, in words, to experiencing the extinction of consciousness:

> *And everything is gone, the body is gone*
> *completely under, gone, entirely gone.*
> *The upper darkness is heavy on the lower,*
> *between them the little ship*
> *is gone*
> *she is gone.*

> *It is the end, it is oblivion.*

But Lawrence doesn't end there:

> *And yet out of eternity, a thread*
> *separates itself on the blackness,*
> *a horizontal thread*
> *that fumes a little with pallor upon the dark.*

> *Is it illusion? or does the pallor fume*
> *A little higher?*

Ah wait, wait, for there's the dawn,
the cruel dawn of coming back to life
out of oblivion.

22.

In *All Is Lost* at the last moment a hand reaches down, Michelangelo-like, to save Redford and the film ends exactly at this point of contact. I am reminded of a line of I. A. Richards's, from the time when I was studying tragedy at university: 'The least touch of any theology that has a compensating Heaven to offer the tragic hero is fatal.' But then so is drowning. And there's no suggestion, anyway, that Redford is meant to be a tragic hero. He's just an unknown person who wakes up one morning and finds himself in a sea of troubles.

23.

Over the years assorted lower back troubles have left me feeling as if I were either as brittle as glass or locked in concrete, sometimes both at the same time. But it's my neck that's been the Achilles heel. Susceptible to every kind of spasm, strain, or seize-up, even while I'm asleep, this long and feeble neck means that I can go to bed at night feeling fine and wake up the next morning having aged eighty years in eight hours. The good thing about this giraffe neck is that it's as recovery-prone as it is injury-prone, always ready to bounce back from whatever has gone wrong and let bygones be bygones. The current crick is small beer compared with stuff that's made me fear that it might be the end of the road tenniswise. It felt like the end in the spring of 2019, in London, when I had what I worried was a recurrence of a wrist injury that had kept me out for a year, ten years earlier. First time around I'd needed an operation (torn cartilage) so I went back to the consultant who'd done the original surgery. He'd seen and fixed thousands of patients in the meantime, but since he was the only person who'd ever operated on my wrist, our last meeting, to me, was adjacent to this one. Like everyone else, he'd put on a bit of weight while I seem only to get thinner with age. He was wearing a jolly tie and one of those striped shirts with a white collar, as popular among men in his profession as they are with those in finance. He pressed and prodded, twisted and stretched, supinated and pronated.

'Does that hurt?'

'Not really.'

'How about that?'

'Not a bit.'

He pressed harder, stretched further. 'Now?'

'Is that all you got?' I said. We'd always got on well, I remembered. While he went on with his examination and manipulations I asked how long the surgery was typically expected to last. He shrugged, still prodding and bending. I said, 'It doesn't come with a lifetime guarantee I suppose?'

'Nothing does. It's all Zara now. Nothing lasts for life—not even life.'

'Actually that's the one thing that does come with a lifetime warranty,' I said. 'It's quality of life that can't be guaranteed.'

Quality of wrist, fortunately, was better than expected. Nothing was torn. A cortisone injection would keep me going. Give it a week's rest, he said, and if everything felt OK I could start playing again. I left the hospital with an unusual sensation in my wrist (throbbing *and* numbness) but a spring in my step, looking forward to tennis and cheered by the sudden irrelevance of another of Lawrence's *Last Poems*:

> *And if, in the changing phases of man's life*
> *I fall in sickness and in misery*
> *my wrists seem broken and my heart seems dead*
> *and strength is gone, and my life*
> *is only the leavings of a life . . .*

24.

'the last fumes of a vaporizing reality . . .'

Between December 1928 and January 1929 Lawrence worked on a long essay for the catalogue accompanying the upcoming exhibition of his paintings at the Warren Gallery. This 'Introduction' took the form of a highly original and partial history of Western art so that, by implication, the history of art was itself an introduction or prelude to . . . his own paintings! Or, to put it into Lawrence-ese, the Western artistic tradition could be said to have achieved a kind of consummation in the paintings he had taken such casual pleasure in producing.

In some ways the essay is an extension and elaboration of sections from the abandoned *Study of Thomas Hardy*—started in 1914—in which he had attempted another survey of Western art. In a chapter called 'The Light of the World,' a particular strain in art is said to have 'reached its climax in our own Turner':

> Ever, he sought the Light, to make the light transfuse the body, till the body was carried away, a mere bloodstain, became a ruddy stain of red sunlight within white sunlight. This was perfect consummation in Turner, when, the body gone, the ruddy light meets the crystal light in a perfect fusion, the utter dawn, the utter golden sunset, the extreme of all life, where all is One, One-Being, a perfect glowing Oneness . . .
>
> If Turner had ever painted his last picture, it would have been a white incandescent surface, the same whiteness when he finished as when he began, proceeding from nullity to nullity, through all the range of colour.

There are pre-echoes of 'The Ship of Death'—'the body gone'—in this passage, which reads like a vision in annihilating white of the

depicted in the later poem. At the earlier stage in Law-
, when he'd been writing his Hardy book, the 'perfect con-
on in Turner' was a sign of something profoundly awry, not in
ter—who perfectly articulated this vision—but in the painter.
Lawrence wrote that he could not 'look at a later Turner picture without abstracting myself, without denying that I have limbs, knees and
thighs and breasts. If I look at the *Norham Castle*, and remember my
own knees and my own breast, then the picture is a nothing to me.' By
dint of its perfection, Lawrence insists, 'Turner is a lie.'

How perfect, then, that Turner tacitly agreed with Lawrence. The
body that, according to Lawrence, had to be denied by Turner's art
in order to achieve this consummation of the spirit, had, as it always must, its own inescapable needs, not only in the artist's life—
Turner fathered two children with his lover Sarah Danby—but in
his work. In 1857, in the course of the huge labour of cataloguing
the deceased artist's work, John Ruskin discovered Turner's erotic
drawings. Made 'under a certain condition of insanity,' these drawings were deemed by Ruskin to be 'evidence of the failure of mind,' a
verdict with which Lawrence would have agreed, though for entirely
different reasons. It was the denial of the urges documented in the
drawings—including studies of female genitalia and of figures cop-
ulating made as late as 1845—that for Lawrence was a cause and
symptom of the degeneration. The life of the body within the larger
body of work—what Lawrence elsewhere called 'the dirty little se-
cret of sex'—became known only after the artist's physical body had
ceased to exist. Ruskin, in turn, denied this by burning the sketches
he'd had the shocked misfortune to discover, thereby briefly transforming the crude appetites of the body into precisely the blaze of
light evoked by Lawrence.

Or so it seemed. But Ruskin's denial may itself have been more
complex than it appeared: an admission or false confession of something that had not actually happened. The claim to have witnessed the
sketches' destruction—framed by a formal, quasi-legal 'and hereby

declare'—might have been Ruskin's way of preserving them. If it was assumed that the offending drawings no longer existed—no longer posed a threat to morality—then they were saved from the threat of the censorious.

Some kind of doubly posthumous belated reunion could take place if one of these denied and apparently destroyed yet, in spite of everything, surviving drawings were used on the cover of a reprint of Lawrence's last major novel, *Lady Chatterley's Lover*.

25.

The dissolution of the physical world in Turner's late works—tangible objects such as castles, palazzi, people, even geographical features hazing into a glow and burst of light—was seen, at the time, as a sign of gradually diminishing capacity, a symptom of 'senile decrepitude.' As early as 1829 Benjamin Robert Haydon claimed that 'Turner's pictures always look as if painted by a man who was born without hands.' By 1838 he was judged 'a talent running riot into frenzies.' If those verdicts seem premature—*The Fighting Temeraire* was exhibited at the Royal Academy the following year—by 1843, after seeing *Shade and Darkness* and *Light and Colour* at the Royal Academy, Robert Browning concluded, 'Turner is hopelessly gone.' Even Ruskin, his most enthusiastic supporter, thought some of the later work 'indolent and slovenly' and regarded paintings made after 1846 as 'indicative of mental disease' or 'evidence of a gradual moral decline.'

With the passage of time these same works came to be seen as visible proof of an artist prepared to 'throw all caution to the wind,' freeing himself both from the material claims of the market and from the artistic chains of the day. Turner, we hear repeatedly, was determined to paint as he pleased without regard to convention or the taste of patrons. Equally determined to get well paid for his work, he felt free to do as he pleased partly because the market for art was changing. Whereas patrons who had commissioned paintings quite reasonably expected the results more or less to conform to their expectations and specifications, there was now a small but steady supply of collectors—wealthy industrialists, or merchants like Ruskin's father—who were willing to pay for works he had created independently. Dealers became increasingly important in facilitating sales, eliciting the desired answer without phrasing the question as crudely as Turner himself: 'Ain't they worth more?' The dematerialisation achieved and celebrated by the paintings bears witness to—and is itself the product of—specific material conditions.

Turner's dedication to capturing the transitory effects of light anticipated and was admired by the impressionists, including Monet and Pissarro who saw his work in London in the 1870s. They valued exactly the qualities that were derided in the press, but popular jokes at Turner's expense—that it didn't matter whether the pictures were hung upside down, that a baker's tray spilled in an art gallery might be indistinguishable from a Turner—suggested he had gone further, had single-handedly moved towards abstraction. 'Sky and water were equated with the paint itself,' wrote Adrian

Stokes, articulating the way Turner looks ahead both to the era of abstraction—when paint becomes the subject of a painting—and, more immediately, to his own 'great last period' when 'the world [is] washed clean by light.' This was the Turner—not just ahead of his time but somehow able to catapult himself beyond the surly bonds of art history—who came, in the twentieth century, to be regarded more highly than the painter of mythical, historical, and seafaring scenes.

The apparent surge towards abstraction seemed even more extreme for a very simple reason. As early as 1806 Joseph Farington deemed *The Battle of Trafalgar, as Seen from the Mizen Starboard Shrouds of the Victory* as 'very crude' and 'unfinished'—an opinion tacitly endorsed by Turner, who reworked the painting and exhibited it again two years later. If Turner's works looked unfinished, writes the biographer Franny Moyle, 'the question of finish was further complicated by the fact that Turner also began to show works in his gallery that his contemporaries generally accepted *were* unfinished, and were apparently displayed as a work in progress.' Some of the late paintings looked abstract because they were unfinished, had been abandoned on the way to becoming *less* abstract, but this insubstantiation helped sustain, substantiate—helped to complete—the case for the artist's reputation as proto-abstractionist. In the twentieth century, with finished and unfinished paintings hung next to each other, the blurring—between figurative and abstract, between finished and unfinished—consolidated the process of dissolution contained within the paintings. Critics 'have been unable to agree whether works like *Sun Setting over a Lake* (c.1840–45) are finished or were abandoned in progress,' reads the catalogue entry for the Tate show *Late Turner: Painting Set Free.** Either the landscape has yet to emerge into view,

---

* If Turner's late works point to the future, the debate about them also sends us in the opposite direction, into the past. Goethe made a defining observation about late style generally when he noticed how Titian 'in his old age depicted only *in abstracto* those materials which he had rendered before concretely: so, for instance, only the *idea* of velvet not the material itself.' Considering some of these 'very late pictures,' the art historian Francis Haskell asks

is yet to come into existence, or, as J. K. Huysmans wrote after seeing an exhibition in 1887, the landscapes in such works 'have been vapourised.' That which is not yet becomes indistinguishable from that which was: a working definition of eternity.

26.

We need to go back to that extraordinary line in Lawrence's essay: 'If Turner had ever painted his last picture . . .'

What an idea: that Turner somehow never quite got round to painting his last picture, never achieved the apotheosis that his work—as many of the quoted commentators insisted—seemed always to announce. In this way, Turner the proto-impressionist and -modernist remained the quintessential romantic, condemned to the corporeal. Of *Norham Castle, Sunrise* (c. 1845) Lawrence writes that 'only the faintest shadow of life stains the light, is the last word that can be uttered, before the blazing and timeless silence.' Consciously or not Lawrence seems here to be echoing Shelley who, in his elegy for Keats, lamented the way that 'Life, like a dome of many-coloured glass, / Stains the white radiance of Eternity.'

Lawrence's suggestion that Turner never painted his last picture can also be viewed as a projection onto the artist and his canvases of the viewer's experience of looking at them. Lady Trevelyan, a friend of Ruskin's, put it simply: 'You never get to the end of a picture of his.'

---

whether they were 'merely left uncompleted at his death or does the tremulous freedom of his brushwork and the sometimes arbitrary treatment of natural appearances represent a "late style," through which the painter sought to convey so personal an impression of his deepest emotions that he was prepared to venture far beyond the comprehension of his patrons?'

27.

Regulus, first shown in 1828, subsequently reworked and exhibited in 1837, has its origin in the story of a Roman consul captured by the Carthaginians during the First Punic War. Allowed to return to Rome to arrange an exchange of prisoners, Regulus advised against such a deal and then went back to Carthage to convey the news of Rome's refusal to his captors. If they were impressed by the way that he had honoured the terms of his provisional release this did nothing to prevent the Carthaginians expressing their extreme displeasure at having their offer rejected: they cut off his eyelids so that his eyes were roasted by the sun of North Africa. And that was just for starters; lidless in Carthage, Regulus ended up sealed in a spiked barrel and rolled around the city for his pains.

There has been some debate as to which of the small figures in the painting might be Regulus (if he is there at all) and whether the scene depicted shows him not on his return to Carthage but about to leave for Rome (with eyelids intact). We don't have to choose between these two options. Freed from documented chronology (before and after) the painting collapses and contains the whole narrative to recreate vicariously, for the viewer, the subjective experience of what we know will befall Regulus and what is known to have befallen him. Even if he is setting out for Rome the barrel is being rolled out in the bottom left-hand corner for his eventual return. Meanwhile the sun is starting to obliterate everything: the planetary source of a macular degeneration that leaves only the periphery of vision more or less intact. At the centre all is bleached out. And that sun—routinely evoked by Lawrence to symbolise consummation—will eventually consume more and more. The picture depicts a 'classic' and recognisable Turner mytho-historical scene in the process of being burned away, of having all the identifiable props—buildings, people—vaporised so that we are left with the all but featureless blaze that remains uniquely Turnerian. Stand here for a while, the picture insists, and more and more of what you see will be obliterated by that which enables you to see—thereby echoing the mock concern of the critic in *Blackwood's Magazine* who asked if Turner's eyes had 'been put out by the glare of his own colours?' So the painting can be seen to represent in dramatic form the trajectory of Turner's art, which culminates in—or boils down to—a blinding scorch and glare. After this you will be left with something like *Sun Setting over a Lake*, an extreme painting, made between 1840 and 1845 but close in every way to the 'last' painting imagined or retrospectively prophesied by Lawrence.

28.

Since Lawrence raises the idea that Turner never painted his last painting we can ask when the potential for that last painting became apparent. Can we extrapolate backwards from that unachieved apotheosis to a moment when such a possibility was first suggested?

Before his death in 1844 William Beckford, one of Turner's earliest patrons, complained that Turner 'paints now as if his brains and imagination were mixed upon his palette with soapsuds and lather.'

I knew vaguely about Turner but only became properly interested in him when I read the essay in *About Looking* in which John Berger reminds us that the artist's dad ran a barbershop. Without offering a definitive causal analysis Berger asks us to:

> Consider some of his later paintings and imagine, in the backstreet shop, water, froth, steam, gleaming metal, clouded mirrors, white bowls or basins in which soapy liquid is agitated by the barber's brush and detritus deposited. Consider the equivalence between his father's razor and the palette knife which, despite criticisms and current usage, Turner insisted upon using so extensively. More profoundly—at the level of childish phantasmagoria—picture the always possible combination, suggested by a barber's shop, of blood and water, water and blood.

So Turner's last painting—as conceived by Lawrence—was simmering in his consciousness long before he had painted his first.

29.

Paintings of eternity have to survive in time, like the rest of us. *Regulus*, hanging patiently at Tate Britain, is not as spectacular as accounts I had read led me to expect. Seeing the original was not a significantly more heightened experience than looking at reproductions in books. It seemed to have dulled over time, yellowed. This in itself is in keeping with what Turner's first biographer called his 'clouding eyes.' Medically, the gradual predominance of yellow in Turner's work may have been due to cataracts caused by his habit of staring into the sun. Cataracts, in this context, seem like the opposite of—nature's attempt to make good or compensate for—the lidless torment of Regulus.

30.

In his eighties John Berger had an operation to remove his cataracts. Two days later he noticed that the white paper on which he was writing had become 'whiter than anything I've become used to seeing.' He recalls the extraordinary whiteness of things in his mother's kitchen when he was a child and of how, 'gradually the whiteness dimmed without my taking account of it.' Post-cataract, 'the whiteness of the paper rushes towards my eyes, and my eyes embrace the whiteness like a long lost friend.' Newly conscious of his rejuvenated eyes, as Lawrence was conscious of his knees and limbs while looking at *Norham Castle*, Berger here responds to Lawrence's larger appeal on behalf of the body. (I'm tempted to say that the long-lost friend *is* Lawrence!) The whiteness has become palpable.

31.

Light and Colour (Goethe's Theory) was exhibited at the Royal Academy in 1843: a square swirl, a trapped centrifuge of colours. 'Red, blue, and yellow,' as Turner explained gnomically to Ruskin.

Goethe on his deathbed eleven years previously is said to have asked for 'more light.' Turner, let's say, *took him at his word*.

So we ask—in turn, as it were—what else died *with* Turner? In English art, an appetite for the visionary—that coarse 'appetite' is more appropriate than any romantic 'yearning'—and transcendental that did not return until . . . Actually, it has never returned. It *bled out* with Turner (who could even be said to have showed it being tugged to its rest); the eponymous annual prize has proved so effective that we can forget this without regret and, crucially, without the sense of loss that might engender it again.

32.

Rain, Steam, and Speed—the Great Western Railway was painted in 1844, in the midst of Britain's 'Railway Mania' when Turner was sixty-nine. It shows a stretch of the Thames he had often painted, at Maidenhead, where Brunel had built a railway bridge across the river five years earlier. To the left is the old Maidenhead road bridge.

The first section of railway had opened in 1825 and lines had spread throughout Britain in the 1830s. So a relatively new phenomenon—the train—characterised by its unprecedented energy, was painted, late in the artist's life, with undiminished intensity and matching force. To reduce the questions suggested by the painting to binary terms: is the train the very engine of progress or an instrument of the destruction of an old, settled, idyllic England where, in George Eliot's phrase, 'the cattle had hitherto grazed in a peace unbroken by astonishment'? Is the picture a lament for the passing of the ancestral Thames and rural life—as embodied by the ploughman, working to the slow rhythm of the seasons—or a vision of the irresistible heroic energy of the railway age? It is both of course.

According to one account, a passenger on a Great Western train saw a man she later realised was Turner leap up from his seat and crane his neck out of the window to feel the tumultuous sense of speed. While this may be no more reliable than Turner's own story of how he had himself lashed to the mast during the storm depicted in an earlier painting, *Snow Storm—Steam-Boat off a Harbour's Mouth*, it vividly demonstrates the purpose of the painting: to convey not an impression but a sensation—of speed. Although we are seeing the train from outside—as if we are watching it hurtle by—we share the experience of the people within it.

If the painting has a documentary value it is in registering a change in the nature of perception—how our perception of time and space is being changed by speed. The energy of the train, in the view of the author of *Vanity Fair*, William Thackeray, was barely contained by the confines of the canvas: 'There comes a train down upon you, really moving at the rate of fifty miles an hour, and which the reader had best make haste to see, lest it should dash out of the picture, and be away up Charing Cross through the wall opposite.' By this reckoning the effect of Turner's painting anticipates that of the Lumière brothers' film of the train arriving at a station fifty years later when the audience recoiled in fear, thinking it was going to come crashing out of the screen and into the auditorium.

It's a far cry from Philip Larkin in his train on that famous Whitsun more than a half century after the Lumière screening when his most distinct feeling, as the train eventually gets under way, is of 'all sense / Of being in a hurry gone.' Historically, that sense of hurry was already long gone. That's the most startling aspect of the last mentioned of Turner's titular features, 'speed': how quickly the railway was assimilated, becoming an attractive, decorative, and rather sedate component of the landscape it was briefly seen to ravage. Although Monet and Pissarro almost certainly saw *Rain, Steam, and Speed* in London, their paintings of railways display none of the calamitous excitement and threat that you sense in Turner; they're more like those idyllic posters advertising the bucolic charm of a day out on the train. The railways that were seen to be tearing through the landscape have become an enhancing part of it: the little trains chuffing happily along are central to the harmony of the scene in the way that the ploughman—a defining presence in Thomas Gray's 'Elegy Written in a Country Churchyard,' a marginal, barely discernible figure in Turner—is powerless to manage in *Rain, Steam, and Speed*.

The impressionists, in any case, preferred railway *stations*—places of social convergence. From there it's a relatively short journey back across the English Channel to the train itself as a *place* from which to make a precise and leisurely survey of how country and city flicker and merge in a way that makes England identifiably English:

> An Odeon went past, a cooling tower,
> And someone running up to bowl . . .

33.

It's easy, while reading 'The Whitsun Weddings,' to fall prey to a serial nostalgia for the train, not only for the period before the ruthlessness of Beeching's cuts, but even for the very idea of a national railway system prior to British Rail being carved up into private rail franchises, all in apparent competition with each other to maximise profit *and* commuter dissatisfaction. Certainly the train, for most of my conscious life, has been an elegiac symbol. My dad said that he used to take me to watch the trains arriving and choo-chooing out of the local station, ten minutes away, at Leckhampton, but some of my earliest actual memories are of playing in the semi-wilderness of the station's abandoned buildings and tracks. Those memories sit next to others, from slightly later, of the bigger and busier station of Cheltenham Spa—of the semi-privacy of compartments rather than carriages, of the phased-out restaurant car rather than the bar-buffet—that lead inexorably to the present, when the last refuge of endangered contemplation, the Quiet Carriage, is disappearing from some lines. So the train becomes the vehicle for every kind of lament, including the lost opportunity of reading Peter Ackroyd's biography of Turner undistracted by ringing phones and one-way conversation: 'I'm on a train!' The best thing to be said about travelling by train is that it's better than being on a coach.

The sinking-heart feeling when boarding a train in England has such deep historical roots that Larkin's 1972 'Going, Going'—'that will be England gone'—is a relatively recent blooming of poetic plaints observable in Gray's elegy or Oliver Goldsmith's 'The Deserted Village.' The difference? 'It seems, just now, / To be happening so very fast,' Larkin writes in tones so marked by a lack of urgency or panic as to seem almost stately. Even for Larkin the full flowering of regret still lies in the future (that *will* be England gone). Wordsworth had the characteristically romantic experience of chancing upon an already ruined cottage; Larkin everywhere sees signs of ruination to come.

The outcome may be no more in doubt or avoidable than death itself in the later 'Aubade' but it is yet to happen, is still in the process of becoming.

Adrian Stokes hinted at something similar in Turner, pointing out that he was working during 'a period when many English towns and villages were astonishingly beautiful, at a moment of poignant beauty inasmuch as the threat of great changes was sometimes implicit.' So perhaps an inversion of Raymond Williams's framing argument in *The Country and the City* is in order and overdue. Noticing that a recent lament for a vanished English landscape reminded him of something he had read years earlier, Williams sought out that earlier reference and then continued to trace the moment of decline—of the just-passed idyll—further and further into the past, all the way to the last station stop, the unblemished terminus of the Garden of Eden.

A reverse research project could document the ways in which fear of ruination keeps getting updated and projected, by increments, into the future, culminating with climate change, which involves the ruination of the very idea of a future. Such an undertaking would need to consider depictions of the post-apocalyptic future in films like *I Am Legend* (2007) and *28 Days Later* (2002). With the exception of Cormac McCarthy's *The Road*, the most striking aspect of these scenarios is the way that they always have, even if only briefly, an idyllic quality: no queues at supermarkets, no traffic on motorways or crowds in central London. Another, often remarked-on aspect of these visions of the dystopian future is that whereas they used to be scheduled at some impossibly distant date the wait time for envisioned sci-fi catastrophe gradually shrank until it was knocking impatiently on the door of the imminent. So it's fitting that anyone involved in such research would have found that their endeavours had been derailed and overtaken by events as they were stranded by the reality of Covid lockdown in the empty streets of London in April 2020, as recorded by the photographer Chris Dorley-Brown.

34.

'*All the kiosks were shuttered, the symbolic train waited, the clock's hand jerked from minute to minute.*'

When my friend and I got the train from Oxford to Lewisham for the Clash gig we knew nothing about the geography of London, had no idea that Lewisham is about as far away from Paddington as it is possible to get. Groping our way back to Paddington on a hopeful combination of buses and tubes took so long that we missed the last train to Oxford.*

Ah, the last train! Fine if your evening happens to come to an end,

---

* We ended up travelling on something that no longer exists: the milk train that used to run in a kind of slow limbo between the last passenger train of the night before and the first properly scheduled service of the new day. It left so early, made so many stops—and travelled at such a snail's crawl between stops—that it was of use only to the stranded.

naturally, so that you can head to the station and catch that train or the faster penultimate one at your leisure. But usually it looms over an evening like a curfew, a threat of social execution. I still remember the time in 1989 when another friend and I took our bikes on a train to Cambridge. We had a nice Rupert Brooke–y afternoon cycling to Grantchester but the real reason for our trip was to see McCoy Tyner's trio (Louis Hayes on drums, Avery Sharpe on bass) at the Corn Exchange. It was fantastic and it was awful because we had to leave before the end, as they were launching into 'Walk Spirit, Talk Spirit,' to sprint to the station in time for the last train back to King's Cross.

In David Lean's *Brief Encounter* Laura (Celia Johnson) and Alec (Trevor Howard) never have enough time. They are always having to hurry for their respective trains, to Ketchworth in Laura's case, and in the opposite direction, to Churley, in Alec's—though they invariably have time, either before or after hurrying, for a cup of tea in the refreshment room at Milford Junction. Except on one notable occasion the trains they are rushing to catch are not the day's last trains—it just looks that way because it gets dark so early: *noir*ishly dark in the station's subway, where the passions of the unconscious erupt amid the mad dash for platforms (but not so dark that Laura can stop worrying that someone might see them snogging). They could catch later trains but habits and patterns of behaviour being as strong as they are, nothing can be allowed to get in the way of their taking the same trains that they did before their almost-affair began.

Or almost nothing. When Alec announces that he is not getting his train, that he is going back to the flat that his friend Stephen allows him to use, Laura resists this temptation and gets on her usual train. Then, as it's about to pull out, she jumps off and heads to the flat. We see her mount the stairs of the apartment block through the iron cage of the elevator and the metal bars of windows but it's hard to say whether she's entering a prison complex or escaping from the simple confinement of married life. The door of the flat opens and she steps inside. Soaking wet from unseen rain, she tells Alec that she can't stop, but she does remove her wet coat and hat. There's a lot of talk, naturally, about how wet she is. Usually she's buttoned up in multiple protective layers—coat, jacket—of refinement and convention. Even now, at this moment of greatest intimacy, there are several remaining layers to preserve her from their desires. There is also the exigency of plot as time once again works against them in the shape of Stephen, returning to his flat unexpectedly early. She hurries out undetected but Stephen guesses what's been going on, leaving Alec morally besmirched and Laura—when he catches up with her later at the station—feeling ashamed and low. Still, this unexpected intrusion has successfully fudged the moral, dramatic, and emotional crux of the film as circumstances have prevented Laura from following in the fatal footsteps of her doomed antecedents Emma Bovary and Anna Karenina. After their very last interrupted meeting at the station she runs out, intending to throw herself under the express, like Anna, but returns to the refreshment room, faint, bedraggled, exhausted. Lawrence believed that Tolstoy pushed Anna under the train to punish her for a transgression he had relished. Noël Coward's script hustles Laura out of the flat, out of harm's way, before she can consummate her folly. The shared conventions of respectability—clothes, the home, husband, kids, the *Times* crossword, *The Oxford Book of English Verse*—hold firm, even when rocked by Rachmaninov's second piano concerto (which hubby Tom naturally asks Laura to turn down when she cranks it up on the home gramophone).*

The encouraged assumption is that after returning to her normal

* Unlike Connie and Mellors in *Lady Chatterley's Lover,* Alec and Laura are of the same class but there is an insistent feeling that it's not just marriage but larger societal moorings that are threatened—in order to be eventually reaffirmed. The enlarged scale of transgression, of falling foul of the standards of behaviour appropriate to one's class, is established as a key—both in the sense that everything will remain locked safely in place and in the musical sense of a note or tone that will define the whole piece—by the very first bit of dialogue in the film, an anecdote about a passenger trying to travel in first class with a third-class ticket. Class trespassers will be caught and punished! This little story is the focus of our attention, is literally foregrounded while the lovers' meeting—their last, actually, before the film flashes back to their first—unfolds discreetly in the background. The socio-sexual status quo just about holds together and hangs on, as has the embattled country itself through the long struggle of the Second World War (though by the time of the film's release, in November 1945, a Labour landslide in the general election will have brought about something akin to a parliamentary revolution).

life of wifely devotion to the family nothing wayward will happen to Laura again. Her days of romantic and almost-sexual adventure have come to an end. But something has awakened or, at the very least, stirred within her. On one of her journeys home, soon after falling for Alec, she gazes at and through her reflection in the dark glass of the carriage window. The brief encounter with him is also what Emily Dickinson calls a 'self encounter.' The ease with which she lies to her husband and friends, the happiness she feels—all of this makes her aware, as never before, of another self that has been revealed *by* remaining hidden: 'Ourself behind ourself, concealed.'

35.

Bear these images—both Dickinson's and Laura gazing at her reflection—in mind when, a couple of stops from here on this meandering milk train of a narrative, we arrive in Turin. There, 'at the beginning of his madness, Nietzsche would rush to his mirror, look at himself, turn away, look again,' writes E. M. Cioran. 'In the train that was taking him to Basel, the one thing he always asked for was a mirror. He no longer knew who he was, kept looking for himself, and this man, so eager to protect his identity, so thirsty for himself, had no instrument at hand but the clumsiest, the most lamentable of expedients.'

36.

At Wymondham station in Norfolk the café has been modelled on the refreshment room at Milford Junction. I thought at first that this might be where *Brief Encounter* had been filmed but it's just derived from the place in the film. Still, it was a nice spot to wait for a train back to London after I'd been at one of the annual parties at a country house near there, the kind of house that Williams writes about so movingly in *The Country and the City*: 'Think it through as labour and see how long and systematic the exploitation and seizure must have been, to rear that many houses, on that scale.' Think it through as hedonism, with seven sound systems in the cellars, decked out with lasers and smoke machines so that the whole subterranean warren is turned into a one-night-only club, and you have the best parties imaginable. Until they stopped happening. They were too expensive to host (even though ticket prices were hefty); there were complaints from neighbours about noise travelling for miles through the big skies over the open fields of Norfolk. And we the partygoers were getting older, though the main effect of this was to raise the party still higher in everyone's affections, as the single best night of the whole year— even if a lot of the people in attendance spent a chunk of each summer in Ibiza having similarly wild nights there.

The format was always the same. We camped in the gorgeous grounds of the house and on Saturday afternoons there would be an aerobatic display featuring vintage planes. Later we'd assemble on the lawn, in the shape of a heart, for a photograph taken from the roof of the house, with everyone dressed up in whatever the year's unifying colour happened to be. The photograph would develop into a large-scale, low-key drinks party and then people would drift away, to eat, to get dressed up and ready for the real action. This started soon after dark, with a burst and spray of fireworks launched from the roof of the house, before the doors were thrown open and we all piled into the cellars. The main room, the Tractor Shed, had the most powerful sound and lighting system but all the rooms were fun, everything about it was fantastic, even those interludes when you found yourself squeezing from room to room along the sweating stone corridors or up the narrow, Schloss-Adler stairs because you couldn't quite lock into the music wherever you were and hoped to find something better elsewhere. Bliss was it in that dawn to be middle-aged! But that was the problem—the dawn came *so* quickly. The entire night flashed by so that within five minutes of entering the cellars you emerged wide-eyed into the waiting daylight, the sturdy trees and the lawn slipping away towards the low mist of the Excalibur lake. It sounds silent, put like that, but the thump of music from the cellars was still audible, adding credence to the neighbours' gripes, making you wonder if you should dive back inside for whatever vestiges of mayhem remained.

37.

One of Martin Amis's characters in *The Pregnant Widow* is 'well launched on the bullet train of his fifties.' I've only just got off that one and onto the connecting train that sends you hurtling through your sixties. Given its ever-increasing, potentially terminal velocity, I'd better start looking around now to make sure I don't miss my stop or leave any personal items behind. Or, since this next train is actually the *same* train, the same one that came crawling out of childhood, maybe I'll sit tight, stay on, and hope no one asks to see my age-stamped ticket. That's what I was feeling just over a year ago at the KitKatClub in Berlin—a city where, at the weekend, there are no last trains; whatever time you leave a club there's always a U- or S-Bahn waiting to take you home. I read somewhere that W. H. Auden believed he was always the youngest person in the room—quite an achievement given the state of that thousand-year-old face—and although that wasn't a delusion I could share I never felt self-consciously old once we were in the club. And then, with Covid, there were no parties, clubs, or trains of any kind to stay on, and I found myself living like a depressed pensioner whose life has flattened out to a walk along the beach, past a couple of girls who glance up and say something about 'that *old man*.'

38.

In 2013 I arrived at Miami airport to give a reading at Stetson University in Florida. My host, the writer Mark Powell, was waiting at the baggage carousel. As we walked to his car he asked if it would be OK if . . . The pause made me worry that he was going to propose something untoward, something seriously *inconvenient*. The thing was, he continued, his mother was arriving shortly in another terminal and would it be OK if we waited to pick her up too? Of course, that was fine, I said, and it really was since her flight got in right on time and soon the three of us were exiting the airport in a cool and spacious car. It was still a bit awkward because, in that scrupulously polite American way, this charming elderly lady insisted on sitting in the back and calling me Mr. Dyer, and it felt so silly to say, 'Please call me Geoff,' that we'd had quite a few exchanges over the course of several miles before I was able to find a way of doing so without sounding inversely grand.

It was going to be a long drive and after half an hour of nice chat Mark asked if we'd like to listen to some music. This seemed a lovely idea and he played a CD, on the car's immaculate sound system, of a woman singing about Tennessee and Dixie—the kind of alt-country bollocks I couldn't bear but that I now fell instantly in love with. It was such a perfect soundtrack that the three of us were suddenly starring in the early stages of a low-budget indie movie in which a tweedy English professor—I was neither tweedy nor professorial but in the film version this would be an understandable adjustment of the facts—is due to give a dreary lecture on Tennyson or Wordsworth at an American college campus but then, due to a series of not-too-dramatic, non-*Deliverance*-style mishaps, ends up going instead on a long road trip with his host and the host's mom, shedding his tweed jacket in favour of cowboy shirt and hat along the way, climaxing with a triumphant reading in Nashville, at the Grand Ole Opry.

39.

That's how I first heard Gillian Welch, in 2013, which means I encountered her embarrassingly late—after David Cameron, even. One of many reasons she is so wonderful is because . . . I was going to say because of her deep immersion in Dylan but since so many people are immersed in Dylan that's not accurate enough. It's because she has taken from Dylan in a very Dylan-like way, not least his magpie ability to pick and choose bits and pieces of Americana from the past. There are also the vocal stretches and slurs (especially on 'Wrecking Ball' and 'One Monkey' from *Soul Journey*), the elliptical nature of the songs, and, on occasions, what seem direct allusions to his stuff. Maybe it's just me but the way she sings 'fortune lady' on 'Revelator' seems like a direct summons, across time, to 'the fortune-telling lady' on 'Desolation Row.' (It's tempting to claim that with this line Dylan actually predicts Welch's future allusion to it.) On 'One Monkey' she drawls, repeatedly, 'Here comes a slow train . . .' It's never made clear where this train might be heading but we can be in no doubt—can hear exactly—where it's come *from*. And then there's 'Lowlands,' a response to either his 'Sad-Eyed Lady of the . . .' or his 'Highlands,' regarded by some as Dylan's own response to the earlier song.

40.

'Nietzsche's great luck,' according to Cioran, was 'to have ended as he did: in euphoria.' Cioran—who ended up hollowed out by dementia—is not referring to the end of Nietzsche's actual life, on 25 August 1900, after more than a decade spent being cared for, at first, by his mother, and then preserved as a helpless effigy by his sister. Elisabeth assumed control not just of her brother's body but, tragically, of his body of work, overseeing the transformation of a writer who had written of 'the accursed anti-Semitism' that had been 'the reason for a radical break between me and my sister'—and whose final, semi-coherent words included the claim that he was 'having all anti-Semites shot'— into someone indelibly associated with Hitler and Nazism. 'Unlucky in life,' writes Richard Wolin in *The Seduction of Unreason*, 'Nietzsche was in many ways even unluckier in death.'

Visitors to the Villa Silberblick in Weimar, which became home to the incapacitated philosopher, his sister, and the archive she controlled, would hear howls from the room where Nietzsche lay upstairs, shrieks that sounded like expressions of psychic agony but which contained no meaning beyond the biological fact that he was alive and capable of producing them, without any tormenting memory or residue of extinguished insight and ruined lucidity. Eminent or especially devoted pilgrims would be taken up to see him, propped or lying 'in a white linen gown, which made him look like a guru,' but also, to us, like himself since it is from this phase of his life that the iconic portraits were sketched by Hans Olde (and reproduced on the cover of the first Nietzsche book I ever owned, the Penguin Classics edition of *Thus Spoke Zarathustra*). In August 1888, in a postscript to a long letter, Nietzsche wrote that 'some people are born posthumously,' but the last decade of his life raises the appalling prospect that posthumous life can start while one is still notionally alive. And he was ready for this: 'One pays dearly for immortality,' he had written; 'one has to die several times while alive.'

41.

So Cioran is referring not to the end of Nietzsche's life but to the phase that came to an end on 3 January 1889 in Turin when he saw a taxi driver beating his horse. Nietzsche flung his arms around the horse and collapsed. He regained consciousness but never his sanity.

In the period leading up to this the sky in Turin had grown brighter in tandem with a massive darkening, as happens when the sun makes looming clouds blaze with radiant blackness. Nietzsche knew he was engaged in something momentous, 'challenging humanity as a whole with [his] terrible accusation,' and yet, whichever way the 'decision' might go, he knew that the accuser would himself receive a correspondingly terrible sentence because 'there attaches to my name a quantity of doom that is beyond telling.' In *Ecce Homo* he bounces between joking—happy to be regarded as 'a buffoon,' he claims that, compared to his Zarathustra, Dante was 'merely a believer'—and sombre contemplation of his 'fate': 'One day there will be associated with my name the recollection of something frightful—of a crisis like no other before on earth.'

Written in less than three weeks, between 15 October and 4 November 1888, *Ecce Homo* teeters like this—brilliantly, frighteningly, absurdly, comically, grandly, sadly—on the very brink of collapse. Light, in the letters written shortly before his breakdown, flickers briefly before being consumed, often in the next sentence, by nonsense and darkness. On 5 January in a burst of impenetrable lucidity he writes to Jacob Burckhardt, 'I am every name in history.' I've no idea what this means but I remember first coming across it, quoted by an author whose name I can no longer recall, in a passage about the scrupulous listing of the names of the dead on First World War memorials. So it seems that this line of Nietzsche's, like so much else that he wrote, has a prophetic quality or, more subtly, the proleptic ability to suggest a time in the future when the past is present as a constant echo.

This is a symptom or at least a side effect of what Nietzsche considered to be his most important idea: the Eternal Recurrence. Every moment of the life we lead, he claimed, will be lived over and over, throughout all eternity. If we give ourselves to this concept, there is no—nor can there be any—end. Since the Recurrence insists that every moment is endlessly relived Nietzsche's final phase of euphoria—a mix of delusion and lucidity—will fade, in an instant, and be followed by the decade spent as a drooling zombie, and then by his boyhood, by the long days and nights of his loneliest loneliness, the constant illnesses and headaches, the renewed hopes followed always by fresh disappointments, the gradually increasing sense of having been catastrophically overlooked (and the attendant, swelling sense of megalomania). The only thing not included in this endless carousel would be confirmation of his eventual posthumous global fame and influence: the satisfaction of knowing that everything he predicted for himself—even in his most delusional moments—would come to pass. The gain? That he would be spared all knowledge of the day on 2 November 1933, when Hitler made a ceremonial visit to the archive where Elisabeth presented him with her brother's walking stick. The prospect of his sister Elisabeth's constant reappearance was, he wrote in *Ecce Homo*, the most 'abysmal' aspect of the Eternal Recurrence.

42.

Many commentators, especially academics, have found the idea of the Eternal Recurrence puzzling. Milan Kundera points out that other philosophers have also been 'perplexed' by a 'mad myth' that he himself finds 'mysterious.' Lacking the necessary training in philosophy I took to it like a duck to water. Paradoxically, the Eternal Recurrence of all things insists that we have only one life. It is a formulation that offers no alternative to our being saddled with and sealed completely within *this* life.

Not only is there no afterlife but, crucially, there is no escape in death, no way of downgrading what happens by claiming that, however terrible life might be, it will at some point be over and done with. It's unprovable and yet, from time to time, always at unexpected moments, we get an elusive sense that we have lived our life before (and, according to Nietzsche, will do so again and again). That was one of the first things that struck me about Nietzsche, the way the Eternal Recurrence offered an explanation of the sensation of déjà vu—the flicker that is both premonition and memory. The strangest aspect of déjà vu is the way that the sensation always extends slightly beyond the moment when we have registered it as such so that it *includes* our saying, 'I've just had a déjà vu,' and we are briefly locked into the loop of the moment just as we are locked into endless loops of life.

The film *Groundhog Day* (1993) flirts with the premise of the Eternal Recurrence but permits a slight improvement or learning over time, with each repetition. The best filmic representation of the idea is Christian Marclay's *The Clock* (2010): exactly the same twenty-four hours forever, with multiple climaxes along the way but no finale on the hour, at noon, or even at the end of the day, at midnight. And no pause. Moments after midnight the same day—the same endless loop of 86,400 seconds—is already rolling round again.

43.

Turin is one of those cities that, for various reasons, I am always returning to. The first time I was there, in the early 1990s, I headed, as
soon as possible, to Piazza Carlo Alberto, where Nietzsche had lived.
A plaque on the wall explained—in my rough translation—that

> In this house,
> Federico Nietzsche
> knew the fullness of spirit
> that challenges the unknown;
> the Will to Power
> that drives the hero.
> Here, as attests his high destiny
> and genius,
> he wrote 'Ecce Homo'
> the book of his life.
> In memory
> of the creative hours
> Spring/Autumn 1888.
> At the centennial of his birth
> the City of Turin placed [this memorial].
> 15 October 1944

So although it was erected after the fall of Mussolini (who, unlike
Hitler, had in his youth been 'a connoisseur and admirer' of Nietzsche)
it honoured him in terms associated with fascism. Still, at least there
was a memorial and each time I returned to the city I passed by it,
sometimes accidentally.

In 2013 I was in Turin for a jazz festival and found that I was stroll-
ing through a familiar square rendered briefly unfamiliar by extensive
renovation. Blue corrugated fencing had cordoned off a section of the
building at the corner of what I realised was Piazza Carlo Alberto. In

a Sod's Law way I thought that the plaque would be behind this cordon, thereby denying the pilgrim the confirmation—the stamp in his psychic passport, the cameraless selfie—he craves. And then I saw it, on the corner of the street where I'd entered the square. The upheaval of building work made it more obvious than ever that a new memorial was needed to free Nietzsche from the war-time, quasi-fascistic bombast of the hero and the will to power. Instead there should be a sculpture of the moment when he threw his arms around the poor horse being beaten by its driver. It wouldn't have to be a realist sculpture but that episode would be the defining part of the commission.

Standing there I conceived the idea of a competition inviting sculptors to come up with ideas for exactly such an artwork. I was already thinking like an influential member of the Turin city council but almost instantly I saw that it would be better if one were mayor of Turin, or, ideally, a dictator with untrammelled powers so as to cut down on the preliminary bureaucratic rigmarole that attends a major undertaking such as this. Perhaps this is where the urge to power starts to make itself felt: the belief that you are right, that it is so obviously the best thing to do—to erect a statue of Nietzsche in a public square—that the opinions of others are no more than a hindrance to be trampled down and clambered over as quickly and ruthlessly as possible.

And it so clearly was a good idea, since in the middle of the square there's already an equine statue—some generalissimo on a horse on a plinth, sword raised, going nowhere but—in the way of these statues—going nevertheless. He's facing the Museo Nazionale del Risorgimento Italiano, wearing one of those old-fashioned whatever-they're-called hats. Turin, like most major cities in Europe, is full of this stuff; putting up third-rate statues like this is part of the project and one of the rewards of achieving nationhood. But this rote bit of statuary would be revived and improved when offset by the Nietzsche statue, which—this was emerging as another part of the brief—would be:

a) at ground level rather than on a pedestal,
b) life-size,

c) tucked discreetly into a corner (in accordance with the way
that Nietzsche created his earth-changing work while living
in almost complete obscurity).

This was a marvelous idea and one to which the council would
be sympathetic because although the square was dominated by this
old statue part of it was given over to a temporary exhibition of eco-
logical posters for public transport (a luxuriously appointed bus with
the caption 'I don't drive, I have a chauffeur') and cycling. Totally flat,
Turin is the perfect city for bikes (or would be if it weren't for the
murderous cobbles and lethal tramlines) so it made sense to claim
that 'cyclists make better lovers' by showing a bucolic scene in which
a bike is lying on the grass surrounded by discarded clothing, including a bra and knickers.

The new Nietzsche monument—which would be anything but
monumental—would be in keeping with this mood, signalling the
transition from conquest of nature (as represented by the military man
astride his horse) to reconciliation with it as the philosopher threw his
arms around the horse's neck. It would also embody the transition in
Nietzsche's reputation from 'hero' and promulgator of the superman
to man of compassion and proto–horse whisperer, even if there's no
sign, in his writing, that he gave a rat's arse about ill-treated animals.
The irony is that although the whupped horsey must have welcomed
Nietzsche's intervention really it was poor Nietzsche who was in need
of help, compassion, and love. Maybe, I thought, as if I were now not
just organising and judging the competition but, in the way of dictators,
submitting my own proposal for what would turn out to be the winning
entry, by a unanimous decision, it would be possible to create a statue in
which horse and man held each other in a mutually consoling embrace.
I walked on, simultaneously animated by this project of public works
and eco-urban renewal and disinclined to do anything further about it
except imagining the grand opening ceremony and unveiling, to be followed by a screening, later that same night, of Béla Tarr's last film, *The
Turin Horse* (2011), which I'd never had the patience to sit through.

44.

It doesn't matter that it's impossible to know exactly what happened in the Piazza Carlo Alberto on that January day in 1889. Attempts to trace the story of Nietzsche embracing the beaten horse back through its various retellings have found no corroboration from reliable witnesses and contemporary sources—the first printed account of the episode did not appear until thirteen years later—but neither has it been contradicted by established facts. There is something appropriate about this since Nietzsche's solitude condemned him to being, in Stefan Zweig's phrase, 'the sole witness' to the tragic monodrama of his life. We are in the realm of myth that sustains its own truth. This version of what happened corresponds to the reality it created—as should the statue commemorating the day's event.

And it should do something else too: recognise Nietzsche's achievement while also emphasising his abysmal failure, a failure and eventual change in fortunes as seismic as van Gogh's. The biographer Curtis Cate gives a detailed account of Nietzsche's publishing fortunes a couple of years before his arrival in Turin. In 1886 half of the print run of a thousand copies of the first volume of *Human, All Too Human* had been sold, which was better than a third of volume 2 and one-fifth of *The Wanderer and His Shadow* (also from print runs of a thousand each). The figures for *Dawn* and *The Gay Science* respectively were 216 and 212 from print runs of the same size. None of the *Zarathustra* volumes had sold more than a thousand copies. Compare that with 1914 when 150,000 copies of a special pocket-sized edition were printed for German soldiers to take into battle.

The cruel irony is that as Nietzsche was on the brink of losing his mind he was on the brink of finding the appreciative readership that had been denied him. In 1888 the Danish scholar Georg Brandes gave a series of lectures on his work. 'Suddenly,' writes Wolin, 'Nietzsche's name was on the lips of all Copenhagen.' That sounds an almost comically modest claim but these lectures were the start of an eventual sea-change in Nietzsche's fortunes and sufficient encouragement, to a writer starved of all acclaim, to persuade him of how widely he was read—and how highly regarded—in the rest of the world: 'I have even real geniuses among my readers. In Vienna, in St Petersburg, in Stockholm, in Copenhagen, in Paris, and New York—I have been discovered everywhere.' Obliged, in *Ecce Homo*, to accept that he had not yet been discovered 'in Europe's flatland—Germany,' he took his lack of recognition there as further proof, in *Twilight of the Idols*, of why 'increasingly, Germany counts as Europe's flatland.' This was in stark contrast to that lofty peak, '6,000 feet beyond man and time,' where the idea of the Eternal Recurrence had first come to him. In *The Gay Science* he injected a note of compromise in his Manichaean opposition of the lofty and the low:

> *Stay not where the lowlands are!*
> *Climb not into the sky!*
> *The world looks best by far*
> *when viewed from halfway high.*

45.

'The greatest weight.'

The first two days of my visit to Turin in 2013 were rainy—Enrico Rava had played in one of the main squares, on Friday night, in a massive downpour—but Sunday was dry, cloudy, warm. I'd sung for my supper the previous afternoon (in the form of a poorly attended reading) and had the whole day to myself before flying back to London later that evening. Sated with jazz, I walked through the city listening to Gillian Welch's 'Lowlands.' With its deliberately plodding drum beat, 'Lowlands' is a song about depression ('what is this weight on my mind?'), about how, after a point, one can become so accustomed to it as to forget one is depressed, can assume this state to be the normal, unenthusiastic response to and condition of life. And not only that: you can come almost to like it, to take comfort in the dead weight of its familiarity. It's like Nietzsche's time in Rome when, in the spring of 1883, he 'merely put up with life'—in sharp opposition to what a recent biographer calls 'the sunlit uplands of [his] permanently joyful mood' in Turin. Possibilities—escape, romance, new vistas—beckon, but while Lawrence was able to declare ecstatically, 'A fine wind is blowing the new direction of Time,' Welch, perplexed, can ask only, 'What is this new sense of time?' If it's a symptom of depression to blame others for your situation, for things that have gone wrong, then it's a sign of potential recovery when Welch acknowledges that 'it's no one else, no fault but my own.'*

There's no uplift at the end, no surge through to the convalescence celebrated by Nietzsche in *The Gay Science*—'a sudden sense and anticipation of a future'—but it's a song, it's sung by Gillian in always-lovely harmony with Dave Rawlings, so its explicit resignation contains a hypnotic reassurance of receptiveness to beauty and all that implies. The song generates the possibility of leaving the Lowlands behind even while staying in them. I walked through the city and, as can happen when you listen to a song over and over like this, it seemed to describe my state exactly. Except, by virtue of song and setting, it became an elevating experience.

46.

On 23 May 1888 Nietzsche wrote to Brandes, 'Now and again I forget I am alive.'

It seems an extraordinary observation about what is a quite ordi-

---

* This could not be more different to Dylan. A sung love letter from Bob is a notoriously dubious tribute to be in receipt of. However desirable you might be according to the attributes listed in a given song, Dylan will always blame you, even if you're just a friend ('you've got a lot of nerve . . .'), it's *always* your fault, you've betrayed him ('with your touch'), stood there grinning while he was down, held him back, and so on.

nary state of mind: if one of the hallmarks of health is that we become conscious of it only by its lack, when we are sick, so we spend a lot of our lives unconscious of the fact that we are alive. Lawrence was utterly opposed to this. 'The only reason for living,' he insisted, 'is being fully alive.' Lawrence, however sick, remained convinced until the very end of his ability to become healthy again. Nietzsche, in Turin, was conscious of this belief slipping away. 'Not only is health lacking, but also the predisposition to get healthy,' he wrote his friend Overbeck on 4 July 1888. 'The life force is no longer intact.'

47.

I returned to Turin in November 2017. The afternoon light was like nothing I'd ever seen: so fragile and sharp that the buildings became both splendid and insubstantial. Every feature in the perspectival recession of arcades and squares was perfectly defined. (I had come from Los Angeles, not from the cloud-shrouded, tired light of London, so it's not as if I was unused to blue sky.) White in the high distance, the Alps were so clear that better visibility, anywhere on earth, was inconceivable. If ever there was a day when infinity might be measured this was it. The lyrical tends to have a slight quality of halation, a faint hint of reverb. This was different, this was the lyricism of the absolute.

The weather was bad when Nietzsche arrived in Turin in April 1888 but then improved to the extent that he 'never believed a town could become so beautiful through light.' By October there were extended stretches of magnificent weather as 'day after day dawn[ed] with the same boundless perfection and plentitude of sun.' In *Ecce Homo* he likened the city to 'a Claude Lorrain projected into infinity, each day of the same boundless perfection.' It was, as he wrote to a friend, 'a real miracle of beauty and light': the blazing light of unending prospects—in the darkening twilight, the shortening days, of his sanity.

48.

'In the metaphysical streets of the physical town . . .'

I was back in Turin for one night, for another gig of sorts, in July 2019. Because of multiple delays I didn't get to my hotel till after midnight—after the event, after the after-event dinner and after-dinner drinks. I had seen nothing of the city so I left my luggage in my room and headed out again. The city was deserted except for a few other solitaries wandering with the tourist's distinctive and determined purposelessness. As one of these figures and I converged slowly on a water fountain it seemed as if we might both be cruising. There was nothing threatening about this almost-encounter; the presence of the occasional human figure only added to the de Chirico emptiness. I have never had such a strong feeling of walking through an artist's work as I did that night, drifting through the Piazza Vittorio Veneto.

I'd not recognised the de Chirico aspect of Turin before, when the crowds of people prevented it slipping from the real into the oneiric. But that's what it had become: a city shadowed by perspective and dreams. It was as warm as late afternoon, the part of the day often depicted in de Chirico's metaphysical city. 'Part' not 'time' of the day because although the hands of the various clocks point to certain numbers there is no sense that they work, that they are capable of moving round the clock face. How could they when, in the unconscious, there is no time? There are trains—or *a* train, it always looks like the same one—but they don't run on time; they keep it.

In 1910, at the age of twenty-one, de Chirico wrote to a friend, 'I am the only man to have truly understood Nietzsche—all of my work demonstrates this.' The claim to exclusive comprehension is something all readers of Nietzsche will recognise, one of the things we all have in common. If you don't feel this way you haven't experienced Nietzsche at all; you've only studied him.

Piazza Carlo Alberto is depicted in the painting *Turin Spring* (1914), with the horse-and-rider statue looming like an augur of . . . Nietzsche's collapse? Of anything you want it to be an augur of really and, besides, in de Chirico *everything* looms. Perspective seems to loom *towards* as well as receding from you. Instead of converging at a vanishing point there are perpetually uncertain *appearing* points. We are looking but there is an encroaching sense that everything we are seeing is also looking at us. 'Silence and calm reigned supreme,' de Chirico wrote in 1913. 'Everything gazed at me with mysterious, questioning eyes.' He was thinking, in this case, about an afternoon in Versailles but the feeling of reciprocity between seer and seen is a feature of many of the so-called metaphysical paintings. '*One must discover the eye in everything,*' he admonished while also stressing the need to 'see everything, even man, as a *thing*. This is the Nietzschean method.' Maybe it is, but it's a line of Goethe's that best evokes the de Chirico effect of recessive convergence: 'Everything near becomes far'—and vice versa.

You could walk through a de Chirico forever and not get to where you think you might be heading and the chances are that, after walking for hours, you would look around and find that the statue you started out from is only a few yards behind you. The landmarks on which you rely to orient yourself serve to make clear how lost, how thoroughly disoriented, you are, especially since each picture is a glimpse of the world also found in another picture. You could put them all together to form a more or less complete visual map of this nameless city, or a city called 'Enigma.' (De Chirico really over-eggs the enigma pudding; in his writing it's always enigma this, enigma that, enigma the other, and, as a consequence, he drains much of the enigmatic from it.) You would still have no idea of its size because it is possible that all you are seeing are a few basic elements—arcades, squares, arches, statues—viewed from different angles. Whatever the city's size it would be impossible ever to leave. The clock in *The Enigma of the Hour* reads six minutes to three but if you came back an hour later both time and turquoise sky would be the same. That might make you think that perhaps you had been away for an entire day—which in turn would make you uncertain about how far you had walked. Time and space rely on each other—or rather *we* rely on them, cross-referencing one against the other—and in de Chirico this is impossible. Everywhere is always the same and the time is always now.

49.

There is no doubting Nietzsche's influence on de Chirico. The unprecedented importance of his discovery of metaphysical art, 'which in spiritual power and painterly construction surpasses anything as yet attempted in the human arts,' is retrospectively announced in tones that echo those of the creator of Zarathustra. His writing is full of Nietzsche-derived phrases, intuitions, and symbols. The dream-space of his city is full of 'dimensions, lines, and forms of eternity and the infinite.' In his descriptions of places we are encouraged constantly to intuit something like the visual equivalent of the Eternal

Recurrence: 'The arcade is here forever. Shadow from right to left, fresh breeze which causes forgetfulness,' he writes in 'Meditations of a Painter.' 'All the gods are dead.' De Chirico succeeded, absolutely, in expressing something that had become clear to him in Florence in 1910. 'The intense, mysterious feeling [he] had discovered in Nietzsche: the melancholy of lovely autumn afternoons in Italian cities' is plain to see. What I don't really see is any Nietzschean *thought* in the pictures. The fact that Nietzsche's was one of the influences that went into conceiving the paintings doesn't mean any of that is going to come out the other side, as it were, in the finished canvases themselves. (No bad thing, of course.) Even the sense of being lost or stranded in time seems more like a manifestation of the perpetual present—'the present alone is the form of all life'—evoked by Schopenhauer in *The World as Will and Representation*. De Chirico directs us to Nietzsche whose long shadow points to Schopenhauer as educator and influence, a mirror sending us back to where we have come from. The feeling of inescapability might be a symptom of the Eternal Recurrence but apart from that and the way the paintings include numerous architectural features of Turin, Nietzsche is there only as an implied presence. Unless, that is, we see the Eternal Recurrence in a more cynical light.

50.

According to the version of events put forward in a novel, V. S. Naipaul was living in a cottage in Wiltshire when he came across a booklet with very small reproductions of a dozen paintings by de Chirico. With their 'occasional applied touch of easy mystery,' the paintings did not make much of an impression on him but one did snag his attention, 'perhaps because of the title: *The Enigma of Arrival*.' The scene is of a Mediterranean or ancient-Roman wharf; 'in the background, beyond walls and gateways (like cut-outs), there is the top of the mast of an antique vessel; on an otherwise deserted street in the foreground there are two figures, both muffled, one perhaps the person who has arrived, the other perhaps a native of the port. The scene is of desolation and mystery: it speaks of the mystery of arrival.'

The painting gave Naipaul the idea of writing something about this strange and unsettling scene. He envisaged a man arriving at the classical port, walking past the muffled figures, and coming 'to a gateway or door.' Having entered the door he would be swallowed up by the noise and life of a bustling city. Gradually the traveller would feel that he was getting nowhere and would need to escape. At some point he would come to a door, open it, and find himself back at the quay where he had arrived—only to discover that above 'the cut-out walls and buildings there is no mast, no sail. The antique ship has gone. The traveller has lived out his life.'

Naipaul did not write this story, a story that was 'more a mood than a story.' He realised that there were perhaps traces of its concerns—or fears—in *In a Free State*, the book he had been writing 'for eight or nine months' after a 'calamity' befell him when another book he had been working on for two years 'did not please the publisher who had commissioned it.' 'I had finally been undermined,' Naipaul writes. 'My spirit had broken.' No dates are given in this fictive rendering of events but, allowing for a degree of inconsistency, the year is approximately 1970. And then, many years after he had seen the de Chirico picture, 'the idea for the story had come to me, again, in my own life . . . another version of the story of *The Enigma of Arrival*.' It was published with that title and with a detail from the painting on the cover, as 'a novel in five sections'—the quotations above are all from the start of section two, 'The Journey'—in 1987.

51.

De Chirico lived till he was ninety but produced little of value after about 1919. That is a very long time to spend living and working in the wake of the slim period of sustained creativity—less than a decade, from 1910—on which one's reputation rests. Some of that extended aftermath was spent in self-forgery. As early as 1924 he did a 'replica' of *The Disquieting Muses* for Paul Éluard and his wife at less than a third of the price being asked by the owner of the original. That was just for starters. The catalogue of the Museum of Modern Art's 1982 show reviewed by Robert Hughes includes a further *eighteen* knock-offs of *The Disquieting Muses*, 'all done between 1945 and 1962.' According to Hughes, 'Italian art dealers used to say the Maestro's bed was six feet off the ground, to hold all the "early work" he kept "discovering" beneath it.' Various attempts have been made to rehabilitate de Chirico's post-metaphysical work—in the Tate exhibition and book *On Classic Ground*, for example—but, as often happens with such undertakings, the main effect is either to consolidate the consensus they were attempting to undermine or to offer documentary proof that the hitherto shared judgement on the later work was, if anything, over-generous.

52.

So Naipaul's abandoned story or fable—abandoned, it seems, before even being attempted—ends up describing the career of de Chirico quite accurately. He leaves the metaphysical scenes behind, enters the heavily populated world of classical excellence, and then tries—in the form of self-derivation—to return to the metaphysical painting. But the ship has left. Art history has moved on; he can't recapture or renew the strange, stilled energy of those first paintings. He is marooned, left behind. His creative life has passed him by so he spends his time recreating the moment of artistic arrival when he conceived the idea of creating these scenes, simultaneously unable to reconcile himself to the idea that such scenes continue to be viewed as his major achievement—and condemned to duplicating them.

And in this light there is some suggestion of the Eternal Recurrence. The problem is the completeness of de Chirico's early success—not in terms of popularity, prices, or critical acclaim—but the hermetic thoroughness with which he created a world. The ships and trains are both illusory—there is no way of travelling elsewhere—and all too real: permanent fixtures. There's no way out of his paintings; they represent a world that is entirely contained by the frame and that extends well beyond it, to another piazza and, by extension, to the edge of consciousness.

53.

Naipaul came back again and again, in book after book, to the story of how he came from Trinidad to London, from the fringes of empire to its metropolitan centre where, through talent, discipline, and extreme vocational dedication, he was able to become the great writer his father had never managed to be. After a while this, for Naipaul, became the only story, the story that contained all others—including, effectively, the ones he had told in all his novels. In one of these late books, A Writer's People (2007), a rather half-hearted combination of reminiscences and reflections, he tells the story of his friendship with Anthony 'Tony' Powell. Powell had been extremely kind and generous to the young Naipaul. After Powell's death Naipaul was asked to contribute a piece about him to a literary weekly; since he had little knowledge of Powell's books and was too busy to start reading them he had to decline, but 'the idea of writing about Powell attracted me, and I asked the editor to wait a little.' Sometime later he duly settled down to read six consecutive books from the middle of A Dance to the Music of Time. The result? Naipaul was 'appalled.' There is 'no narrative skill,' the 'failure is extraordinary.' Perhaps, he reflects, 'the friendship lasted all this time because I had not examined his work.'*

---

* Powell was famously snooty, turning away a plumber who had the temerity to turn up, one freezing January, to fix a burst pipe at the house of a Mr. Powell, pronouncing it to rhyme with 'towel' rather than 'Lowell.' But with the eternal and unassailable advantage of his Brahmin birthright and superior literary talent Naipaul could out-snoot anybody. Thus he reports that at the ceremony for an honorary degree Powell 'and his wife Violet had taken

54.

About ten years ago (actually, on checking the dates, it turns out to have been fourteen) I abandoned *A Dance to the Music of Time* after volume 5: *Casanova's Chinese Restaurant*. No one could say that, after twelve hundred pages, I hadn't given Powell a chance, though that's effectively what my father-in-law did say. It really gets going in volume 6, he claimed, though I suspect that, had I announced my retirement after *The Kindly Ones* (volume 6) he'd have pointed ahead to volume 7, *The Valley of Bones*. I got the impression that it was going to keep going without ever getting going. Neither witty nor entertaining except in that passing-the-time sort of way that is almost synonymous with wasting time, it seemed entirely devoid of merit. Powell's prose from the outset was on some low-wattage, upper-crust, energy-saving setting, capable of being maintained, with minimum expenditure of effort, over the immense distance of the twelve-volume haul. There was no sense, as there is when climbers set off from base camp, that a steady pace is established because more exertion will be required as the summit is approached, in the thin air of the death zone. This, clearly, was going to be a plod along the flat, with only the slightest inclines. I had no inclination to continue. My only regret, when I gave up on it, was that I had not abandoned it sooner, ideally before I'd even started.

But something—not least the memory of Perry Anderson's epic two-parter on Powell in the *London Review of Books* in 2018, which I'd also abandoned, halfway through the first instalment—made me think that the Covid lockdown might be the perfect opportunity for giving the *Dance* another chance. This meant starting from the beginning since any qualities residing in the remains of the sequence could be properly appreciated only while the resonances of the ear-

---

many photographs. They had especially enjoyed meeting the minor poet Philip Larkin.' *That* is some major snootage.

lier volumes were reasonably fresh in my head. So I set off on the same twelve hundred pages that I had not enjoyed, that had led me to believe that there was no point continuing with the remaining seven volumes, reading again five novels that I wished I hadn't read even once. There was something purposefully pointless about this that chimed perfectly with the larger feeling induced by lockdown.

I gave up again, this time after only three volumes. They seemed, if possible, more thoroughly devoid of merit than they had first time around.

55.

The preceding is not the prelude to a serious critical reappraisal of Powell. But it does introduce a subset of this book's larger theme of quitting: giving up on reading books. I've given up more than once on *The Man Without Qualities*, Proust (one vol. out of seven, twice), *The Brothers Karamazov* (I've just checked: a 2012 receipt from a restaurant in Bologna was preserved between pages 80 and 81; thought I'd done better, more recently than that), *The Ambassadors* (gripped, each time, by the conviction, at once blurry and insistent, that my reading glasses were somehow changing prescription mid-sentence), and most of Faulkner. It seems I read *Light in August* when I was twenty (the annotations prove it) but gave up on re-reading it after fifty pages when I was sixty. *The Sound and the Fury* was an absolute doddle: three pages was enough to persuade me I'd never make it. I believe people who say that *The Sound and the Fury* becomes great when you get to the second part or, ideally, when you read the whole thing for the second time; what you rarely hear is how to get through the first part for the first time. If only I'd read it, *The Man Without Qualities*, and all of Dostoevsky when I was in my early twenties. Strange, the way it was easier to read difficult books when one knew less about books and reading. And what a curious status Dostoevsky has: one of the greatest, everyone agrees, but the best time to read him seems to be when you're in your late teens, while your taste is in the process of being formed—by the experience of reading writers like Dostoevsky. (We talk of growing out of certain writers and books—*The Catcher in the Rye* or *Catch-22*—but perhaps they record, like height marks on the door frame in a childhood home, how far they've helped us grow beyond ourselves.) I've not only taken *The Brothers K* on several trips abroad in the last twenty years, I've made a point of taking no other books as a way of forcing myself to concentrate on this one, but the only thing that tactic obliged me to do was to seek an alternative in the meagre, overpriced English-language section of the nearest book-shop in Bologna. It's looking increasingly likely that I'll go to my grave without ever having had *The Brothers Karamazov* experience.

56.

You would think that works made late in an artist's life would mean more to you as you get older. It seems no bad thing that I started listening seriously to Beethoven's late quartets when I was roughly the age he was when he composed them. Even if they were and will forever be beyond my comprehension musically, I was ready for them in other ways. At twenty-five I didn't even try *The Wings of the Dove* or *The Ambassadors*; I deliberately left late James—let alone what one scholar calls '*late* late James'—for later, and now it's too late.

I look at my shelves, at James and Joyce, at the edition of *Ulysses* that I read as an undergraduate (one of only two oversized Penguin Modern Classics from those days, the other being Camus's *The Rebel*). I could get rid of it—though there's no way I will—as I'm never going to read it again. (*Finnegans Wake*? Never read it and will probably never even *open* that sucker again.) What is the ratio of books that had seemed impregnable when young but that opened up to you later compared with those that you could somehow have got through when young but that become impossible later? About one to five, I suspect. How about books where a delay of however many years improved my responsiveness? I remember a four-year wait between attempting Joseph Brodsky for the first time and completely falling for him but that was from the age of twenty-four to twenty-eight, a period of time that now seems negligible, part of the *same* phase of my reading life.

Something similar happened with Louise Glück: I made only limited progress with *Poems 1962–2012* when it came out but, prompted by her Nobel Prize win, I went back to it and am now within her austerely embodied consciousness, its gaunt sensuality and granite lyricism. The unapproachable intimacy of her work almost insists on some kind of hesitation on the part of the reader as an appropriately faltering response. Holding the book in my hands, I'm reminded of the way my dad would sometimes bring home magnets from work—not the red horseshoe-shaped ones but solid metal blocks. Arranged one way they would jump towards each other and become clamped tight; but if I turned them around the air between them acquired an eerie and invisibly squishy quality, strong enough to prevent my hands from bringing them together. I feel occasional residues of that resistance now, when I am at the mercy of Glück's pages. The reason for this, I think, is because that claim about my being within *her* consciousness puts things the wrong way round. She, of course, is in mine and has been implacably reconfiguring it. That's something that happened so frequently—think back to the huge and subtle effects of reading *Middlemarch* for the first time—in your teens and twenties you were scarcely even aware of it. As you get older it feels not like an upheaval exactly—as it did when I got my first wallop from Nietzsche—but as if something belatedly fundamental is going on. The best way I can describe it is via Cioran's wise observation that the further one advances in life the less there is to convert to. Some writers are so strong, with so distinctive and profound a vision of the world, as to affect you in the psychic space where that urge—to convert—might once have resided. You respond to that power even as you know that conversion would be a regression, a stupid insult to the writer in question.* I had a similar reaction to Rebecca West (*Black Lamb and Grey Falcon*) and (appropriately) Annie Dillard.

And I insist: nothing has really changed in my readerly disposition or overall ability during the eight-year pause between buying and properly reading Glück. Extending the time frame again, I can't think of anything that I am able to read now that I was unable to at thirty except, perhaps, Len Deighton's *Bomber* and that's because I was ready to *lower* my hitherto strict entry requirements (in terms of stylistic and literary merit) rather than because my ability to do any kind of heavy lifting had been raised, thereby enabling me to get to grips with books that had previously been beyond me. There are writers and books that I came to later—almost everything by Jean Rhys and Eve Babitz; Mavis Gallant's stories; several novels by the undervalued Elizabeths, Bowen and Taylor; Larry McMurtry's *Lonesome Dove*; James Jones's *The Thin Red Line* (to see how it compared with Terrence Malick's film)—but I would have enjoyed these at whatever age I'd encountered them. Surely there's some example of how, some *way* in which, my readerly strength has increased? There's Shirley Hazzard's *The Transit of Venus* but, looking inside, I see that the twenty-plus-year hiatus between my first feeble attempt and realising that I was reading a masterpiece extended from the early 1980s to 2004, too early to be assigned to a phase or syllabus of late reading. (Though I did just read it for the third time, almost shaking because of the power coursing through every page, every paragraph.) I'm looking along my shelves again. *Son of the Morning Star*, Evan S. Connell's book about Custer? There was a thirty-year gap between being sent the paperback and reading it but I would have loved it if I'd got going as soon as it arrived in the post— wish I had done, actually, since the print is so tiny . . . The only possible candidate is Ivy Compton-Burnett, whom I might have struggled to make sense of when I was young, but I suspect that I'd have been

---

* To his credit, Lawrence, who attracted admirers like a magnet, tended to fall out with people as soon as he detected any whiff of the convert about them.

lured in by the pathological comedy. She's a scream, as they say, but you never know with comedy; I mean you always know when it works but you never know *what* will work. Seriously, do Powell fans laugh during scenes like the one where Widmerpool gets sugar poured over his head at whichever party it is in whichever volume it is, or is *recognising* that it's a comic scene reward enough? Seeing that something is meant to be funny while having no urge to laugh is a recipe for misery. Compton-Burnett's novels are like those of P. G. Wodehouse, with Jeeves and Wooster stranded at the precise moment, in Gaspar Noé's film *Climax*, when the cast begin to notice that the punch has been spiked. Since this dread realisation can be expressed only within the clipped register of class and period a repressed mania holds way. I say this with a conspicuous lack of authority because it was only recently that I got round to trying an actual Wodehouse. I was looking forward to having a good old chortle, but after a hundred pages hadn't chortled once. Feeling this readiness to chortle starting to turn into a reluctance to chortle, hardening into chortle-resistance, I gave up and—sticking with the *W*s—re-read some Joy Williams stories instead. If you don't find her funny then there's no point even *having* a sense of humour. A philosophical system built out of her work would completely remake the world, but that world would be exactly how it was—hilarious, awful, wonderful—before the makeover.

In 'Train,' Danica, a young girl, asks the father of her friend if she and Jane will be friends forever. They are sitting in the empty Starlight Lounge of a train heading to Florida from Washington. It's late. Drinks are no longer being served but Mr. Muirhead is nursing a last Bloody Mary. He replies, 'Definitely not. Jane will not have friends. Jane will have husbands, enemies and lawyers . . . I'm glad you enjoyed your summer, Dan, and I hope you're enjoying your childhood. When you grow up, a shadow falls. Everything's sunny and then this big goddamn *wing* or something passes overhead.' This is not the answer Dan was expecting but she accepts it with a simple 'Oh.'

Crammed near to Williams is Edith Wharton, whom I'm glad I didn't read when I was young (when I undoubtedly had the capacity to do so) because of the bliss of doing so at sixty when, partly because of that wing or whatever it is, such pleasures are less frequent.

57.

Although I might have been *capable* of reading certain kinds of books when I was younger the fact is that I didn't—because I was too busy reading fiction. And while you write the kind of books you want to read this doesn't mean that you read the kind of books you write. More often you read the kind of books you're incapable of writing, whoppers like *The Power Broker*, Robert Caro's twelve-hundred-page biography of Robert Moses; Richard Rhodes's *The Making of the Atomic Bomb* (weighing in at close to a thousand pages); Brenda Wineapple's *Ecstatic Nation*; Henry Mayer's biography of William Lloyd Garrison, *All on Fire*; Jill Lepore's *These Truths* . . . It's always time well spent, reading whoppers like these. You learn so much. The problem is how little of that 'much' is retained after finishing them. 'Little' is sometimes a euphemism for 'nothing.' What I do remember, quite clearly, is blahing on to a friend about Tony Judt's *Postwar* only to falter, mid-pitch, because I couldn't remember whether it was a whopping great history of the world since the Second World War (I did at least get the war right) or just of Europe. Yes, yes, it's Europe, I remember now. And I remember why I had trouble remembering. I'd read Ramachandra Guha's history of *India After Gandhi* right after the Judt so Europe got briefly muddled up with India and out of this confusion emerged a mental alliance that came to embrace the entire post-war world.

I also remember what a slog it was getting through *Postwar*, but even though I remember few details of that slog I definitely feel, in some way, that I know more (about Europe or whatever) than I did before I slogged through it—it's just that in order to convey this knowledge I'd have to slog through it again. Or through more books covering the same period or the period leading up to it (Ian Kershaw's *To Hell and Back*, say, which I *have* read). That's the other thing about the process of knowledge absorption as you get older. You can't get it all on one plate, in a single helping. You have to read about the same events, slog through the same subjects, in multiple whoppers, so that Mayer's account of Garrison is qualified and shaded by David W. Blight's recent life of Frederick Douglass. It's not only that one account of India's campaign for independence will stress the intransigence of Gandhi and another his inspirational importance, that one book bunks where another debunks and a third rebunks. Knowledge has to be laid down in the brain in overlapping and criss-crossed layers. You need the underlay before you can have the carpet and then—then you can abandon the analogy because it's completely unsustainable. Everything has gradually to become a kind of sediment in the brain, its ocean floor—a place so dark and mysterious that the fish aren't even really fish, just creatures without eyes or brains, flattened by the dead weight of water-knowledge pressing down on them.

58.

One of the signs that Nietzsche's marbles were starting to roll in Turin was the belief that as soon as he wished for something that wish would be granted. On the basis that he need only think of a person for a letter from them to arrive 'politely through the door,' he came to believe that 'there are no coincidences any more.' While troubling, this was an extension of his creed of *amor fati* whereby, as he wrote in *Zarathustra*, every 'so it was' is turned into 'thus I wanted it.'

Towards the end of *The Colossus of Maroussi* Henry Miller is taken to a soothsayer in Athens who tells him that he has a great destiny in store. This comes as no surprise to Miller but he is startled by the soothsayer's ability to have foreseen it. Back in America, writing about the encounter a year later, he is conscious both of the dangers that lie ahead and of how everything has fallen into place: 'one fulfilment, one realization after another, has occurred with an almost clock-like precision. Indeed, I am almost terrified for now, contrary to my life in the past, I have but to desire a thing and my wishes are gratified.' It is an extraordinarily precise and entirely appropriate echo of Nietzsche.*

If Nietzsche demonstrated the potential for delusion in such an exalted state Miller's power to have the world conform to his desires makes him circumspect to the point of caution or inhibition. 'I am in the delicate position of one who has to be careful not to wish for something he really does not desire.' (This might be a misapprehension on Miller's part; one of the lessons of the Room in Andrei Tarkovsky's *Stalker* is that it's not what you think is your deepest wish that comes true; your deepest wish is *revealed*.)

As Miller muses on the soothsayer's findings he mentions that he had hinted to a few friends in Paris that he 'would one day give up writing altogether, give it up voluntarily—at the moment when I would feel myself in possession of the greatest power and mastery.' Those same friends doubted this but Miller was convinced that he would 'pass from art to life.' 'To continue writing beyond the point of self-realization seems futile and arresting. The mastery of any form of expression should lead inevitably to the final expression—mastery of life.'

Well, good for him. I wouldn't have minded if he'd given up earlier, partly because I left it so late to start reading him (having been persuasively urged against doing so by Kate Millett in *Sexual Politics*). Trying to read Miller for the first time at sixty is like taking up squash. I should have started earlier, when I might have been susceptible to what he was up to and before the liberties he took with the novel form became universally available. But even that might not have been early enough; maybe I needed to have read him an entire generation or two earlier.

Right after *Maroussi* I gave up on *Tropic of Cancer* after fifty pages,

* Although I didn't know about the extent of Miller's knowledge of Nietzsche when I read *Maroussi* I guessed that he must, at some point, have been drenched in him. Then I looked up the numerous books he'd written later in life, including *The Books in My Life*, published when he was the age I am now. I have it here on my desk. At the end is a list of one hundred books. Nietzsche is one of a dozen or so authors identified not with a particular title but for 'his works in general.'

which meant there was no chance of even starting on *Capricorn*. This in spite of the fact that the *Tropic* books had been reissued as Penguin Modern Classics—with nude drawings by Tracey Emin on the covers—and the times are ripe for a Miller revival given the current vogue for autofiction. The lasting value of *Tropic of Cancer* probably resides in the lines from an 1841 entry in Emerson's journal—occasioned by reading a disappointing novel—that provided Miller with his epigraph:

These novels will give way, by and by, to diaries or autobiographies—captivating books, if only a man knew how to choose among what he calls his experiences that which is really his experience, and how to record truth truly.

59.

Changes in taste—what one ends up liking or disliking—are not arbitrary; the general trend of personal aversions and affections tends to conform to broader demographic norms, even if particular instances are not shared. The signposts vary but the overall direction is the same. For a man of my age this means a reluctance to stray far from the military history section of bookshops, with an ever tightening focus on the Second World War. I'm conscious also of a steadily increasing aversion to a certain *tone*. After re-reading *The Portrait of a Lady*, I thought I'd take a look again at Cynthia Ozick's essay collection *What Henry James Knew* and identified almost immediately with what she was saying—identified with and felt proud to be part of 'times and habits far less elevated in their literary motives (and motifs) than [James's] own.' Maybe Ozick had interesting things to say about James but that high-minded tone meant that I'd never find out what they were. Something similar happened, albeit more gradually, over the course of Czeslaw Milosz's essay collection *To Begin Where I Am*. When you go to a lecture you sit and listen while someone holds forth and it's fine if they do so from on high. But the moment anyone steps away from the lectern and off the podium the default rules of speech are reasserted. No one wants to be lectured at once a lecture is over. In Milosz's case he sort of *converses* with the reader from on high, as if that's where he habitually dwelt. It's not even self-regarding; it's more a well-marinaded assumption of the high regard in which he is held. Fair enough, you might say, the guy won the Nobel Prize. How could I forget, given that he mentions it so often? *Not* in a boastful way, of course, but the thoughts, reflections, and meditations end up being instinctively expressed in what Martin Amis (writing about José Saramago) called 'Nobelese.' It's what happens when high-mindedness becomes second nature, as if you don't just make yourself a cup of tea in the morning, you make yourself a cup of Nobel tea to have with your Nobel eggs and rashers of Nobel bacon.

In his book *Slight Exaggeration* Adam Zagajewski recounts a time in the late 1990s when Milosz called him on the phone and, in a voice filled with 'deep melancholy,' said, 'please tell me honestly, have I ever in my life written a single good poem?' If this conversation had taken place in person, over beers, rather than over the phone, and if the two writers had been English, Adam, face as straight as a ruler, would surely have replied, 'Well, now that I think of it, Chezza, I don't think you have.' And that would have cheered up his pal immediately.

Not that anyone should live without the sympathetic encouragement of friends. In 1979, after receiving a letter in which Larkin asked, 'Do you think I'm going batty?' Martin's dad, Kingsley, replied promptly: 'You'll never go mad.' But I suspect Larkin would have been still more cheered by a letter he received from his old friend a few years later, in 1982, congratulating him about a 'not v. good' TV programme that he'd been featured in: 'Made people like Ted Hughes and Peter Porter and John Ashbery look like cunts.'

The pleasure afforded by this passage is in sharp contrast to how I felt after reading about another writer, French, being filmed for a TV programme. The cameraman happened to be called Albert so when the director of the show unceremoniously called out 'Albert, go that way, hurry up,' the still-young Nobel laureate was quick to demand respect: 'C'est Monsieur Camus, s'il vous plaît!' How devastating to learn that Camus became *grand*, possibly the single most repulsive characteristic—inevitably abetted by humourlessness—this side of tendencies that may be subject to criminal prosecution. Better to be pompous than grand; the former at least has a redeeming suggestion of the ridiculous and, since the intended self-inflation is always perceived as auto-deflating, is fundamentally a comic quality. (I might have backed myself into an unexpected logical corner where, by virtue of the comic safety valve supplied by pomposity, someone who is both grand *and* pompous—the two are natural bed-mates, after all—is preferable to someone who is simply grand. Hmmm. The thing about 'grand' is that it comes in a surprising variety of shapes, sizes, and modes, some of them not immediately recognisable as such, and can thrive in unexpected conjunction with other unlikely characteristics. I can think, but prefer not to, of writers who are grand *and* chippy.) If the tradition of becoming grand is something that unites the republic of France with *le Royaume-Uni*—in England you can occasionally become aware of someone biding their time, testing the waters to see if the moment of potential investiture has come, when they can get away with it—then one of the joys of America is that, like polio, this scourge has been effectively eradicated. Strangely, what is objectionable as a character trait can become an appealing feature of prose. Someone who had met the ageing Rebecca West told me she was 'rather grand,' which sounds entirely plausible since there is an intimate, endearing grandeur to the prose of *Black Lamb and Grey Falcon* that is appropriate to the immensity of the undertaking. Might women be less prone to a touch of the grands than their male counterparts? One hopes so even in the face of direct evidence to the contrary (Naomi Wolf threatening to storm out of an interview on *Newsnight* because Brigitte Berman had the temerity to *disagree* with her) and its capacity to mutate so that there are recorded sightings of what might be termed daffy-old-bird grand. Still, the following observation/advice is made with the boys in mind.

After a stage in a man's life—especially if a degree of eminence has been achieved—it is essential that he retain some residue of how he saw the world as a fourteen-year-old.* Camus retained within him the 'unconquerable summer' of his childhood in Algiers but I have in mind something distinctly English (and less serious than Harold Wilson's famous joke that, politically, Tony Benn had immatured with age), something along the lines of Larkin's explanation to Amis, in 1981, of the kind of mail he received now that his reputation as a poet was attracting students to Hull: "'Dear Dr. Larkin, My freind [sic] and I had an argument as to which of us has the biggest breasts and we wondered if you would act as—'"

All accounts stress the awfulness of Larkin's later life. Well, it was wretched by anyone's standards, but even Amis junior seems to underestimate the chthonic depths of humour in Larkin—which is surprising, given his consciousness, in Time's Arrow, of 'the mortal hilarity that sniggers behind everything we do.' (There are dying echoes here, textual and contextual, of the siren call of Larkin's 'Ambulances': 'the solving emptiness / That lies just under all we do.') Larkin's life was so miserable as to be a complete joke (a 'farce,' as he termed it) and therefore a self-contained source of both dejection and consolation. Unlike Naipaul, Zagajewski recognises Larkin as 'a genuinely great poet' but he is wrong to regard him as a 'cynical' one, even bearing in mind the additional and ostensibly supporting evidence of the correspondence in which the dismal farce is scripted and enacted. No book makes me laugh more than Larkin's Selected Letters. It's not simply the gags, classic though many of them are: 'I am having an ineffectual economy drive. It consists of not buying other people

---

* Like I say, I had the boys in mind but when I think of my sweet-natured mother-in-law who is eighty it's so easy, still, to picture her as a giggly thirteen-year-old growing up in Arkansas. So a version of the same point applies. And there is a negative—and no less endearing—manifestation of the same condition in Vivian Gornick, who recounts, with relish, a psychic injury her mother inflicted on her when she was eight. In The Odd Woman and the City, a memoir published when she was just shy of her eightieth birthday, Gornick writes that she 'grieved over [this] incident for fifty years.' (And came back to it again, five years later, in the aptly named Unfinished Business!) The opposite of grand, Gornick's view of the world—her tonal relation to it—is determinedly from street level. That and a constant, self-replenishing sense of grievance—injustice if you want to give it ideological heft—helped keep her sprightly.

drinks.' And remember, always: a sense of humour is about so much more than being funny; it's an entire relation to—and a view of—the world: 'Yours is the harder course, I can see,' he wrote to Judy Egerton in the lead-up to a typically desultory Christmas in 1958. 'On the other hand, mine is happening to me.' It came to him early, this irrefutable philosophical position, but maybe it always does. You can cultivate a sense of humour insofar as you can learn to laugh, in public at least, at the right times (usually after a telltale delay while the dull brain grinds through the process of pattern recognition: 'Ah, I see, a joke was being made') but if you haven't got one by adolescence then you're not going to acquire one in the way that you might diligently go about developing abs of steel. (Larkin, naturally, ended up with a belly that looked 'like something inflated with a bicycle-pump.') Equally, it's not something you ever lose, like the ability to ride a bike or, as Larkin put it, 'like the Cheshire cat, of which, as you will remember, the last thing to go was the smile.'

During the various lockdowns, as more time was spent communicating with friends via text or email, something entirely unprecedented occurred. From time to time we found ourselves asking, 'Is that a joke?' or having to clarify—'I was joking!'—in a way that had never been necessary, even with the most deadpan delivery, in face-to-face life. This extraordinary ability of email and text to filter out jokes offered a vision of how boring it must be, the hellish (and easily offended) life of the humourless.

60.

Wouldn't it be marvelous if it were possible to be a serious writer without taking oneself at all seriously? Not just *socially*, that's easy (even if some not very serious writers find it impossible, an affront); I mean while actually doing the work.

I think there's a tendency to write
jottings about one's own psyche,
and call it a novel. My book,
though . . .

—Shirley Hazzard

01.

Right after my own breakfast today—a not ignoble soft scramble—in the course of looking up something in Michael Ondaatje's *The English Patient*, I came across the titular patient's notebook entries about winds:

> There is a whirlwind in southern Morocco, the *aajej*, against which the fellahin defend themselves with knives. There is the *africo*, which has at times reached into the city of Rome. The *alm*, a fall wind out of Yugoslavia. The *arifi*, also christened *aref* or *rifi*, which scorches with numerous tongues. These are permanent winds that live in the present tense.
>
> There are other, less constant winds that change direction, that can knock down horse and rider and realign themselves anticlockwise. The *bist roz* leaps into Afghanistan for 170 days—burying villages.

Literature is not a packed nightclub operating a one-in, one-out door policy but I am conscious that a VIP like this (with the *P* standing for 'passage'), while scoring well on a Beaufort scale of quality, no longer commands the easy admission to my affections that it once did. It's been bounced to the margins of my tonal receptiveness by Eve Babitz, who knows the winds of Southern California 'the way Eskimos know their snows.' In 'Sirocco' she remembers one particular night 'when the Santa Anas were blowing so hard that searchlights were the only things in the sky that were straight.' That is superb, but it's not in Babitz's nature to make a *writerly* meal out of a wind, or of anything else for that matter, except gossipy lunches at the Chateau Marmont.

Joan Didion, having sketched the physical and psychic toll taken by the Santa Anas—'drying the hills and the nerves to the flash point'—in her 'Los Angeles Notebook,' has, as we would expect, to 'lie down.' As flexible as Didion is brittle, Babitz, ten years later, is breezily intoxicated: 'The confusion, the roly-poly of the winds made me hilarious. Nothing can keep me sober when everything is flapping around for dear life.'

Lawrence, in a letter from January 1929, jotted down a pre-emptive, impatient, and very English counter to the English patient's seductive taxonomy: 'The mistral is an even nastier wind than the tramontana or the maestrale, which is saying a lot. We've all more or less got chesty colds from it.'

Whatever else one might object to in Lawrence—and there's a lot—he is *never* precious. If preciousness is something to which I have become increasingly allergic then Babitz (who, throughout her writing life, remained in the closest possible touch with her fifteen-year-old self, and who, as a feminist, believed that 'deep down inside every woman is a waitress') offers a universal antidote: 'Janet and Shawn too were nice but I thought that of all the days in my life that were rotten, this one in Palm Springs was probably going to be the worst. In a frivolous kind of way, of course.' Nietzsche, with his life-altering insight that earnestness is the sure sign of a slow mind, would surely have fallen in love with Babitz (who greeted with derision the Dionysian 'hogwash' spouted by her one-time lover Jim Morrison).

02.

The problem of preciousness is especially acute in certain strains of nature writing where it can often be spotted, wandering around hand in hand with earnest *meditations* on this uniquely wonderful—uniquely precious—planet of ours: 'a wet ball flung across nowhere,' in Dillard's hard-to-beat phrase. I want to look after this wet ball and keep it spinning through space to the best of its abilities for as long as possible, but the effect of reading prose-prayers to the natural world—either because it's been maimed by us or, conversely, because it has the capacity to heal us—served up by a writer like Terry Tempest Williams is to make me cherish my inner yob, to nudge me towards a radical Trump-ist position whereby we should at least be open to seeing if it might make sense, economically, to auction off the Grand Canyon to a conglomerate specialising in golf courses and strip mining.* If the intention of writing like Williams's is to help us move up to a higher level of appreciation and oneness with the universe then that intention is better served—negatively—by the crudest rap.

03.

'Now: let us raise the fucking tone.'

The courts where I play tennis, by the microplastic-threatened ocean in Santa Monica, are next to a public basketball court. I really like the scene there, like cycling past it, I mean, though what I like even more is knowing that one of tennis courts one through five is available so we won't end up on court six, right next to the basketball. The basketball court is properly democratised to the extent that it looks like the exercise yard of a zero-security prison where racial loyalties have been entirely dissolved and marijuana recognised as an effective way of reducing tensions. It's all tattoos, armpits, weed smoke, and shouting over a soundtrack provided by rap on a boom box or whatever they're called these days. So the occasional arguments and constant shouts are underwritten by a soundtrack of heavy beats, mothafuckah this, and bitch that. The music has an urban power, which I like even though it sometimes means it's difficult to concentrate on playing

---

* I'm tempted to spread the blanket to cover *any* prayers. I've not read as many as Don Paterson, who took the trouble of wading through an entire anthology of them. In the process of confirming a prejudice of his own he also confirmed one of mine: 'prayer really is the lowest form of literature.'

tennis, and when I say urban I don't mean 'Black,' I mean *urban* because that quality is even more striking given that, a hundred yards away, there is the pristine blue and pounding breakbeat of the Pacific. I know there are multiple strands of rap, but the version favoured here is not conducive to the development of fine feelings, of the ability to discern more finely, or indeed to any notion of refinement. It's a constant, unsubtle inducement to crudity of relations with—and responses to—the world. Back in the 1950s people voiced similar fears about the musical gyrations of Elvis Presley, which now sound rather quaint, so it's possible, I suppose, that *this* music will one day lose its insistently brutalising character—if the world, in that time, has become even more brutalising and horrible, which it may well do if this music has its sway. Theodor Adorno, in his *Introduction to the Sociology of Music*, writes that chamber music 'practices courtesy.' That's nice in itself but, being Adorno, he goes further and says that 'the social virtue of politeness helped to bring about that spiritualization of music which occurred in chamber music and presumably nowhere else.' (Adorno was apparently oblivious to Indian classical music.) So: courtesy, politeness, and spiritualization. It's inconceivable that the music pumping away at the basketball court leads to this trinity of qualities. And not only that. Listening to this music eats away at the powers of concentration necessary to appreciate Puccini (whom I've never really listened to) or to read the late novels of Henry James. Might the habits of mind of basketball and tennis players alike be elevated by recordings of *Tosser*, or a setting to music of *The Golden Ball*?

04.

For all I know this implausible change of musical policy has been successfully implemented—I've not been near the courts because of the latest in a series of creeping career-ending injuries. Ailments and injuries might well be the physical equivalent of dreams: endlessly fascinating to the person experiencing them, torpor-inducing to anyone expected to endure listening to or reading about them. Context is all. Few things make for more gripping reading than Joe Simpson overcoming a mountain of injuries in *Touching the Void*. But what about aches and pains, ice packs and ibuprofen, and desperate visits to the Lourdes of chiropracty? This book must not be allowed to become an injury diary or sprain journal, but the truth is that with my hip flexor proving stubbornly physio-resistant, I made an appointment with a highly recommended and correspondingly highly priced Chinese doctor. He spoke no English so we embarked on a slightly cumbersome procedure whereby I communicated my problems to an assistant who then translated this information for the doctor—in another room—whose verdict would then be relayed back to me by a reversal of the same method. The assistant was a fit-looking guy of about thirty to whom I presented a list of ailments and aches before presenting a more rounded assessment of my condition.

'Let's suppose that, in addition to the two of us sitting here there was an eighty-year-old man shuffling slowly around the room. If I'd seen you six weeks ago and you had asked me with whom I most identified . . .'(For some reason the knowledge that he was the translator generated an urge to speak an English that was, in the circumstances, not only superfluous but quite preposterous.) 'Given this choice, either you or that old man, I would not have hesitated. "You," I would have said. Now I am not sure.'

Being young, the awful pathos of this was lost on him, but not on me. I felt an immense welling-up of self-pity that was also a form of inverted self-aggrandisement, a declaration of infirmity as strength that was not devoid of abject pride.

To my surprise the Chinese doctor, looking kind, wise, old, and fit (a by no means poor advert for the efficacy of his own services), returned without the assistant and indicated that I should lie on the table, on my back. I kept my eyes closed as he stuck needles in various places in both legs. Then he left me lying there. The insertion of needles had barely hurt at all but I became conscious of an extraordinary feeling of heat spreading out through the gates and alleys, the ley lines of the body. When I opened my eyes I saw that it was because a heat-lamp was toasting both knees.

After half an hour the doctor came back and pulled out the needles. I sat up and moved to a chair, as did the doctor who waited patiently and benignly while his verdict and prognosis were rendered into English by the assistant. The news was good, he said. The doctor could treat me. This treatment, in addition to fourteen sessions of acupuncture, would involve eating beef tendons, tuna, and barley soup in the morning. I also had to drink some tea that came in a gallon container costing seventy-five bucks and take dozens of pills that looked like ball bearings, the first pot of which was to be given free as part of an introductory offer. While the good doctor's words were being conveyed I was busy calculating the total cost of this deluxe healing package, which, as far as I could tell, would come to just south of three grand. I left with my free pills and my gallon container of murky-looking tea, and didn't go back again.

The hip flexor remained an issue even after I started playing again, before eventually curing itself courtesy of lockdown-induced rest, which, somewhat like the Treaty of Versailles, kicked the can down the road and created the conditions for the host of other problems arising from my return to action months later.

05.

That hip flexor became a problem because I kept playing when I should have stopped, when the pain was mild. Quitting like that actually requires the self-discipline normally associated with persistence, with continuing to slog away at a book you're reading without pleasure. Playing through the pain is invariably a recipe for further, more painful pain—but how about *reading* through the pain? As the exchange with my father-in-law about *A Dance to the Music of Time* suggests, it's always possible that you've made a mistake, that you've quit too soon, that if you'd kept going for one more page you might have turned a corner and found yourself not only enthralled but immersed in a work that is suddenly revealed to be of high literary quality. That's why, having decided to bail out, you tend to give the book another couple of pages to redeem itself—or for you to redeem yourself.

The parachuting metaphor makes me think of stories from the Second World War when a pilot selflessly tells the rest of the crew to jump while he holds the flak-ravaged Lancaster as steady as possible—and then somehow succeeds, in spite of leaking fuel and the loss of two engines, in nursing it back to an airfield in Lincolnshire. The reader who has jumped winds up either dead (pitchforked by incensed farmers) or languishing in a German POW camp for the rest of the war, nursing two broken legs, with nothing to alleviate the pain except *Biggles in the Baltic*. A postcard eventually arrives from Blighty telling the story of what happened to the doomed plane that turned out not to be doomed, the so-so novel about a bombing raid over Germany that turned into 'a rattling good yarn and a powerful condemnation of the senseless violence of war.' The injured prisoner shifts uncomfortably on his bunk: 'If only I'd stuck with it.'

Often you fail to stick with it because of a lack of readerly stamina rather than a lack of strength on the part of the writer, but it's always tempting to convert the former into the latter. What is widely held to be a great book doesn't mean it will be experienced as such by you—and the failing may well be yours alone. But just because something's a classic doesn't mean it's any good. Status is not a guarantee of quality. My Penguin Modern Classics edition of a certain book quotes Walter Allen's opinion that 'a good case could be made out for considering it the greatest novel in English of this [the twentieth] century.' Since that's an experience no one in their right mind would want to miss out on I will milk the suspense no longer: it's *Nostromo*, a book I waded through forty years ago, when I had the stamina of a youthful ox and the dumb faith of a bespectacled lamb, a book that has stayed with me because nothing I have read since has been quite as boring as *Nos*-frigging-*tromo*. That's not true, obviously, but the horror, the horror of trudging through *Nostromo* is something not easily forgotten. I've got my copy here—the cover showing a close-up of the face of a dark-eyed 'Zapata' by Alfredo Zalce—and can feel the remembered dread emanating from its pages, over every one of which my eyes dutifully grazed.

06.

Football fans sometimes leave the stadium early, either to beat the crowds or when it's obvious that their side is on the wrong end of a caning. But there *is* always a chance of things being turned around in the dying seconds. Manchester United's 2–1 victory over Bayern Munich in the 1999 European Champions League final, when Bayern's ribbons were being tied to the trophy, is the most spectacular instance. Are there comparable examples of films or books, of persistently poor quality, suddenly turning themselves around—by which I really mean turning around the reader's judgement—in the last minute or on the last page? Is such belated critical redemption even possible? (William Golding's *Pincher Martin* has the most dramatic last-line reversal but it is entirely gripping from the first page.) I thought of *Nostromo*, thirty-four years ago, during the first two hundred pages of a book I was constantly on the brink of abandoning. I was in the market, back then, only for literary experiences and this book read like a thriller, an indifferently written thriller, a thriller indifferent to the idea of literariness that, a full six years after leaving Oxford, still defined my notions of what was and was not worth reading. The setting was pure Conrad, pure *Nostromo*, 'an imaginary Central American Republic called Tecan,' according to the *Evening Standard*, 'a country in the grip of a right-wing dictatorship.' I can't remember what kept me reading; what I do remember is that quite suddenly, when one of the main characters goes scuba diving in chapter 15, halfway through my distinctly unattractive Picador paperback, two things changed. First, I realised that I was reading a great book; second, that my ideas of what greatness might look like—might read like—had been fundamentally reconfigured. Great literature didn't always read like . . . literature. The book was *A Flag for Sunrise* by Robert Stone and I was gratified, a few years later when, in a little Q and A, Salman Rushdie said that he'd had an almost identical reversal of opinion while reading it. I always think of *A Flag for Sunrise* when I'm about to give up on a book; it's kept me going through many a bad passage (one of Stone's characters quotes Nietzsche's famous line about suicide getting him through bad nights) in many novels but I've never enjoyed a more dramatic mid-stream conversion.

When I re-read it in 2013 the literary merit of *A Flag for Sunrise* was evident early on—its apparent shortcomings had been mine—but it stands for the possibility of any book becoming unexpectedly excellent after the point at which one might have expected to jump ship.

07.

With books you can *usually* tell after a couple of chapters if something is terrible. But what about films? How long does it take for a film's lack of quality to become apparent? About thirty seconds, sometimes less. The opening shot can be enough but typically you need two or three edits to discern the lack of any hope of rhythm, to perceive that the director's 'vision'—if one can dignify it with that word—has been entirely determined by, and possibly even aspires to, cliché. I have a special fondness for those occasions when the silent kettledrum of the opening claim—'A film by X'—intended to announce the start of the latest work by a self-identified *auteur*, has torn itself to pieces by the time the credit sequence has unfolded. In books there is always the possibility of later transformation. Film is an unforgiving medium. There is not even the possibility of redemption after the first botched minutes. Perhaps that's one of the reasons why redemption is such a stalwart of cinematic plot and theme.

The reverse situation, of books or films falling apart in the final stages, is all too common. In action thrillers a massive deterioration in the final ten minutes—when the bullets are flying and the bodies falling—is almost a convention of the genre. An assumed escalation of excitement manifests itself as the exact opposite: a steady slackening of interest as the violence, killings, and explosions proceed to an increasingly tedious denouement.

And what of those movies that have come to an end but then keep going, on and on, so that the poor viewer is like an exhausted hiker confronted with one crest of hills giving way to another and another? The most ludicrous manifestations of this are films in which the villain or monster, having been finished off, somehow recovers from mortal injuries—De Niro's Max Cady, that tattooed Lazarus, in Scorsese's 1991 remake of *Cape Fear*—to return for a final assault on the life of the hero and the patience of the viewer.

Even more insidious than instances like these, where plot and action having been completed to everyone's satisfaction are extended by gratuitous resurrection, are those films, typically less plot-driven, in which the camera movement—pulling back so that the specific human drama (in which we lost interest a while back) is seen to shrink within the wide-screen context of the landscape at large: a view of road, hill, forest, or prairie that gradually fills the screen—lulls the viewer into thinking that things are coming to an end, that the credits are about to roll, that the cinema is about to be exited and a bar soon to be entered, only to find that, as with Haydn's Joke Quartet (op. 33, no. 2), this expectation has been deliberately raised in order to be thwarted, that the end is merely a slight pause, a turning of the cinematic page introducing another chapter that makes the induced thirst rage more furiously.

08.

To reprise the claim of Boyle's narrator in *Budding Prospects*, I've always been a leaver and walker-outer of films. Some people prefer to see things through to the end. You've paid so you might as well get your money's worth. It requires a small effort of will to get up, to disrupt and irritate people sitting in the same row. The slight discourtesy of this—groping and shuffling past, treading on a foot, or becoming entangled in the strap of a handbag—is appropriate since you are effectively breaking the contract that was tacitly signed when the ticket was bought. The assumption of everyone involved in the film's creation is that once you're in you're in and will stay the course.

It's a very different situation with TV series. You're free to stop at any time, mid-episode, mid-season, or at the end of the first, second, or third season. Hence the feeling that so much of the ingenuity and intelligence of writers and directors—to say nothing of the technology that means the next episode will automatically start before you've had a chance to locate the remote—is designed to keep you bingeing. As soon as I became conscious of this, after two episodes of the first season of *Homeland*, I stopped watching, but it's not always as easy as it seems. After sitting through the whole of *The Undoing*, starring Nicole Kidman and Hugh Grant, I felt I'd been fleeced. Actually, it was even worse than that; I *knew* I was being groomed and played halfway through but went along willingly with the unforced abduction of time and brain. Even with the best series you buy into the convention that nothing has consequences so drastic that they can't be undone after a couple of episodes or the start of another season. Wonderful though *Succession* is, it doesn't matter which of Brian Cox's leery and pampered offspring are in or out of favour at any given climax since further permutations of bestowal and banishment are bound to follow. In keeping with the precedent of Arthur Conan Doyle and Sherlock Holmes at the Reichenbach Falls, the certain death of Malotru (drugged and unconscious in a blazing building in Ukraine) at the end of season four of *Le Bureau* is only a prelude to his resurrection and relocation in season five. Every end, to paraphrase T. S. Eliot in the last episode of the final season of *Four Quartets*, is a new beginning.

09.

At any poetry reading, however enjoyable, the words we most look forward to hearing are always the same: 'I'll read two more poems.' (The words we truly long for are 'I'll read *one* more poem' but two seems to be the conventionally agreed minimum.) It's lovely hearing this. You can feel a sigh of relief passing through the audience, especially if the previous couple of poems have been precedent-setting sonnets clocking in at under a minute each. After long months in the sea of poetry the shout has gone up from the crow's nest: 'Land!' We're almost there, we've made it, can practically taste the scurvy-healing lager being poured in a bar afterwards. But then these two last poems turn out to be the opposite of the sonnets that had served as a double false dawn before the concluding multipart epics, the felt duration of each is twice as long as *The Ring and the Book*.

Which raises a question: why did we come if, while being here, we would end up being so preoccupied by no longer being there? Could it be that our deepest desire is for everything to be over with? We want encores—value for money, bang for our buck—but however vigorously we've been clapping and clamouring for more there is invariably a sense of relief when it becomes clear that the band, despite our collective imploring, are *not* coming back, that the house lights have flicked on (bringing the last residue of applause to an immediate, slightly impolite halt), and that we can apply ourselves single-mindedly to getting a good place in the stampede for the exits.

'Beneath it all,' writes the minor poet, 'desire of oblivion runs.'

10.

How we love the idea of the last. The last stand (Custer's), the last flight (of the *Memphis Belle* or Concorde), the last four songs by Richard Strauss, the last . . . anything really: *of the Mohicans* (Fenimore

Cooper), *of the Just* (André Schwarz-Bart), *September* (Elizabeth Bowen), *Tycoon* (Fitzgerald), *Letters from Hav* (Jan Morris), *Picture Show* (Larry McMurtry), *Record Album* (Little Feat), *Days of Disco* (Whit Stillman), *Year at Marienbad* (Alain Resnais), *Resort* (Pawel Pawlikowski), *Emperor* or *Tango in Paris* (both Bertolucci). Last but by no means least, there are the generic literalists such as Dennis Hopper, David Markson, or Peter Reading, who served up, respectively, *Movie*, *Novel*, and *Poems*. (Obviously there are posthumously published collections of *Last Poems* by many poets, including Lawrence. Published in 1994, a full seventeen years and multiple books before his death, Reading's *Last Poems* presents itself as the discovered last manuscript of a vanished poet. According to the foreword it is unclear whether the final two incoherent and indecipherable pages were intended 'to appear in their present form, or whether they represent drafts towards an unrealized work in progress.')

The combination of last and summer occupies a special and lasting place in our consciousness. Pasternak nutshelled it (*The Last Summer*), the BBC branded it (*Last of the Summer Wine*), and Alan Hollinghurst built *The Swimming-Pool Library*, his first novel, around 'the last summer of its kind there was ever to be.' This was 1983, a summer of unbridled gay carnality and hedonism before the AIDS epidemic. It was lent a larger resonance by an earlier last summer of 1914, rendered forever glorious by the catastrophic darkness that followed as the lights went out all over Europe: 'The glorious summer of 1914, to which Stefan Zweig would always think back in later years, when he uttered the word *summer*,' according to Volker Weidermann in *Summer Before the Dark*. Weather being simultaneously part of and thoroughly indifferent to history, there were, of course, plenty of great summers to come, one of which appeared hot on the heels of the war: 'the cloudless, golden, incomparable summer of 1920.' Others that spring to mind are 1966 when England won the World Cup at Wembley, the summer of love in San Francisco in 1967, the second summer of love—or loved-up-ness at any rate—in England in 1989, and 1996 when England got to the semi-finals of the Euros, but these were localised or demographically selective affairs (I didn't go to a single rave in 1989 and watched all of the 1996 tournament on TV, in Rome); 1914 was the epochal summer, after which the entire world shifted on its axis.

11.

Lastness is oddly self-perpetuating. For a while at least, one last thing generates and leads to another, to its viral perpetuation and renewal, as in Billy Collins's poem 'The Last Shepherd':

> *The last shepherd realized he was the last shepherd*
> *When the last sheep in his flock*
> *Which happened to be the last flock on earth . . .*

The end can only be postponed, not averted, but it's sometimes not as final as previously envisaged, as the ultimate turns out to be the penultimate, ante-penultimate, or ante-pre-penultimate: a curtain-raiser for a succession of further encores and finales.

Few things more powerfully illustrate this—or our hunger for lastness—than the cavalry battle. 'Since the days of the Franco-Prussian War,' writes Ulrich Raulff in *Farewell to the Horse*, 'historians have never tired of constantly declaring a new "final" cavalry battle in human history.' We could rephrase this and say that Raulff never tires of telling us that the Battle of Omdurman, for example, 'is yet another of those cavalry battles often credited as being the *last* of its kind in history,' or that Komarów on 31 August 1920 'was host to a cavalry engagement which—yet again—has been described as "perhaps the last pure cavalry battle in European history,"' or to sum up, 'that since the tail end of the nineteenth century, the cavalry has seen a great number of final battles and died a great number of deaths.' Clearly, this satisfies a need—and, in the process, generates further need.

Ideally these cavalry charges are futile instances of tactical blundering—as in our national version memorialised by Tennyson in 'The Charge of the Light Brigade'—or doomed proof of technological and historical obsolescence (as when the charge is against tanks). The heyday and tactical supremacy of the cavalry charge seems, in retrospect, to have been fueled by the magnitude and frequency of its later repeated failure. The fate of Custer and the 7th Cavalry was especially wrenching because instead of a last charge there was only its opposite, a last *stand*. Some accounts claim there was not even that, that what occurred was more akin to 'a rout, a panic' than a 'concerted "last stand."' Either way, two things were guaranteed: that the fascination with what happened at the Little Bighorn would never end, and that Sitting Bull's victory would serve as a prelude to revenge, to the massacre of Native Americans at Wounded Knee.

12.

The demise of the Plains Indians was intimately connected with the fate of the buffalo. As late as 1871 a herd of four million was seen in present-day Kansas. 'The main body was fifty miles deep and twenty-five miles wide,' writes S. C. Gwynne in *Empire of the Summer*

Moon. 'But the slaughter had already begun. It would soon become the greatest mass destruction of warm-blooded animals in human history.' Whereas the Indians had used every part of the animal for nutrition, clothing, or some other practical function—bladders, logically enough, were used as water containers—white hunters were interested only in the skins. To that end thirty-one million were killed between 1868 and 1881, and by the late 1880s the buffalo was on the brink of extinction.

The great visual elegy for the lost majesty of buffalo and Indian in the midst of a sublime and idyllic wilderness is *The Last of the Buffalo*, by Albert Bierstadt. (Custer lunched at the artist's studio before heading west for his last campaign.) The painting was finished in 1888 when there were only about a thousand buffalo left. 'I have endeavored to show the buffalo in all his aspects and depict the cruel slaughter of a noble animal now almost extinct,' Bierstadt said. But one aspect of the mass slaughter is not featured. Although there are skulls and bones all around (an acceptably Arcadian touch, far more pleasing to the eye than the vast pyramids of skulls documented in photographs) the dead animals are like enormously furry, dormant, or stuffed versions of themselves. The Plains are not littered with the exposed and grisly heaps of stinking and rotting flesh left behind after the hunters had stripped them bare. So while it's a beautiful painting, it is, Robert Hughes insists, a beautifully constructed lie: 'It shows no white hunters with Sharps rifles. The blame for the ecocide is put on the Indians themselves.' This is not entirely misleading but the title of the painting—and Bierstadt's explanation of what he was attempting—is slightly at odds with the evidence presented *within* it. The Indians are not blamed; in fact the picture avoids any blame—which might itself constitute a failing for which the artist is to blame. The two starring buffalo—one engaged in active combat with the Indian on his Géricault horse, the other staring gamely towards the viewer (punctured by arrows but still with some fight left in him)—are far from the last. In the background there are plenty more roaming over a composite landscape—made up of various views Bierstadt encountered on the Landers expedition of 1859 when, relatively speaking, the buffalo were in rude health. Indians and buffalo are still locked in adversarial harmony, as symbolised both passively or negatively by the bodies of horse and rider lying amid—and partially hidden by—the dead buffalo, and actively by the way that, at the dramatic heart of the painting, the wounded buffalo is goring the Indian's horse: a goring in keeping with an overall lack of gore. In this wide-screen vision of paradise in the process of being lost there are still way more buffalo than there are Indians to slaughter them. The depicted ecosystem can remain in perpetual balance since the landscape looks like it goes on forever. Rather than a scene of terminal scarcity, this is a world of abundance and boundless possibility (though even to introduce that notion is to be reminded of the manifest destiny by which buffalo and Indian were facing extermination by the time of the painting's creation). So the amalgamated landscape of the painting is the staging for a condensed and composite history whose actual outcome—catastrophic for Indian and buffalo alike—has already been decided but that can be internally denied or kept at bay, excluded from the all-inclusive illusion of the picture frame.

Since that sounds like a description of what is to come in the form of the filmic Western one would think that Bierstadt had a big hit on his hands. Well, it was big (six feet by ten) and he had it on his hands in the sense that the American committee for the 1889 Exposition Universelle in Paris rejected the painting that Bierstadt considered 'among my best efforts.' 'There is something corrupt, something calculating and extreme in Bierstadt,' writes John Updike—as if describing a producer of movies—and Bierstadt had miscalculated badly. Taste and fashion in art had moved on. Van Gogh was already in the last year of his life, the Nabis in Paris were beginning to offer their intimate, small-scale glimpses of nuanced interiors before the blazing heyday of those much loved wild beasts, *les Fauves*. What Bierstadt termed the 'unpleasant episode' of the Exposition Universelle marked the end of the career of the foremost painter of the American West with the poor buffalo ('an ugly brute to paint') standing as a forlorn but still cuddly symbol of the decline in his creator's fortunes.

In another way Bierstadt's vision lived on, in reverse, as it were. If *The Last of the Buffalo* looks cinematic that is because the movies' visual ideal of the western landscape, the real and fictitious—in a word, mythic—landscape of the Western, 'owes its origins to the inventions of Bierstadt.'

13.

In his essay 'How the West Was Won or Lost,' Larry McMurtry tells the story of 'a straggling band' of Kiowa Indians who come to the ranch of Charles Goodnight and ask for a buffalo from the herd he has been building up since the late 1870s. Goodnight, one of the original Texas cattlemen and a veteran Indian fighter (who provided a mold for the character of Woodrow Call in *Lonesome Dove*), 'thought they wanted to eat it. What they really wanted to do was to chase it on their skinny horses and kill it with lances, in the old way, one last time.' Or at least, McMurtry concludes, 'that's the story that is still told in the Texas panhandle.' He also mentions that the incident forms the basis for 'a fine story,' 'The Last Running,' by John Graves. Graves briefly returns to his own story and its origins in the book *Goodbye to a River*, about a last canoe trip along the Brazos River. In this retelling of his fiction 'a scraggly band of reservation Comanches, long since whipped,' turn up at Goodnight's ranch and, having persuaded him to give them a buffalo, run it before them and kill it 'with arrows and lances in the old way, the way of the arrogant centuries.' Like McMurtry, Graves acknowledges the apocryphal nature of the episode, how he came across it in slightly different versions (one of which involved a different rancher). It 'may not be true,' he writes. 'But it could be true—ought to be.'

We're here in the kind of territory mapped by Roberto Calasso who, in *The Marriage of Cadmus and Harmony*, writes: 'The repetition of a mythical event, with its play of variations, tells us that something remote is beckoning to us.' Remote and, in the remote stretches of the American West, ever-present. Hence Graves begins his discussion of the Goodnight story and its variations in a style that is declarative and distinctly Texan: 'A tale exists.'

Unlike the story of Nietzsche and the Turin horse it is possible to track this tale back to a specific source. Goodnight invited Indians to his ranch several times to take part in hunting buffalo from the herd he had cultivated, including the occasion in October 1916 when three Kiowas using traditional weapons and wearing traditional clothes—as stipulated by the host—brought down a buffalo that was then barbecued and served up for 125 guests the next day. Attended by 11,000 spectators, the event was such a success that another of these authentic last hunts was staged two months later, this time for a documentary film, directed and produced by the elderly Goodnight, called *Old Texas*.

This is not to say that the Graves-McMurtry story begins with the grainy and quaint-looking footage from the same year as the Battle of the Somme (both the actual event and the documentary of that name with its re-enacted scenes of violent death). The film itself has roots that reach back way beyond the verifiable occasion in 1878 when Goodnight agreed to give Quanah Parker, the last chief of the Comanches, and his men 'two beeves every other day until you find out where the buffaloes are.' That sounds a reasonable outcome of a cordial encounter but the amount of history that lay in the six or so feet between the two men as they looked in each other's eyes was as vast as the Texas plains. The 'something remote' evoked by Calasso is within touching distance: either a fatal blow or a handshake. McMurtry *measures* that distance by quoting Goodnight, who, when asked 'near the end of his long life' if he was a man of vision replied, 'Yes, a hell of a vision.' In McMurtry's own words, he 'saw the end in the beginning.'

14.

In my last year at Oxford, unsure what I might do after graduating, I made a few half-hearted applications for postgrad studies. Not because I wanted to set out on the long, dreary, and utterly pointless slog of a doctorate, but as a way of postponing the need to embark on the life of being something other than a student. The only thing I could think of proposing as a possible area of research was 'how novels end.' If this seemed like an under-researched area that was because I had not researched it at all. There was no theoretical under-pinning or framing, I had no idea what this project might be expected to uncover, and I can't remember anything of substance that my 'proposal' contained. I had heard of—but not read—Frank Kermode's *The Sense of an Ending* and I mentioned *Great Expectations*, with its revised and ambiguous ending ('no shadow of another parting'), might even have suggested that this represented some kind of turning point in the history or development of something or other, but I was not interested in making a contribution to knowledge; I was interested in getting a grant.

To this end I took a train to Birmingham, where I had a meeting with David Lodge, who was surprisingly encouraging, and I applied to a university in Canada, but everything fizzled out before it had even properly fizzed. With my formal education and academic aspirations at an end I drifted into the life of unsupervised and unfocused study to which I was perfectly suited: signing on the dole, reading a lot, listening to music, going to the cinema, and drinking beer. Gradually I weaned myself off the dole but essentially my life has continued on the same trajectory—a trajectory, if such a thing is possible, without direction or purpose—ever since.

I *say* that but then I realise that there are so many little things that substitute for the lack of a larger goal that continue to crop up in the course of one's journey through life. I put it ponderously like that be-cause what I have in mind is something like the ambition, conceived as I turned sixty, of never buying shampoo again. I don't mean giving up washing my hair; I mean not *paying* for shampoo. I can afford to buy shampoo; I've got the cash to go out to CVS right now and buy it by the crate-load but I prefer to filch bottles from hotels. That's how it started, modestly enough, but then my wife and I were in a hotel in Marfa, Texas, where instead of little bottles of shampoo, a large dispenser of high-quality product was fixed to the wall. It so happened that we had brought our selection of daily vitamins in a glucosamine container, so we pumped the contents of the dispenser into that and made off with four times the amount of shampoo we would happily have settled for had they not tried to stop us taking any at all. Thereafter, we always travelled with a couple of empty containers and came to hope that there might be a dispenser rather than a selection of little bottles. We were held in check by the hundred-mill limit imposed by airlines on liquids in hand luggage but on one occasion we drove back from the Skyview hotel in Los Alamos (the town in California, not the home of the Manhattan Project) with two water bottles of shampoo and conditioner. That's when things really took off. We soon had enough shampoo to open a salon. It was a good feeling, knowing we had this product reservoir—I liked opening the under-sink cupboard in the bathroom and looking at the mix of original sample bottles from Bigelow and the confusing array of vitamin containers we'd decanted the shampoo into, but what I really liked was the ongoing project of constantly accumulating more and more shampoo. We had rules and we had everything under control—if we were invited to a friend's house for dinner, we never took along an empty aspirin bottle so that we could siphon off some Aveda shampoo while using their bathroom—but within a year this incremental project had acquired the form of a grander ambition: *never* to buy shampoo again. This was now a quasi-Pharaonic undertaking—not a life's work exactly but something I would continue doing for the rest of my days. I've used the first-person plural throughout this account but in truth my wife, although happy to squirrel away shampoo, never committed to it with anything like my single-minded zeal. There were three reasons for this. One, she has a fulfilling job that occupies a large part of her consciousness. Two, a slight propensity for scalp eczema means she likes to buy Nizoral (unbelievably expensive) to keep this at bay. Three, after getting into a protracted lather about her hair smelling fishy, she discovered that I'd left a capsule of omega-3 oil at the bottom of one of our shampoo containers.

Like so much else, this admirable mission was brought to an end by the coronavirus pandemic, also in three ways: with all trips cancelled I was unable to top up our supply of shampoo; I was always having to wash my hair at home (rather than at the hairdresser when I was having it cut or in hotels); and the fact that I was unable to get a haircut meant that, as it grew longer, I was having to wash it twice (rather than once) a week. As coronavirus hardships go this barely merits a mention (the financial impact of having to buy shampoo is incalculably small) but I mention it precisely *because* it's not worth mentioning. The shampoo project was one of the things that had made my life enjoyable and worthwhile, and gave it a purpose that was suddenly either taken away or made to seem entirely pointless. There were lots of things like this and now almost all of them are gone. I've never had any big goals, ambitions, or dreams but I've always had so many little schemes, dodges, scams, hobbies, and interests on the go that I've never felt the lack of a larger purpose or the need for loftier consolation.

'That the profoundest mind must also be the most frivolous one,' was, Nietzsche said, almost a formula for his philosophy. One of the most profound minds of our time, Annie Dillard, has voiced her disappointment with philosophy's failure 'to address what some called "ultimate concerns,"' most of which can, in her opinion, be boiled down to a single question: 'What in the Sam Hill is going on here?' In its homely way that does indeed sound like a big question but bear in mind that, as a young graduate student, Dillard devoted much thought to Thoreau's *Walden*, trying to work out what kind of book it was. At one point she decided it was 'really a book about a pond.' My shampoo ambition might seem pond-like, like pond-life behaviour, and it was, in a way, but it was one thread among many that, taken together, formed a net, the gain of which was so huge as to be not only life-enhancing but life-*defining*. So although we came back from Marfa with both a pot of shampoo and a new project of obsessive shampoo acquisition we didn't go there *for* the shampoo. That would have been pathetic. We went because we needed a few extra tier points to maintain our Gold status with BA and found we could do this by taking just one more flight, from Los Angeles to El Paso.

It's not just shampoo or air miles and it's not just me. (That's the whole point of—and justification for—writing about yourself; indulged in conscientiously, with sufficient rigour, it's *never* just about you.) Take tennis players and towels. Or, to rephrase that slightly, watch them take towels at the end of a match. For the low-ranked or qualifiers getting into a Slam represents a rare and much-needed towel bonanza but even the top players make sure, after strapping on their sponsored watches in full view of the TV cameras, to scoop up as many towels as possible—the Australian Open ones are particularly desirable—before trudging off court. Pre-Covid they would toss their disgusting, sweaty wristbands into the crowd—such largesse!—and occasionally throw in a towel for good measure but most of the time they'd make their exit looking as if they'd just finished looting a branch of Bed Bath & Beyond. It's possible that, after showering, they dump the odd dirty towel in the locker-room laundry basket but I suspect that they regularly head back to the hotel and then the airport with bags stuffed full of towel-swag. They're multimillionaires, many of them, but they've still got their eye on the main towel chance. Especially if they lose and are in need of all the tear-absorbent consolation they can get their hands on. It's a perk, an athletic leftover from the ethically unquestioned heyday of imperial plunder. Any successful player has a trophy cabinet; Roger and Serena probably have designated towel rooms, maybe even separate towel *houses*. Like the great aristocratic families who take pains to ensure that generations of offspring will continue to enjoy the unearned benefits of inherited land, the titans of the tennis meritocracy bequeath to their children and grandchildren lives freed forever from the realm of towelling necessity.

As for me . . . Like a team that managed to stay in the Premiership with a draw in the last game of the season only to go down the next, we were relegated to Silver a year after the Marfa run had enabled us to cling onto Gold. Since we're not flying anywhere now it doesn't matter, but that, obviously, is not the point. 'The action is the juice,' as Tom Sizemore tells De Niro in Michael Mann's *Heat*.

15.

'After this I'm out.'

It's a cliché of thrillers: the bank robber plotting—or lured back for—one final heist. I'm thinking of the scene in *Heat* when De Niro gathers Sizemore and the rest of his crew to ask if they want to take part in an already compromised and risky score—they all, for different reasons, say they're in—but there are numerous other examples. In every one of these the chances of success are not just slim but irrelevant. Like Peckinpah's Wild Bunch they go ahead even though they know that it will result not in a fabulous haul of wealth but in failure, imprisonment, or death. That 'even though' is misleading, of course. They go ahead *because* of the near-guarantee of failure. Now, this is not an original or profound psychological observation but I am going—I *went*—ahead with it anyway because I like the idea of all those unseen—because unmade—films in which a criminal mastermind or some member of his crew decides to stick rather than twist (often a pre-synonym of bust). He quits while he's ahead. The film then concentrates not on the score, with its predictable and bloody denouement, but on this person's happy, contented, and law-abiding domestic life. There are no regrets or doubts. Nothing and no one turns up (as in David Cronenberg's *A History of Violence*) to shred the comfortable present by the excoriating claims of the past. One morning, drinking coffee at home, in his garden in Santa Monica, he reads in the newspaper about how, as the result of an anonymous tip-off, police foiled an attempted bank raid that resulted in every member of the gang being shot dead. Unlike the paper, his expression is impossible to read. I like that but then I want to push it further and do without both the tempting offer of a last comeback *and* the prior criminal career. How about a film concentrating instead on a thoroughly contented life with no violence or crime lurking in the background? The life, that is, of most people in the audience for these last-roll-of-the-dice films, for whom such films are part of the culture that reconciles us to our uneventful lives—and eventual deaths. So here's my pitch. A man in his sixties, living in the suburbs of Paris, who has dutifully attended every film in a complete Éric Rohmer retrospective at the Espace Saint-Michel, is getting ready to go to the final film in the series: *Full Moon in Paris*, a movie he has never seen before, about Pascale Ogier moving into her boyfriend's apartment in the boring suburbs and her frustration at having to catch the last train back after parties in the city. And then, just before he is due to catch the RER into Paris, he decides to stay home.

16.

But what if it was a different film or a different retrospective? What if he failed to see . . .

A book about last things, this is also about things one comes round to at last, late in the day, things one was in danger of going to one's grave without having read or experienced. So it's possible that, at the eleventh hour, as the final deadline for making changes looms, I will add a section of breaking news or a postscript about how, contrary to what was said on page 75, I've finally managed to get through *The Brothers K*, the whole of Proust, or *The Man Without Qualities*. Milan Kundera in *Testaments Betrayed* evokes the period of modern musical invention as 'a sky ablaze at the end of the day' but that sky also glows with discoveries made by the listener—or reader or viewer—just before nightfall. It's not only the ability to create; the capacity to *appreciate* also needs to be nurtured, sustained, and celebrated so that one does not become reduced to and defined by aversion, indifference, or hostility. The trick—which is no trick at all—is to be able to enjoy the cultural and ideological 'pisscuntment' expressed by the ageing Kingsley and Larkin while developing an easy, un-outraged immunity to it.

So let's celebrate the fact that I've finally seen Michael Powell and Emeric Pressburger's *The Life and Death of Colonel Blimp*. How had I not seen it before? I must have been put off by the title, by the expectation that it was a Blimpish film. My first experience should have been at a cinema—I have a vague memory of screenings at the Ritzy in Brixton that I made no attempt to attend in the 1980s, when the film was restored and re-released—but my wife and I were obliged to watch it on my computer, during lockdown.

For the first hour there was such a profusion of things going on that we had no idea what we were watching. It had the energy of screwball (with the associated feminine independence personified by the first of Deborah Kerr's three lovely incarnations); it looked, at times, like a musical; it was funny (slapstick), mesmerising, bonkers, splendid. But right from the start, with the swerving tracking shots of army motorbikes and trucks on manoeuvres, it had such a strong rhythm (encouraging the impression that it might burst into a full-blown musical) that, even while it seemed chaotic, crazy, it never seemed out of control. There was a sweeping visual *command* but with so little time to decipher what that order might be we followed, not blindly but open-eyed, allowing ourselves to be swept along. It was a joy. And then—I'm saying nothing new here—it becomes so moving. In London in November 1939 Theo Kretschmar-Schuldorff (Anton Walbrook), the German friend 'Blimp' met in Berlin almost forty years earlier, is being aggressively quizzed about his status as an enemy alien. When his application is rejected he delivers a long, direct-to-camera soliloquy about the Nazis and why he left Germany to come to England. He has just finished when the uniformed 'Blimp'

(Clive Wynne-Candy, played with boundless generosity of spirit by Roger Livesey), whom he has not seen for twenty years, strides into the makeshift office and agrees to stand surety for him 'with everything I have, sir.' And then . . . the screen dissolved. I wasn't crying, I was sobbing.

This great film does not need me to sing its praises but, without doubt, *I* needed it. The extraordinary thing was that I'd been able to go about my business, living a normal life, with this huge *Blimp*-shaped hole at its centre. For all this time I'd been an incomplete person. What if I hadn't seen it? Well, nothing, in the same way that nothing *happens* if you don't read Jane Austen or listen to *A Love Supreme*, but your life will be defined in some ways by these and other lacks. (Some lacks are easy to diagnose, as when Nietzsche realised that the 'perpetual lack of a really refreshing and *healing human love*' was in some ways warping his life—as its presence animates Blimp's.) Athletes routinely speak of being able to compete at a high level; the strange thing about these huge cultural lacunae is that one can function—OK, *compete*—at a high level of cultural cognition and discernment while lacking what one belatedly realises is a vital component of that cognition. I should have seen *Blimp* years earlier but there is, I suppose, something appropriate about the way I was seeing it at something close to the age of Blimp himself at the film's beginning and end.

17.

If I was late to the party, Michael Powell was nothing if not precocious. The last—and first—and therefore, in his own words, 'the only director alive who has ridden in a cavalry charge,' he 'always held a grudge against Tony Richardson . . . for directing *The Charge of the Light Brigade* instead of me.' The charge took place in 1915 when a cavalry regiment was on manoeuvres near Powell's family home in Kent. 'Micky' had been told he could not take part—'too dangerous'—but he and his pony, the gallant Fusby, managed to join in even though his sword 'was only an ashstick with a handguard on it, one of a pair my brother and I used to fence with.' Powell was ten at the time.

18.

'The Old Man ceased: he saw that I was moved . . .'

'Sobbing' in the middle of *Blimp* was unusual but I've become steadily more prone to crying as I've got older. Those Martin Luther King Jr. speeches, the interview with the Freedom Rider Jim Zwerg from his hospital bed in Montgomery, Alabama, or newsreel footage of the *Hindenburg* going up in flames ('Oh, the humanity!') are guaranteed to make anyone cry but I was leaking tears when the German commander addressed his defeated troops during the last episode of *Band of Brothers*. Any manifestation of citizenly behaviour has the potential to get me going. Just this morning a young woman was interviewed on the radio about her participation in one of the Covid vaccine trials in the U.K. That set me off because she was such a model *citizen*. Declarations from France asserting the values of the Republic in the face of terror attacks will do it too. As will words like 'doctor' or 'nurse,' or the letters 'ICU,' 'PPE,' or, more broadly, 'NHS.' And then there's sport. The deaths of Nobby Stiles and Maradona, Willie Borland's match-winning nine-darter, everything to do with Roger (winning or losing), any display of sportsmanship . . . Soon a mere lack of cheating will be enough to leave me blubbing. Literature has become a Pavlovian tear fest. Not just obvious things like the makeshift memorial carved by Woodrow Call after the death of one of his men in *Lonesome Dove*: 'CHERFUL IN ALL WEATHERS, NEVER SHERKED A TASK. SPLENDID BEHAVIOUR.' If I start quoting any of the poetry I learned by heart at school and university—the end of *Paradise Lost*, chunks of Hardy, Tennyson, or Shakespeare—my eyes think I'm peeling onions at the funeral of a much-loved pet.

Wordsworth in his ode on 'Intimations of Immortality from Recollections of Early Childhood' writes of thoughts that 'often lie too deep for tears,' but there seems to be an underground reservoir of tears within poetry—including Wordsworth's—that lies at a deep level of my formation. Not at the deepest level of earliest childhood—which is precultural in terms of learned susceptibility to the printed word—but, as it were, at the layer resting just above that. With age these depths come brimming to the surface. It's as if the insulating layers of the years have, in the process of their accretion, worn thin.

No painting, however much it means to me, ever makes me cry.

19.

One of the less remarked-on features of Burning Man is its capacity to move participants to tears. You might think you're going for a good time but you end up blubbing because of the profundity of the experience.

I went for the first time in 1999 and then missed just two years before going for the last time in 2005. I was conscious, even as I bought a ticket and made plans to go, of a tendency to do things one time too many. I used to love going to Hadrian's Villa near Rome. If I was in Rome I'd always want to go Hadrian's Villa. The last time I was there, at the villa, my friend Sergio said, 'We are never coming 'ere again!' and I had to admit he was right. When my wife and I went back to Zion, in Utah, in 2017 we knew, from day two of a scheduled five, that we were doing something that we had already done too often. (She also claims we've done Death Valley to death but I'll be dead before I get tired of going there.)

It's hard to know for sure that you shouldn't have done something until you've done it one time too many and I'm glad I went to Burning Man in 2005 because I knew, afterwards, what until then I'd only suspected: that a phase of my life had come to an end. I had no regrets. Every Labor Day weekend in the following years, I was happy whatever I was doing, even if it was nothing, secure in the knowledge that if I felt hungry there were places where I could hand over money and, in exchange, be provided with food. These places are called restaurants and frequenting them was a source of deep satisfaction. Knowing I wasn't at Burning Man was enough.

And then in 2018, after an absence of thirteen years, I returned to the restaurant-less desert of Black Rock City. I knew the festival had become much bigger in the intervening years, during which I occasionally met people who said it was now 'too commercial.' (None of these people, needless to say, had ever actually been.) There were multiple reasons for returning, including the death in April of co-founder Larry Harvey, who I'd become friendly with. Given the impact of the festival on so many people's lives the avoidance of a personality cult had always seemed an important achievement in itself; but this year was bound to be an emotionally charged celebration of and memorial to Larry. Also, my friend Gerry had asked me to participate in a film he was making about the festival. Most of my contributions ended up on the cutting-room floor but, in anticipation of what was assumed to be my starring role, he had arranged for me to fly, rather glamorously, on a charter from Burbank into Black Rock City Airport. Waiting for the plane I thought back to the period from 1999 to about 2001 when I felt even more finished as a writer than I usually do. I'd always written about what was most important to me and nothing was more important to me than Burning Man—which was impossible to write about because it was beyond words.

The flight itself was a treat but I kept saying to myself, 'This phase of my life is over, I shouldn't have come.' In Black Rock City the more extravagantly you dress the more pleasure you give to everyone around you—'you fit in by standing out,' as one of my friends had said to reassure me while I waited in the long line, in a state of high anxiety, to get into the KitKatClub—but on the plane, in that suspension between the default world and the hard-to-conceive reality of the playa, I felt ill at ease.

All reservations melted away when I saw the dust-blasted figure of Gerry waiting for me at 'immigration' and although there were afternoons when I wished I wasn't there—hunkered down in my trailer, waiting for dust storms to pass—most of the time there was nowhere else in the world I wanted to be. Even during the dust storms I was happy reading Zagajewski's *Slight Exaggeration*. The trailer was decrepit—the shower didn't even pretend to work and the generator was powerless to power anything except a single light that took a dim view of the sunken wreck of the sink—but I had it to myself and just being able to shut the door, to have a barrier between myself and everything going on outside, was enough. And what was going on outside, in the festival at large, was better than ever.

20.

Cycling back to my trailer one afternoon I stopped off at the large bell tent of the Jazz Café, where one of their history of jazz seminars was in progress. During these seminars the hosts would give a little talk and then play some representative tracks on the amazing sound system. This particular segment was devoted to free jazz and a track was playing from Coltrane's *Meditations*. At the end of the track, moved to testify by both the music and the participatory spirit of Burning Man, I got up and gave an impromptu lecture to the six or seven people slumped on sofas about the quartet version recorded two months earlier. No one seemed very impressed and the organisers looked more than a little miffed by this self-invitation to sit in and pontificate.

21.

On Friday morning the Black Rock Philharmonic played at Galaxia, the just-completed temple—construction had been delayed by high winds and dust storms. The whole orchestra was decked out in an assortment of functional desert wear and crazy costumes. There was lots to look at but whenever I go to hear orchestral music I follow a strict code of conduct, always keeping my eyes on the most attractive Asian violinist. In this instance, the policy was beautifully rewarded: she was wearing a bikini—black as her hair, in skimpy homage, presumably, to the more formal attire usually deemed appropriate for such occasions. The performance lasted an hour and included a solo piece by a cellist—T-shirt, shorts, hiking boots—I'd seen playing out in the playa, by a tunnel of hooped lights, a couple of nights earlier. On that occasion he'd been accompanied by a dancer who, at the end of the piece, collapsed to the ground in the way of performers who want to show that they have given their all. We applauded for a long time, feeling, after a while, that he was perhaps milking it a bit by lying there for so long. The cellist walked over to give him a hand up, so they could walk off together, but then this help took on a more urgent character and soon several people were gathered around, giving the dancer CPR. Next there were rangers cycling up and then the blue and red flashing lights of arriving paramedics. The dancer had suffered a heart attack and, at the time of this performance at the temple, was in intensive care in Reno.

Towards the end of the programme the orchestra played the Ode to Joy from Beethoven's Ninth. There will never be a more joyful performance, precisely because it was a bit ramshackle. Not wanting their best instruments to be ruined by the sun and the corrosive dust of the playa the musicians played instruments deemed expendable. The orchestra as a whole had not had a lot of opportunities to rehearse together. And, most importantly, this being Burning Man, those of us watching were participating by singing wordlessly along. All of this had the tear-inducing effect of de-institutionalising the ode and pulling it back from what Adorno called an oration to mankind, freeing it from the ceremonial shackles of openings of European parliaments or the Olympics or whichever franchise of the Enlightenment was being celebrated and enshrined. Normally one ends up feeling excluded by virtue of the monumental fellowship proclaimed; here, in the vast open air, we were enfolded within it.

22.

In turn the music had its effect on the venue. Temples are built in order to worship a particular deity and in accordance with long-standing architectural conventions guaranteed, by tradition and shared belief, to maximise the chances of communicating effectively and appropriately with that deity. The experience you have is therefore determined in advance. And those temples have been built, often over an extended period of time, to *last*. Over the course of centuries they acquire an atmosphere or feeling as a consequence of devotees' behaviour, rituals (prayer, hymns), and architecture being locked into a stable and enduring relationship. This is why Nietzsche deemed churches, even in the anticipated days after the lease had expired on the belief system that had inspired their construction, to be unsuitable places of contemplation for free spirits: 'they are houses of God and ostentatious monuments of some supramundane intercourse; we who are godless could not think *our thoughts* in such surroundings.' (Larkin, in 'Church Going,' quietly and memorably demurs.)

Each year the temple at Burning Man is built from scratch to a new design. It conforms to no architectural blueprint other than safety-code requirements—ability to withstand gale-force winds and so on—and the necessity that on the Sunday night it will burn. It is built and then, in the brief span of its functioning, has to acquire, with extraordinary rapidity, qualities that have usually deepened over hundreds of years. The nature of those qualities is entirely dependent on what people bring and how they behave. Although each year's temple is dominated by tributes to the dead, it could, by virtue of pure democratic will, become a shrine to the KKK, to anti-vaxxers, to Shining Path . . . anything. Unusually responsive and susceptible, it is not architecturally predisposed to any outcome except by two constants. There is always some kind of shrine dedicated to the memory of those who have died. And the temple is always built by a team of volunteers, each with his or her own particular skill, who are all dependent on one another.

In *Slight Exaggeration* Zagajewski relates one of the 'mad metaphysical theories' of his friend Joseph Brodsky, who claimed that religion would 'include more infinity after breaking with the great natural religions.' Zagajeswki—whom I knew slightly, and who died while this book was being written—is skeptical, insisting that we need 'to sustain the infinity contained in existing religions, to nurture it, just in case, like the embers of a bonfire, stirring it, kindling it, in hopes of raising a greater flame.'

It is remarkable how effectively the structure develops its spiritual power: how quickly it *becomes* a temple in the fullest—rather than simply structural—sense as a conduit to infinity. A condition of this unusual acceleration is the shared knowledge and acceptance that in a few days it will burn.

23.

Before that, on Saturday, the Man himself is burned. I had strict instructions about how the night would proceed—would *not* proceed—from the producer of the film in which I had gone from starring to supporting to cameo role. Now, it seemed, I was about to become a kind of minder with limited portfolio. It was very important, she said, not to let Gerry take any 'naughties' (quaint usage) until after the Burn, *after* filming was complete, and AFTER all the camera and sound equipment had been safely stowed. This was reasonable advice but when we had joined the crowds at the huge perimeter around the Man—we were right at the front because of the film—I found it impossible not to mention to Gerry that I was feeling absolutely wonderful about everything, that I was so happy to be here with him and to be part of his film. After this heartfelt announcement he would not take no for an answer, insisting that, as the director, he outranked both me and the producer, so I was obliged to hand over his share.

We were all waiting for the Burn but there was none of the impatience that you feel when waiting for a concert to start and so, in a way, we were not waiting at all. Just having everyone gathered round like this—the entire population of the city, all the crazy vehicles, everyone with their already-shared experience—was an event itself.

The Man, made of wood and blue neon, was the centre of the world. Throughout the week he had stood with his arms by his side. And then, as we waited for the Burn, his blue neon arms were slowly raised. Oddly, this indication of imminent departure and farewell was a gesture, also, of welcome. The open arms replicate the way the city, arranged like a geographical clock face, is open to the desert from the spatial equivalent of 10 to 2. So it's not like a closed circle—of wagons against potential threat—or the quadrangle of an Oxford college, which is predicated on exclusion, on the belief that the quality of what goes on within is enhanced by what is kept out. That was a reasonable notion in the context of England in the Middle Ages but not here—and, in my experience, not in Oxford either. The raised arms are a benediction, and an acknowledgement that there is no need of the Man anymore—for a year at least. The power and beauty of that gesture, those arms stretched out to include everyone in the city! It contains all the religion I will ever need in this life, or any other—and, of course, there *is* no other. The same thing happens every year but the feeling of belonging, of communion, was especially powerful this year because Larry Harvey had passed away.

The blank face of the Man, arms raised above the desert, reaching into the night:

'It is like a prayer to what is empty,' writes Tomas Tranströmer in a poem from *The Half-Finished Heaven*:

> *And what is empty turns its face to us*
> *and whispers:*
> *'I am not empty, I am open.'*

I'm glad I went back in 2018. I believed again, absolutely, but I knew, this time, that I would never go again.

24.

In 2001, late in the evening of what had been a very busy, scorchingly hot day at Burning Man, my wife began to feel unwell. We gathered up our things and walked away from the sound system where we'd been dancing. We walked, we sat down. If we sat down she wanted to stand up; having stood up she needed to sit down. She wanted to shut her eyes but worried that, if she did, she'd fall asleep and never open them again. We kept walking, out into the playa, in the direction of the temple, but she was becoming more and more frightened. When we thought things couldn't get any worse, they did. We came across something that we had not seen before: a huge, 2001-style black monolith on which was inscribed a detailed account of her condition, both mental—'visions of people or things that do not exist'— and physical. The last line was not reassuring: Death is Imminent.

I tried to steer us casually away from this object as though it were a poorly executed artwork of only minor interest but it exercised an awful fascination. That's putting it mildly. We were transfixed, convinced by the truth of a prognosis that became harder to refute with every second spent gazing at it. A splendid art car—some kind of giant fish—swam by, breaking the spell. I tugged my wife away from the scary sign and we walked back towards the city, to the reassuring medical tent—reassuring partly because she was in a lot better shape than people deep in the snake-pit of the screaming heebie-jeebies— where she ended up on an IV drip. In the morning she was wobbly, exhausted, weak, had what she called 'a full-skull headache,' but compared with the mounting terror of the night before she was feeling better.

On the way out of the festival the following day little messages of about five words were written on signs lining the dirt road. These signs were spaced at ten-yard intervals so that sentences emerged, most of them reminding us to drive slowly or safely, to avoid creating dust. We crept along in a patient line of cars. The theme in 2001 was The Seven Ages of Man, from Shakespeare. In the midst of the functional messages about driving and dust was the start of a small sequence I recognised immediately: 'Our revels now are ended . . .' It was the beginning of Prospero's famous speech from the close of *The Tempest*. I knew the speech by heart but now, as we drove slowly past, the lines unfolded in a new way, each measured phrase framed and isolated by a single sign. Cadence followed majestic cadence, exactly describing the indescribable wonders of which we had been a part:

> *Our revels now are ended. These our actors,*
> *As I foretold you, were all spirits, and*
> *Are melted into air, into thin air;*
> *And, like the baseless fabric of this vision,*
> *The cloud-capped towers, the gorgeous palaces,*
> *The solemn temples, the great globe itself,*
> *Yea, all which it inherit, shall dissolve,*
> *And, like this insubstantial pageant faded,*
> *Leave not a rack behind. We are such stuff*
> *As dreams are made on, and our little life*
> *Is rounded with a sleep . . .*

It was the most intense literary experience of my life and it happened at Burning Man.

25.

Prospero's announcement is actually premature—or at least I had misremembered which revels were ending; he's referring to the masque rather than the play as a whole. Still later, at the end of act 5, he announces his intention to retire to Milan 'where / Every third thought shall be my grave.' That sounds proportionally right. But what might occupy the remaining two-thirds? One-third will be a random and uncategorisable jumble of things, much of it so trivial as to make one wonder if there is any ordering in the cognitive reckoning of the life of even so powerful a figure. Did I forget to pay Asclepius for that rooster I owed him? Did I leave the light on downstairs in the living room? Who edited *The Vintage Book of Amnesia*? Whatever happened to the prescription sunglasses that I lost in 2000? . . . The other third, however, leaves us in no doubt that there is indeed an implacable or-der. These thoughts will be of sex: memories of afternoons and nights spent in bliss, in cities and rooms across the world. These are among the all-redeeming moments Nietzsche had in mind when he first hinted at the idea of the Eternal Recurrence in *The Gay Science*: the moments you would happily live, over and over, throughout all eternity. Unfortunately for him there were no experiences of this kind in his own life. For the rest of us our memories will be intermingled with those of lost opportunities, of times we were too shy or unsure to move towards an initiating kiss—and these thoughts will themselves be touched by death since they will be taken to the grave. If Prospero has access to a phone or email in Milan—surprising, in a way, that no ISP called itself Ariel—he will surely call up or drop a line to someone from his past, in her sixties now, and remind her of a Saturday night in Johannesburg when they went to a club and of the following night, a Sunday, when they drove around for over an hour looking for a place that might still be open, still serving drinks but, he suspected, driving (in a city where no one drives around for the sake of it) mainly for the excuse of being, as it were, accidentally together.

'That night,' Prospero will write, pointlessly, 'I so wanted to kiss you.' Or: 'If I had asked, would you have come home with me?' There are three possible answers, though the first two amount to variations of the same thing: either 'No' or some expression of what is clearly a struggle to remember the night in question (since even at the time it had no special significance at all). And then there's the third answer: 'I kept waiting for you to . . . ,' or, 'Of course. Why didn't you?'

Which of these answers would be the more depressing? Strangely, the last, those permutations of 'Yes,' because the first two—polite or astonished variants of 'No'—would at least confirm that his instincts at the time had been correct, that more than shyness was holding him back, that inhibition was a correct response to a vibe or its lack even though the vibe seemed palpable, that he was never someone who imposed himself on women, even when he was most inclined to misinterpret his desire as being not only reciprocated but partly generated by theirs. He was someone who, as he grew older, still occasionally fell for women and these were some of the best moments in his life, and even Prospero, with all his art, remained as powerless as he had been as a fourteen-year-old first becoming conscious of what would become a life-absorbing preoccupation. And even if he doesn't write or phone he will replay that strange evening spent driving, sticking faithfully to the script of what happened right up until a moment when he should have moved to kiss her. How stupid! What would have been the harm? What was the worst that could have happened? The worst was exactly what *did* happen, that she had dropped him off at his house—with the possible addition of what might have been five minutes of awkwardness in the car. What foolishness. What life-denying timidity. If only he could relive his entire life and just change that evening (that evening and others like it), that sequence of events and see if it (they) might have turned out differently.

26.

With this in mind I realise that I will have to return to Burning Man, not in real life—that will never happen—but here, now.

Shortly after his arms had been raised fireworks erupted overhead and the Man began to burn. This was in 2018, the year Gerry was making a film there. The heat was immense, the fire so bright it was like staring, with dilated pupils, at an earth-hatched sun. The heat became so intense that even at a safe distance it felt like our eyeballs were being seared.

After that and after the film equipment had been safely stowed we set off on our bikes. We were part of a large group that formed and re-formed in various permutations but at some point it boiled down to three of us: a guy called Ted, Gerry, and me. Ted was thickset, bearded, in his mid-forties. His station wagon—turned into a cosy-looking nest where he slept—was parked next to my trailer. At some point, at one of the big sound systems, Ted decided that, although already tripping heavily, he needed to go back to camp for more acid. This seemed singularly ill-advised. The chances of being able to find us again were minuscule. There were probably five thousand bikes parked here, all flashing and pulsing with LEDs, twinkling and blinking with fairy lights, and many of the landmarks we relied on to orient ourselves were themselves flashing, pulsing, and mobile. A few nights before, sober as a befuddled judge, I had spent an hour trying to find my crappy bike—having paid scrupulous attention to where I'd left it—from a similar but smaller sprawl of bikes. 'I'll find the bikes and you,' Ted said, but I knew we had seen the last of him.

'It's probably best,' I said to Gerry, 'if we forget that he even existed.' But twenty minutes later, there he was again! Given the state he was in it was one of the most impressive feats of search and recovery ever attempted. We went to other things, had loads of adventures. It was a magical night that went on forever and flashed by in no time. Slowly, it began to grow light. Flares were drifting quietly back to earth from the sky, grey now rather than black. The Man, of course, was nowhere to be seen. We decided to head home.

It's always quite a production getting ready for bed at Burning Man. I had used the Porta Potti, brushed my teeth, washed some of the dust and sparkle off my face, put a plastic bottle by the bed, ready for peeing in if I woke up. I was in my underwear, about to put on my eye mask and my ear-plugs in when there was a knock on the door. I guessed it would be Ted and knew exactly what had happened. In his confused state he had somehow locked himself out of his car and I was going to get involved in un-fucking this situation while he was bombed on acid. I opened the door. Yep, it was him, but he didn't look at all confused.

'Well,' he said. 'Both of us know. The sexual tension between us has been palatable.' He meant palpable but, in the circumstances, this was a minor lapse and it did not seem appropriate to quibble. 'You know it, I know it. Now, I've never done this before but it's Burning Man and I want to do it. We both do.'

I had been feeling loved-up all evening, but most of our exchanges had been just banter or saying 'Wow,' and the rest had involved ad-dled indecision-making about where we might be heading next. The only erotic interludes during our long night of adventure had occurred when we had—when *I* had—been silently entranced by girls dancing. He was far gone on acid, which is not a drug, in my experience, to make one feel sexual. For my part, while I wasn't anything like as high as I had been, I was feeling more *conscious* of how high I was, stand-ing in the doorway of my functional trailer, in full daylight, than I had been earlier, caught up in the delirium of music, lights, and people out there in the depths of the interstellar night. So this encounter felt like opening the door on a Sunday morning to find a salesman trying to interest you in buying something you had no desire for—though this being Burning Man where nothing was for sale, the something was being offered for free. And that offer, that something, was being gratefully accepted, right at this moment, all over Black Rock City. If I had given expression to a complex mathematical theorem that was forming hazily in my head I would have said that there were probably ten thousand women at the festival, to whom, if they'd showed up at this very door and made a similar suggestion, I would have responded, 'You're absolutely right, that is indeed palatable. Please wipe your feet and step right in.' Making allowances for a degree of confusion on his part, I sought to emphasise the comedy of this *misunderstanding* while he persisted in viewing the situation and its potential with a romantic clarity that was the opposite of my own clearer clarity. We negotiated for a bit and then I shut the door, feeling several things.

First: relief that I didn't have to get involved in the nightmare task of somehow prying open his locked car. Second: good about myself. After a certain age—I had turned sixty in June—any expression of attraction or even interest is more than welcome. What I didn't feel, what I didn't take, was any kind of umbrage. I was flattered. But I was also conscious that he was entirely wrong. There was no sexual tension between us and this made me think about occasions when I had made a rejected move on someone. On a few occasions I had been pretty sure the invitation would be declined but wanted verbal confirmation of what I had intuited. Sometimes you make a pass *in order* to be turned down.

I got up at about lunchtime. Quite a few people from the camp had already left. Absent camper vans, trailers, and cars meant that the densely packed neighbourhood of the city was already looking more open, suburban. Ted's station wagon was still there but there was no sign of life within it. He finally emerged in the late afternoon, looking only slightly sheepish as he ate a bowl of cereal. I pulled up a folding chair. While we chatted I was waiting for him to broach the subject of the previous night's proposal, was rather looking forward to hearing how he felt about it in the fierce light of afternoon. I thought the moment had come when he said, 'I just want to say . . .' There was an interesting, cereal-munching pause before I learned what it was he wanted to say. 'You're a really terrible dancer.'

27.

In the course of a long writing career, from mid-twenties to mid-seventies, the best work usually comes somewhere near the middle. James Salter is a highly unusual case. Based directly on his experience as a fighter pilot in the Korean War (and how many novelists can claim that on their CV?), his first novel, *The Hunters* (1956), was undoubtedly the finest. There followed several others, the best known of which—partly for its squirm-inducing sex scenes—is *A Sport and a Pastime* (1967). Then, at an age, eighty-seven, when, if people are writing at all, the results are regarded with dog-on-its-hind-legs indulgence, Salter produced a strange and unsettling novel that seemed a summing up of much that he had groped towards in his long middle period.

All That Is begins aboard a ship shortly before the American invasion of Okinawa in 1945. It's a combination of tight close-ups of several characters and rather clunky historical scene-setting ('kamikaze—the word meant "divine wind"') about the 'great' battle about to get under way. The word 'great'—as in 'Okinawa, the great island,' or Midway, 'the first great carrier battle'—crops up four times in the first page and a half. An unconscious declaration of intent and ambition or—and this is another peculiarity of the Salter case—a sign of gaucherie? Praised by peers for his sentences, Salter's seem more than a little awkward, even *after* you give yourself over to their distinctive rhythms.

The battle begins, we're caught up in the action, and then—another weirdness—one of the two characters we've zoomed in on disappears overboard, and we don't see him again until much later, for the briefest of cameos. The novel will trace the life of the other sailor, Phil Bowman, as it unfolds over the course of the next several decades. 'If he had known when he was fifteen how completely women would color his life,' writes Annie Dillard of one of the men in her novel *The Maytrees*, 'he would have jumped ship.' Bowman, by contrast, would have signed up for life.

He goes to Harvard, moves to New York, lands a job in publishing. In a bar he meets a beautiful woman from a rich family who live amid the 'steeplechase hills' of Virginia. As Bowman falls under her spell, so we glide into the long trance of Salter's narrative. It's the 1940s, when people's exposure to the almost-religious mysteries of sex was dependent on having it (the situation now is almost entirely reversed). The erotic bliss recorded in these pages will be a main theme not just of this phase of Bowman's life and marriage but of the book as a whole. Much later, by which time Bowman is divorced and involved with a Greek woman, he will realise that 'everything he had wanted to be, she was offering him. She had been given to him as a blessing, a proof of God.' A transient blessing, it turns out.

Granted 'a life superior to its tasks' by his work in publishing, Bowman finds himself increasingly at home in that industry's version of glamour. The absence 'of a tangible centre in life around which things could form' is a price he is willing to pay—in the form of dinners and evenings alone—as necessary preludes to 'the first word, the first look, the first embrace' and the attendant surges of lyrical renewal that follow. 'He woke in the early light. It was strangely silent, the waves had stopped breaking. A long vein of green lay in the sea.' Christine, the woman next to him as he wakes, betrays him utterly. He has no regrets and harbours no thoughts of revenge though there follows a somewhat disturbing sexual episode when he runs into Christine's college-age daughter Anet, whom he gets hopelessly stoned on charas and seduces (in a chapter entitled 'Forgiveness'!). He then takes her to Paris on an impromptu honeymoon where, after a few days, he abandons her while she sleeps, leaving her without money but with a note: 'I'm leaving. I can't bother now to explain. It was very nice.'

When the book was published these scenes bordered on the unacceptably creepy, without the redeeming, outrage-inducing, satirical justification of the devastating episode—in a school classroom!— prior to Bruno's breakdown in Michel Houellebecq's *Atomised*. Now that it has moved so entirely beyond the imaginative pale I find myself marvelling at Salter's code of unflinching fidelity to the state of moral sanctuary and artistic grace afforded by the novel (even while he concedes, a couple of pages later, that 'the power of the novel in the nation's culture had weakened').

28.

W. H. Auden famously said that Tennyson had the finest ear of any English poet, and his hearing, it seems, did not decline with age. Late in his long life, walking along a beach on the Isle of Wight, he passed two girls sitting on the sand, one of whom recognised him. 'What,' said her friend. 'Did that old man write *Maud*?' Tennyson stopped, turned, said, 'Yes, *this old man* wrote *Maud*,' and resumed his walk.

Talented young writers could tell the story of a man or woman's life, from youth to age, as it unfolds through time and history. They would, however, lack two of Salter's advantages: signs of dimming or faltering of narrative control, which are also evidence of unwavering faith in the strengths of this diminished capacity; and the conviction—similarly unwavering—that infuses Bowman's story with the unrepentant consciousness of advancing age.

29.

Playing tennis is such a big part of my happiness. Let's say I play twice a week for a maximum of two hours per session. That's only 4 out of 112 waking hours but as a percentage of my weekly allotment of well-being it's way in excess of that figure, even when offset by the number of hours—16? 20?—spent feeling wrung out and utterly depleted afterwards. The glow of those 4 hours suffuses the whole week, but for the last month a shoulder problem meant that I was unable to play or do the press-ups I was doing mainly to strengthen my shoulders.

I'm on the way back now, ready to play tennis again, to regain lost fitness and slowly build up the rapidly atrophying sense of physical attractiveness (within the severely compromised self-image of a man over sixty). It's one thing to have drifted to the fringes of the sexual marketplace, but to feel that you have been permanently excluded from re-entry is a dreadful prospect. The only thing worse is if this is a result of self-expulsion whereby you have retired from that marketplace on the self-fulfilling grounds that, since no one in their right mind could ever be attracted to you, it's in the best interest of everyone concerned if you stop having any sexual take on the world—any sexual identity—at all. But even if this worst-case scenario is avoided there are plenty of other scenarios to avoid, some of which are even worse. Isn't it better to opt for early retirement than to risk having the dread epithet 'creepy' applied to oneself? 'Creepy' is like the dye used to stop people voting twice in elections, that renders stolen bank notes worthless. Get called creepy once and you are henceforth behaving like a creepy guy. So you've got to watch yourself. But here's the rub. An interlude of self-reflection—am I being creepy?—is enough to cast a shadow of creepiness over everything you do and say. There you are in the morning being charming and funny—not even flirting—with the attractive woman in her early thirties serving bread at the bakery and by the afternoon you're a creep. Why? Because of that slight hesitation, that *I-wasn't-being-creepy-was-I?* worry you felt on the way home, clutching your still-warm baguette. Concern about avoiding potential creepiness can render you creepy. How does this happen? Like everything else, it just creeps up on you.

30.

'I think it's all over with me. I don't think I shall write any more.'

Jean-Michel Basquiat, Emily Brontë, Keats, Sylvia Plath, Raymond Radiguet, Egon Schiele, Franz Schubert, Francesca Woodman, numerous rock stars and jazz musicians all died young, leaving us to wonder about the work they might have gone on to create.

But what about those writers, artists, and composers who, at whatever age, having published one book—or finished a few paintings or compositions—decide to call it a day? Within this already narrowly defined group I have in mind a particular kind of quitter. Not those who were forced out of the cultural marketplace against their will by circumstantial injury (which, in the arts, usually means insufficient time or money). I am thinking both of people who found that time had been called on them in less obvious ways, who discovered that they didn't have the inspiration, motivation, ambition, or stubbornness to carry on; and of those who decided that, on reflection, one work—great, mediocre, or bad—was all they had in them, all they had to say, all they needed to express.

Maybe the phenomenon of the one-book writer is contained by that very phrase. However many books you publish nothing can compare with the moment when you first see the first copy of your first book. It is an epochal event for everyone concerned, even if *that* phrase—'everyone concerned'—boils down to just one person: the author. You go from being someone who dreams of being a writer, from someone who has, by definition, *worked* as a writer during the composition of the book, to being officially recognised as one. And that can be enough. Paradoxically it can be enough especially for someone who so venerates the *idea* of being a writer, whose commitment to the labour of writing could be sustained only by the intensity of the desire to have their status—cancelling out a previous lack of status—confirmed. They get over the finishing line of that first race, achieve their PB, collapse, and retire. The long haul, by contrast, does away with the finishing line, giving you a lifelong, ringside seat—actually, a seat *within* the ring—from which to assess your life and abilities, even to register the gradual decline of those abilities, leaving you free to collapse in your tracks at any time.

As a young man the narrator of Enrique Vila-Matas's *Bartleby & Co.* published a short novel, but for the past twenty-five years has written nothing. That changes when he begins a 'diary that is also going to be a book of footnotes commenting on an invisible text.' Taking inspiration from Melville's scrivener, who responded to all requests with 'I would prefer not to,' he embarks on an essayistic survey of writers such as Rimbaud or Robert Walser who, for whatever reason, stopped writing. And so, 'after twenty-five years of silence,' he starts writing again, 'about the last secrets of some of the most conspicuous cases of creators who gave up writing.' The resulting anti-canon is capacious, its implications troubling, as the question 'why I do not write inevitably leads to another, much more unsettling question: why did I ever write?' For all the book's playfulness, the stakes for the prolific

Vila-Matas were high. 'I wrote *Bartleby & Co.* because I was strongly attracted to the drive toward negation and wanted to abandon literature,' he said in an interview. 'This was paradoxical because by thoroughly occupying myself with those who had quit writing I was able to succeed in continuing to write.'

31.

One of the best accounts of a writer quitting after one book—a book of short stories—forms the basis of the third novel by a writer who went on to write many more books, three of them devoted to a fictional writer who gave up writing. Frank Bascombe, the narrator of Richard Ford's *The Sportswriter* (1986), hasn't given up writing entirely; he's given up on fiction and literature for the more routine satisfactions and security of writing about sports. From time to time in the early part of the novel Frank mulls over the reasons for giving up midway through what was intended to be his second book, a novel provisionally entitled *Tangier*. Looking back on what happened—on what didn't happen—he realises 'I didn't exactly know I'd stopped writing.' For a good while he'd go to his office and do something that seemed like work but 'the fact was, I was washed up. Sometimes I would go upstairs, sit down, and not have any idea of what I was there for, or what it was I meant to write about, and had simply forgotten everything. My mind would wander to sailing on Lake Superior (something I had never done), and after that I would go downstairs and take a nap.' The remarkable thing about this, about this description of how a writer gives up writing, is that it doubles as a description of how writers can *continue* writing. Everyone—except John Updike and Joyce Carol Oates—has had multiple days like that.

Even as he maps the circumstances of his stopping writing fiction—including being asked to write about sports during this long phase of prolonged inactivity—Frank is unable to answer to his own satisfaction the question of why he stopped writing. He lists a number of reasons and then concludes 'there are those reasons and at least twenty better ones. (Some people only have one book in them. There are worse things.)' Later he will come to a tentative conclusion, that he is unable to sustain the thing that 'real writing requires': 'that you merge into the *oneness of the writer's vision*,' which is exactly what Ford accomplishes in *The Sportswriter*. This vision is achieved largely as a result of voice, and that voice, needless to say, is the one that Frank has derived through his work as a sportswriter: 'a no-frills voice that hopes to uncover simple truth by a straight-on application of the facts.' Overall, Frank is neither displeased nor even slightly embittered by what's happened to him. He may be disappointed but that is itself part of what he sees as a condition that if not universal is very widely shared. And besides, 'It is no loss to mankind when one writer decides to call it a day.' It would have been a terrible loss, however, if Ford had decided to call it a day before he wrote that sentence, the book with that sentence in it.

For the record, Bascombe, the man who gave up writing to become a sportswriter, has, by *Independence Day*, the second volume in the series, given up sportswriting to sell real estate.

32.

Within the group of writers who stop after one book is another small but susceptible demographic: those who had the good fortune to experience what in the military is called catastrophic early success. It's more usual for a writer to use the platform of early success to establish a productive career (Norman Mailer with *The Naked and the Dead*, Zadie Smith with *White Teeth*) but for some it's an experience they never quite recover from. They almost certainly intended to write more but with sudden acclaim and unexpected wealth, without the lash of economic necessity driving them on—or the need to prove critical neglect or hostility undeserved—they gradually allowed themselves to drift away from the graft of the desk in favour of lucrative and pleasing invitations: to teach, judge prizes, or read all over the world. In America you don't even need to have experienced massive success in order to succumb to this; game things well enough and you can coast for decades—retreats, fellowships, teaching gigs, talks, and grants—on the basis of the promise of your first book of stories, all the time claiming that you are working on the big novel that will more than justify the protracted wait for its completion. Sometimes the book *is* completed, thereby vindicating and perpetuating an entire economy of support. Sometimes the author of that initial book of stories lives on the ghost of promise for the rest of their days, conscious, however comfortable the living, that they are working a hustle of which they are both beneficiary and victim.

Back in 1938, before this enviable system of inducements was established, Cyril Connolly, in *Enemies of Promise*, sought to examine the multitudinous ways in which writers give up, the many things that help put them to sleep. The 'pram in the hall' has proved the most famously enduring of impediments but promise itself can also prove lethal: 'Whom the gods wish to destroy they first call promising.'

33.

In almost every case even the most abrupt cessations happen *gradually*. The one-book writer often has a second book, almost always of inferior quality: an afterthought. J. A. Baker, whose reputation is entirely synonymous with *The Peregrine* (1967), followed it up, a few years later, with *The Hill of Summer*. The purpose of the one-book writer's second book is to serve as a sort of confirmation that it's all over. For anyone reluctant to accept this conclusion, at any point in their creative life, there is a resumption of torment. Lying in his hospital bed in *Reach for the Sky* (one of the inspirational films of my childhood) Douglas Bader is about to drift painlessly into death; as soon as he determines to resist—to live—the agony of his shattered legs comes surging back. Connolly pointed out that 'all true artistic indolence' is 'a pain not a pleasure.' Iris Murdoch, who in the mid-1990s is reported to be suffering from writer's block, tells Martin Amis at a party that 'being unable to write is very *boring*.' 'In the old days depression wasn't so bad because I could write about it,' Larkin wrote to a friend in 1979. 'Now writing has left me, and only the depression remains.'

When Amis says goodbye to Murdoch at the party he reassures her that her trouble is not permanent. It's actually terminal. As it was for Larkin—'a turned-off tap'—and as it will prove, at some point, for everyone. Until then highly successful writers whose latest work is eagerly awaited by publishers and readers alike prefer not to admit, in public at least, that they can't do it anymore. Truman Capote led everyone to believe he was still at it, still writing *Answered Prayers* even after there was little chance of his or his publishers' prayers being answered. It's more usual, if you stop writing, that no one cares or even notices.

34.

Cioran writes that every misanthrope, 'however sincere, at times reminds me of that old poet, bedridden and utterly forgotten, who in a rage with his contemporaries declared he would receive none of them. His wife, out of charity, would ring at the door from time to time.'

When, I keep asking myself, will publishers stop sending manuscripts and galleys, pestering me for blurbs? Even as I say this I know that after six months—make that six weeks—I'd be worrying why no one asked me for endorsements any more. I'm only wise enough to realise this because of these lines of Cioran's.

35.

Don DeLillo's 1991 novel *Mao II* wrings multiple twists and thematic turns out of the story of Bill Gray and the novel he's been writing, off and on, for twenty-three years. 'The work has burnt him out. He's burnt out,' explains his editor, Scott. 'Bill walks five feet from his desk and doubt hits him like a hammer in the back. He has to go back to his desk and find a passage he knows will reassure him. He reads it and he's reassured. An hour later, sitting in the car, he feels it again, the page is wrong, the chapter is wrong, and he can't shake the doubt until he gets back to his desk and finds a passage he knows will reassure him. He reads it and he's reassured. He's been doing this all his life and now he's run out of reassuring passages.' And yet: 'When the sun comes up, he shuffles to his desk.' Asked when he might finish the book, Bill himself replies: 'Finish. I'm finished. The book's been done for two years. But I rewrite pages and then revise in detail. I write to survive now, to keep my heart beating.' All of which means, as far as Scott is concerned, that the worst thing Bill could do is actually *publish* the book. The publisher could make millions but 'it would mean the end of Bill as a myth, as a force.' By *not* being published, the book could define an idea, a principle: 'That the withheld work of art is the only eloquence left.' A little later the conversation drifts back to a discussion of whether the novel as a form is finished—overtaken 'by the emergence of news as an apocalyptic force'—and whether this particular example of it might be finished. 'I'll tell you when a book is finished,' says Bill. 'When the writer keels over with a great big thump.'

That's not what happened to DeLillo. *Underworld* was his last—and truly great—big thump. Thereafter his trajectory was in line with the title of Beckett's story 'Lessness' as he made a slow and wobbly glide towards the 128 pages of *The Silence*.

36.

The relationship between quitting and continuing exists in every conceivable permutation and exception. As *The Sportswriter* focuses on a writer who quit after one book, Henry James in his story 'The Middle

Years'—first published in 1893, collected in *Terminations* two years
later—focuses on a writer who, as the title suggests, is washed-up
mid-career. Dencombe has received a copy of his "'latest," perhaps
his last' book, *The Middle Years*. For several years he has been conscious 'of ebbing time, of shrinking opportunity; and now he felt not
so much that his last chance was going as that it was gone indeed.
He had done all that he should ever do, and yet he had not done
what he wanted.' After unwrapping the book he begins reading and is
gradually 'pacified and reassured. Everything came back to him but
came back with a wonder, came back, above all, with a high and magnificent beauty. He read his own prose, he turned his own leaves, and
had, as he sat there with the spring sunshine on the page, an emotion
peculiar and intense. His career was over, no doubt, but it was over,
after all, with *that*.' This feeling of satisfaction and fulfilment soon
gives way to something else, 'a glimpse of a possible reprieve,' the
sense that perhaps all is not yet spent. And not only that. Perhaps it
is only now that he has come into true possession of his talent. What
he needs is an extension, and so, as he turns the last pages, he sighs,
'Ah for another go!'

What follows is like a slight precursor of Italo Calvino's *If on a
Winter's Night a Traveller* as Dencombe encounters someone else
who is reading an advance copy of *The Middle Years*, who turns out
to be a passionate admirer of his work. Dencombe enjoys withhold-
ing his identity from this fan as they talk but then suffers a sudden
collapse.

37.

While Dencombe is briefly uplifted by the experience of reading his
recent work a condition of being able to go on creating late into one's
life seems often to be an inability to see what, for readers, is the
most distinct quality of this later work: its deterioration in quality.
Immersed in writing *Across the River and into the Trees* an excited

fifty-year-old Hemingway told his publisher that he was once again writing as if he were a twenty-five-year-old. Some of the reviews, when the book was published in 1950, would have annihilated a twenty-five-year-old—or anyone less besotted by their own mythos: 'It is not only Hemingway's worst novel,' decided *The Saturday Review of Literature*, 'it is a synthesis of everything that is bad in his previous work and it throws a doubtful light on the future.' The future would hold further success—with *The Old Man and the Sea* and the Nobel Prize—and prove more dreadful as Hemingway, whose method and goal was always to write 'one true sentence,' gradually found himself flailing in one of DeLillo's, from *The Silence*: 'Everything that was simple and declarative, where did it go?'

38.

Willem de Kooning, in the years 1983–86, enjoyed a sudden surge in productivity, averaging almost a painting a week—a cause for celebration that was also a source of concern. 'He might still draw with authority or create a serious composition at the easel. But he would no longer be capable of judging the result. The increasing production suggested, in any case, that he was no longer quite himself.' In the years to come, as these early warning signs gave way to the devastation of Alzheimer's, assistants would project drawings onto canvas for him to paint over and around, line up tubes of paint (to tempt him to expand his colour palette), and point him towards parts of the canvas—'holidays' was their agreed term—that he'd forgotten to fill in.

39.

These are extreme cases—of extreme decline and extraordinary persistence—in every way. Milder and universal symptoms of ageing mean that you can't run as fast as you used to, that your knees hurt more and for longer afterwards. If you're sitting at your desk writing you are spared the obvious signs of mental wear and tear. Your knees might ache (from prolonged immobility) but the brain is not in pain even if it doesn't seem to be functioning quite as well as it once did. Consciousness of the brain not working as it once did is often foreshadowed by fear that this *might* soon be the case. 'I have a considerable talent, perhaps as good as any coeval,' Faulkner wrote in a letter of 22 April 1944. 'But I am 46 now. So what I will mean soon by "have" is "had."' (Young though forty-six seems, one wonders if the deterioration kicked in, syntactically, while he was writing this letter.) As the fear becomes justified it also becomes familiar and, as a result, less fearful. Hard to believe, but even Updike, in his mid-seventies, confessed: 'With ominous frequency, I can't think of the right word. I know there *is* a word; I can visualize the exact shape it occupies in the jigsaw puzzle of the English language. But the word itself, with its precise edges and unique tint of meaning, hangs on the misty rim of consciousness.' You may consult the thesaurus more often ('with shamefaced recourse,' as Updike admits) but it's possible that you can continue to write at the same speed, with the same ease—it's just that the sentences lack many of the qualities that made the prose of twenty or forty years earlier such a joy to read: 'Its carefree bounce, its snap, its exuberant air of slight excess.' (The irony, of which he was fully conscious, is that Updike describes the creep of imprecision and verbal fatigue with customary precision and an appropriately slight diminution of sprightliness.) 'No amount of learned skills,' he writes, can substitute for the youthful conviction 'of having a lot to say.' And when you're older? In the course of his unfinished novel *The Garden of Eden*, Hemingway imagined the difficulties of a young writer, David Bourne, but succeeded in describing his own:

> He had started a sentence as soon as he had gone into his working room and had completed it but he could write nothing after it. He crossed it out and started another sentence

and again came to the complete blankness. He was unable to write the sentence that should follow although he knew it. He wrote a first simple declarative sentence again and it was impossible for him to put down the next sentence on paper. At the end of two hours it was the same.

40.

Larkin greeted the news of a forthcoming bibliography of his work with ironic relief. 'Apart from everything else, it will prove an excellent excuse for not writing anything else, which as far as I can see I am unlikely to do in any case.' Falling deeper into poetic silence Larkin resigned himself to writing letters to friends, boozily accepting that his brain had 'virtually packed up' before taking the next step and writing—in a letter—that he didn't 'seem to write letters these days, or anything else for that matter.'

With cruel and tender playfulness Carol Ann Duffy puts the matter more succinctly in 'Alphabet for Auden':

When the words have gone away
there is nothing left to say.

But that doesn't mean you stop saying, even if it means saying what's been said before—not by somebody else, but by yourself.*

* 'I can't go on. I'll go on.' It was a promise easily kept, not to end this book by quoting these, the last words of Beckett's *The Unnamable*. I mention them down here in the ditch like this because I've always wondered why there was a full stop at the end. Wouldn't it have been better if 'on' had been left suspended in unstoppable space? My Calder edition of the Beckett trilogy ends with that last full stop at the bottom right-hand corner of the last page. I'm guessing this is deliberate. If that full stop were removed a tiny adjustment to hyphenation and justification would mean that 'on' came right at the end of the very last line of the last recto page of the book, suggesting that the narrator had indeed gone on but that a mistake in binding or an act of vandalism by an irate reader meant that the subsequent pages—all the subsequent goings-on—had gone missing.

41.

Writers need to strike a balance between exercising a degree of critical vigilance over their work in progress and not allowing that editorial surveillance to cauterise the flow of words. It's a very delicate operation, requiring constant recalibration throughout a working life. Generally, it's assumed to be a bad thing when the writing dries up, when writers stifle their own creativity. But what if the flow depends on a critical obliviousness for its survival?

In a 1991 piece about snooker Martin Amis observed in passing that he was able to read and write, 'to a high standard'—a claim no one, at the time, would have dared dispute. Two questions then: first, how did he come to write *Yellow Dog* and *Lionel Asbo*? By force of habit, I suppose, by keeping doing what he'd been doing for decades. The second question is trickier: what did he think when he *read* them?

Let's assume that by the end of a day spent working on *Yellow Dog* or *Lionel Asbo* Amis had still been able to thump out as many words as he could in his pomp, while writing *Money* or *London Fields*. Assume, also, that he kept going, didn't become discouraged by reading back what he'd come up with each day until he'd completed a version of the book. But then, when he read back what he'd written, could he not see that something more than work was needed?

'I think you can start to lose your power in language with age,' says Rachel Cusk in a *Paris Review* interview. Implicitly referring to her novel *Second Place* she mentions an idea she has about

> the late work of visual artists being almost like an egg that breaks open to reveal the true visionary self. And that cannot happen in language, because with age, language betrays you. Language shows how old you are. It shows so many things about your identity in the first place, your social class. But as you get older—you see it happen, you see writers suddenly become slightly embarrassing or lose touch with the story of life.

Is this prognosis terminal, with no hope—no possibility—of remission? Even when telling the story of one's own life? Even if this *became* one's subject?

42.

After writing these paragraphs about Amis I made another of the occasional promises that accompanied the composition of this book—and I've kept it. I promised to retain that passage even if it was undermined by the long-anticipated book he was writing about Saul Bellow, Christopher Hitchens, and Larkin. *Inside Story* is his strongest book since the memoir *Experience* (2000), which it strongly resembles despite being offered as a novel. Twenty years earlier Julie Burchill wrote that she 'would have become his slave on the spot' if Amis had entitled that memoir *My Struggle*. So now she is in a form of chattel bondage, though the struggle is the Knausgaardian one whereby the fiction is apparently and deliberately indistinguishable—at least to those who don't have access to the documentary record—from the life and lives it depicts. If the book's exclusive revelations—about his girlfriend Phoebe and his dad, Kingsley, about Larkin, his dad's friend, and his mum—have been invented or heftily reshaped with a view to narrative enhancement rather than faithfulness to the facts, its success as a novel depends on all traces of the fictive being craftily buried. While ostensibly clearing out his pockets, Amis turns *Inside Story* inside out, into a novel, thereby improving the reader's experience and covering his tracks. But if a novel is expected either to live up to certain formal prerogatives or, more ambitiously, to generate its own, then *Inside Story* is a messy and leaky one. A gallon mixture emptied optimistically into a big plastic bag—with holes to prevent the suffocating liabilities of memoir—it lacks the cohesion of the Knausgaard project, which successfully created the mould from which it was in the process of being made. That is what the Knausgaard books are *about*. Amis's books, from *Money* onwards, have been all about the voice. Linguistically *Inside Story* has a lot of the old (young) swagger and verve, especially in the bits dealing with Amis's love life in the 1970s. It's fun to read, even when it's also a bit embarrassing to read (as when we are whisked off on a junket to France where his beautiful and brainy wife 'Elena' is receiving a literary prize).

Now, fun is never to be underrated, especially since fun was what had been missing from recent Amis novels, a lack I'd felt acutely because reading Amis usually made me conscious of how much more fun I was having reading him than I'd had in the course of reading anything since, well, since the last Amis. I cantered through five hundred pages in five days during a sudden cold snap in Los Angeles, lying on the sofa with a rug over my knees, having fun all the time, conscious that I'd have had more fun if I'd done it in three, maintaining the same pace but over a course shortened by two hundred pages—roughly the ratio by which most of Amis's big books should have been cut. Which brings us back to that syndrome whereby Amis is not the best reader of his own stuff. Amis, who insists that he doesn't need editing, is an editor's dream—not because it's all comma-perfect and requires no work but because it's so easy to see what needs to be cut. If asked I'd have advised cutting some of the advice on how to write.

Now, there was a paragraph here of about 120 words followed by a section on how to edit. I got rid of the latter after the book had been copyedited, mainly because I decided to add—and make room for—something else. (It will become clear, later, why every addition has to be balanced by a deletion of equal length.) With a bit of renumbering of sections, that was easily and invisibly mended. But reading through proofs I realised that what was originally in this paragraph should also be cut. It had to go even though substantive changes to proofs are an irritating disruption. How could I have failed to see what was now so blatant?

43.

The best bits of *Inside Story* are to be found in the many passages where the prose is not showy for its own sake but when it's the expression of acute observation. Alex Clark, reviewing the book in *The Guardian*, dwelt on the way that at one point Amis 'activated the kettle.' A clever way, she thought, to avoid saying that he put the kettle on: an example of how, even in the most routine domestic setting, the author can't pass up a chance to indulge in a bit of low-level verbal stunt-flying. But how about another similar action or activation, albeit one loaded with narrative expectation, when Martin visits the ageing Phoebe at her London flat? 'I pressed the steel nub and within a couple of seconds the lock buzzed and weakly rattled.' Those last five words—including the strongly rationed adverb—are enough to prove that Amis is a great writer in the sense of one able fully to render experience in words. When this happens we are not just reading the words but seeing—or, in this case, hearing—the world. Parts of the book are devoted to the decline of Bellow, who, for Amis, has been the best observer of the contemporary world. Even if that's a critical estimation one finds impossible to share there's no denying the extreme and simple pathos of the moment when Amis looks at the ageing Bellow and notices his 'eyes oystery with time.'*

44.

I couldn't finish Hitchens's memoir *Hitch-22* (the writing was bulging-over-the-waistband flabby, falling *way* below the exacting standards by which Amis judges anyone else's prose), enjoyed his essays (with reservations),† and admire unreservedly the columns filed during his final illness (and collected in *Mortality*). I never met him but saw him

---

* John Updike, another of Amis's heroes, uses 'oysterish,' in a very different context, in *Memories of the Ford Administration* (page 15 of my Penguin paperback).

† A quick word on those reservations about the essays: as contrarian and polemicist, Hitchens often set up his essays as confrontations or contests with their nominal subject. Even his celebrations had a combative element in that the person to be praised—Orwell, say—had to be elevated at the expense of not only detractors but also those who were mistaken or muddled in their admiration. In both cases reading Hitchens was like watching a boxer who, as he makes his way to the ring, can't resist taking a pop at someone, including those lined up to cheer him en route to the site of intended engagement.

speak, always impressively, on several occasions. Two things struck me about the late surge in his reputation, before the final super-surge of 'the year of living dyingly.' First, public-school confidence and voice, combined with the ability to lob in quotations from Macaulay, go an awful long way to persuade Americans that they're in touch with some lost essence of England. Certainly it goes a lot further than a recip-rocal arrangement—private school and quotations from Emerson—might grant an American in England. Second, Hitchens became quite famous for supporting the invasion of Iraq (not so clever) and still more infamous for being—wait for it—an *atheist*. How to react to this radical stance except with the single word of astonishment that the young Martin greeted the scene when Paul Theroux, in one of his books, has sex on a train? '*Cor!*' Coming out, as it were, with *God Is Not Great* in AD 2007 was hardly the leap into the intellectual or ethical unknown that proclaiming the death of God had been for the madman in Nietzsche's fable or that the life of 'Shelley the atheist' had been earlier in the nineteenth century. My dad, who never read a book in his life, was a vehement hater of Christianity for broadly the same reason that he was anti-royalist, or anti anything else for that matter: i.e., financial. For him the most powerfully symbolic mo-ment in any church service was not the blood of my blood nonsense (my knowledge of what goes on in these places is a little vague) but the taking of the collection. On the few occasions we were obliged to be in a church he not only refused to contribute a face-saving penny; he didn't even try to make it look as if he had. I asked him how it had taken hold, this trenchant opposition to the church, and he explained that when he was in the army he became friendly with a chap who was 'anti-Christ.' Let it be entered in the record then: Hitch and Mart have fun doing their priest-baiting, but my dad *met* the anti-Christ.

45.

'I have been (among other follies) a hard liver as well as a hard thinker . . .'

While my dad would have seen eye to eye with Amis and Hitchens on issues theological two other matters would have been met with his utmost disapproval and disgust (for exactly the same reasons as those already given): the smoking and drinking. The entrenched belief that smoking was cool, even rebellious, always seemed—and not just to someone like me who's never had a cigarette—the single most uncool thing about Hitch and Mart. As for the booze, the amount they put away, even while Hitch was ill, is something to marvel at. Amis is adamant that it's only those who undergo 'personality change' while drunk who are 'the dipsomaniacs, actual or potential. All else is just heavy drinking.' That's reassuring in roughly the same measure that Scott Fitzgerald took solace in the way that he got shit-faced so quickly; surely that proved he wasn't a real alky? But let's take Mart at his word and say that in *Inside Story* he and Hitch appear to be functioning heavy drinkers—legendarily high-functioning in the case of Hitchens, who could consume vast quantities, before lunch, and then go on to write a thousand-word piece or duff up anyone hoping to out-drink—I mean out-*debate*—him, unchanged and apparently unimpaired.

For the last five years I've kept a record, in my diary, of how much I've drunk each day. The goal was to have at least three nights a week completely off the sauce, though most years I surpassed the required 150 nights. I've never had the intention or even felt the urge to quit drinking but each year I've drunk slightly less than the year before—until this year when Covid caused things to jump off a cliff. We had dinner with neighbours in Venice Beach on 18 March where I drank two beers and half a glass of wine. And that was that. Weeks and weeks went by without a drop and then months and months. There was nothing difficult or deliberate about it, partly because I'd only ever been a social drinker—though I was, for a very long time, *very* social—and suddenly there was no social life at all. It wasn't till 30 June that we next went to the house of some friends where, in the garden, I had three glasses of lovely champagne. One night short of fifteen weeks with not a drop to drink! The disappointing thing about this sabbatical was that I didn't feel any better—even after three months—than I routinely did after the usual three nights off. There was no cumulative build-up of lucidity, well-being, or energy. On the other hand, the long lay-off did not render me suddenly susceptible to the effects of booze once I got a sniff of it again. Those glasses of Moët didn't leave me legless and howling for more, as determined as Denzel Washington in *Flight* to glug down anything I could get my paws on. There was no sense of having fallen off a wagon I had accidentally boarded and stayed on only because there was no reason not to.

Alcohol *wants* you to become an alcoholic—it wants you to want more. But I've always been surprised by the way that, even if I've been drinking a lot, it's a very easy habit to break. After a couple of days the craving for booze goes away (except when eating or, more precisely, *after* eating, as a way of getting the taste of food out of my mouth). This is one of the things I'm looking forward to in the last however-many years of life: drinking less so that I never have to give up drinking.

46.

And what about getting stoned? When Larkin, the final member of the trio of writers in *Inside Story*, saw 'a couple of kids' etc. . . . . he knew this was the 'paradise / Everyone old has dreamed of all their lives.' He was thinking of sex—Larkin was always thinking about sex—but if he'd been living here in California and writing 'High Windows' fifty years later he'd have been thinking about not just Tinder but marijuana. There's never been a better time to smoke pot. It's so great, you don't even have to *smoke* it. That's what stopped me infiltrating the cool crowd at Oxford in the 1970s: having to smoke those revolting, tobacco-stuffed, English joints over which a tiny lump of hash had been ritually crumbled. I tried a couple of times but always felt nauseous because of the tobacco, because I'd never smoked a cigarette. It was only after college, when I discovered pipes and bongs, that I managed to get stoned, but while these useful accessories did enable me to achieve that mythical grail—at once all-pervasive and oddly elusive—the taste was revolting and my throat was always left feeling like a scalded cat's, like a cat with a sore throat. But I got the hang of it and smoking pot became a joy, enhancing every aspect of my life, including work. There were plenty of occasions when I thought I couldn't write something and then, while stoned, an idea wafted into my head. Every experience could be enhanced by being stoned (except the ones that were diminished by it): listening to music (almost a 100 per cent success rate), sometimes reading (poetry mainly), having sex (if one could remain focused), eating certain foods (as long as they had no potential to become revolting), walking in nature, visiting art galleries, sacred sites, or war memorials. Even getting stoned could be enhanced—by getting more stoned. I always got stoned at parties; it made me wittier, only rarely made me think that I might be thinking that I was wittier than I thought I was, thereby opening the door to an infinite feedback loop of self-inquisition. I could even handle taking the night bus home after parties, the slur of lights through the window-drizzle, the perpetual lurk of London yobbery.

And then, as skunk came first to dominate and then entirely monopolise the market, I lost the appetite for it. I liked skunk for a while, for the totality of immersion, the *Gesamtkunstwerk* effect, but then it became a conduit to paranoia, dread, and what seemed like a premonition of traumatic head injury—though even this had a positive side as, in the nick of time, I dug a story called 'Skunk' out of the rubble of skunk-paranoia and skunk-dread.

When we moved to Los Angeles I fully intended getting back on the horse and resuming my life as a pot-smoker. As a gesture of commitment I invested in a state-of-the-art vaporiser, glamorous and silver-sleek, looking and packaged as if it were designed by a hipster offshoot of Apple. And there was no need to buy pot from dealers—something else I'd come to dislike—as one could register for a medical card. This process was frankly farcical but, having told the 'doctor'—whom one would not have wanted to consult for something as life-threatening as a mouth ulcer or stitch—that one was having trouble getting to sleep or staying awake or that one's slippers were the wrong size, it was pleasant to take one's card to a dispensary and be advised by a consultant who, frankly, was often not the best advert for mari-juana use, in order to have a properly curated high even if the actual high ended up being one one didn't actually care for. Things got even more convenient a few years later when the need to visit a medical dispensary was itself dispensed with. A branch of MedMen opened up on nearby Lincoln Boulevard in Venice. Then another branch opened even nearer by on Abbot Kinney. That's when Larkin's line about par-adise really hit home. I passed this always-busy store almost daily, on the way to do or buy something else, even though Abbot Kinney is full of stores no one in their right mind would ever buy anything from, and every time I walked up Abbot Kinney all I ever did was lament the passing of Axe, a restaurant I'd first eaten in years before I moved here, remarking to my companion at the time that this was the best mashed potato I'd ever eaten, though this may have been influenced by the way that we'd got incredibly stoned somewhere miles away and the drive to Venice had been so nerve-shredding that I was, at some level, relieved to be alive and able to eat anything, let alone this ut-terly sensational mashed potato. Walking past MedMen the first few times I was surprised that they had chosen big ugly red lettering for the storefront design. I'm guessing it was to get as far away as possible from all of the associations of traditional pot use even though pot cul-ture has generated an aesthetic that extends well beyond *The Fabulous Furry Freak Brothers* and Bob Marley T-shirts. Although the MedMen sign (red) connotes anything *but* marijuana (green) once inside you can describe exactly the marijuana experience you want, which, in my case, is always the same: clarity above all else, but not *just* clarity.

'Clarity accompanied by laughter,' I clarified the first time I stepped inside this new frontier of narco-retail. 'Free-flow of ideas. All-round enhancement of the senses. Ability to inhabit even the most demanding passages of Beethoven's late quartets. Laughter. No tiredness or dopey feeling, no heaviness, and no next-day fogginess either. That, young man, is the kind of high I am in the market for.' And the respectable-looking young man I said this to claimed he could make it happen.

'Buddy, we'll get you rocking out to the *Grosse Fuge*,' he said. MedMen has exactly the products to do this and anything else, the multitudinous strains with their fun names all broken down and itemised either as sativas or indicas. And so I would get whatever was recommended but always, eventually, whatever had been cho-sen ended up making me heavy-headed and the longed-for clarity would give way to unwanted fogginess. The experience was made-to-measure but it never quite fit. Even if a bespoke suit fits perfectly that doesn't mean the person stuck inside it feels comfortable. I gravi-tated towards the sativas but they made me anxious, while the indicas made me sluggish and the hybrids made me anxiously sluggish or sluggishly anxious. Either way it was never quite right. Despite all the subtle varieties of high promised by the impressive roster of pots on offer there was always one consistent effect, namely that after a while they all made me wish I was un-stoned, and so the intervals between getting stoned grew lengthier and the conditions in which I could attempt breaking this marijuana drought became more stringent. It was important that there had to be no social interaction whatsoever. If I was going to a concert, if I had collected my ticket and knew exactly where I was sitting—had, ideally, already rehearsed the route from ticket booth to seat before stepping outside again—then I could quickly have a couple of hits on my sleek vaporiser before taking my seat and sinking into a performance by the Necks at the Blue Whale or the evening of jazz-metal by Burning Ghosts all the way across town at the Zebulon (where there were no seats). These successes aside, it was only fifty-fifty whether gig-going was enhanced or di-minished by getting stoned. Sometimes I could lock into the music for a while (Gillian Welch at the Orpheum) before drifting off (Stars of the Lid at the Regent) and mainly what I would drift into was thinking about whether I would rather not have been stoned, whether the music had merited getting stoned or, in the case of Zubin Mehta conducting Brahms's Fourth with the L.A. Phil—too frail to stand, he waved his wand from a chair—if we are being utterly frank, whether it merited coming to at all. The standing ovation at the end was a sort of get-well-soon expression of collective good will, designed to get the old boy back on his feet—or at least off the stage so we could get in our cars and listen to Brahms at home.

In tandem with my increasing reluctance to get stoned or, more exactly, my relief when I'd thought about getting stoned but had opted not to, two potentially contradictory tendencies made themselves felt. First, with evidence of the Green Rush all around, a rapidly escalating sense of regret that I'd not got a financial stake in the booming business of legal marijuana. Second, a gradually escalating hostility to marijuana generally. I came to dislike the smell wafting everywhere in Venice, wafting from the boardwalk to Abbot Kinney, wafting from the ocean to the Inland Empire, possibly as far as Oklahoma, like some THC update on the Dust Bowl. There's no getting away from it. Everywhere reeks of marijuana, marijuana that is far too strong and rots people's brains. It's far too strong and it's difficult to resist the conclusion that smoking this mind-rotting pot is rotting people's brains, making the mentally unhinged even more unhinged and further deranging the already deranged. It's not just that it's far too strong. Increased strength might be taken to mean that less is needed to create the desired effect but even a small amount creates a fundamentally different effect, an effect that is the opposite of desirable. Changes in degree become changes in kind.

One of the reasons I always think twice—*twice?* More like fifty times!—before getting stoned, before deciding not to, is the driving. It's not just that being stoned impairs my ability to drive in L.A. Right from the start being in L.A. was enough to impair my ability to drive. I found driving here nerve-shredding anyway but being stoned also made *being* driven nerve-shredding, especially since so many other people were driving while stoned, driving while their ability to drive was impaired, making it more and more dangerous and more and more nerve-shredding, so that I'd always be calling out 'Careful!' or 'Watch out!' to my driver (my wife), who claimed that these constant and unprovoked exclamations of alarm made us more accident-prone, so I'd force myself to remain silent as we approached—as we did, with astonishing regularity—the latest flashing-light apocalypse of a crash-site on the I-10, prompting me to think back to our London life, to how relaxing and safe it was to get the tube from Ladbroke Grove to Baker Street and then walk down to the Wigmore Hall to hear the world's premier quartets and soloists, and it seemed incredible that, in all the years we'd lived in London, we'd gone there precisely once, to what turned out to be such a disappointing recital of something by someone that all I could think about was the crippling lack of leg room.

But it's not so much fear that's the issue; it's a propensity for confusion or, more precisely, what I fear is the confusion induced by getting stoned. I used to have an excellent sense of direction, I used to *pride myself* on my superb sense of direction, but marijuana has shredded wherever it is in the brain that deals with navigation, geography, and orientation, and I often struggle, these days, to get my bearings. I blame it on marijuana because that is preferable to the alternative, which is that I am starting to show signs of Alzheimer's and it's possible that this underlying fear—of Alzheimer's—is contributing to the lurking readiness to become anxious and unhappy if stoned. I'd need an MRI to confirm these hunches but one thing is for sure: the main part of my brain that marijuana has damaged is the part that responds favourably to marijuana—and there's a reassuring side to this too.

There are people who still like to get high in their sixties but in many ways it's a young person's game, getting high. I take heart from the fact that a lot of people my age have shared my deepening aversion to marijuana, a process that is the opposite of the addict's agonised withdrawal from hard drugs. What's involved is a gradual acceptance that we no longer like something we've had a hard time accepting we no longer like. Unlike tennis, say. I still love everything about tennis. I love cycling past the moronic stores selling vapes and bongs on the boardwalk, past the miasma of pot wafting from the stoned skatepark, down the stoned cycle path alongside the stoned ocean, all the way to the courts themselves, near the basketball court, the basketball court mentioned earlier, where so much pot is being smoked that playing tennis on court six is like playing in a giant open-air bong, but this unwanted adjacency of tennis and marijuana reminds me of the times in London when, if I got stoned at a party in the evening after playing tennis in the afternoon, I'd end up replaying points in my head, and if a friend I'd played tennis with earlier that day was also at the party, we'd both relive defining passages of play and it was great, like being a pro player back in the days when they'd all go out partying together after matches. Anyway, that's all in the past now. I just don't like marijuana anymore and at some level I can scarcely even remember what it was like when being stoned lit up the world, releasing the latent glow of things. It's difficult not to feel, like Wordsworth, that there has 'passed away a glory from the earth,' which is not at all the way to feel in California, the land of glory, one of the last places on earth where the glory fades each day, where everything glows, where the blue sky that shows nothing—though whether sky this blue can be counted as nothing remains a moot point—is nowhere and is endless.

And then along came Covid, which meant that you'd need nerves of steel to avoid falling prey to paranoia while stoned. This being California, however, MedMen was deemed an essential medical service and remained open throughout the lockdown.

47.

All this talk of booze and pot makes me aware of another of the potential contradictions that riddle this book. For while I have vivid memories of scrambling out of poetry readings—and films and concerts—the rush was motivated in large part by time being called, by something I forgot to mention in opposition to that long list of lasts beginning way back on page 102, namely last *orders*. We wanted the reading to be over with because we needed *more* time in the pub. The best years of my drinking life, years when I was in peak boozing condition, were dominated by the hated eleven o'clock curfew. It's impossible to exaggerate the misery this caused generation after generation of drinkers in England. That's why occasional lock-ins at the Effra in Brixton felt like heaven. A few members' clubs in central London stayed open late but that was capped by another tacit curfew, the deadline of the last Victoria line trains back to Brixton at about 12:20. It was one of the joys of going to Paris, being able to stay out in cafés as late as you wanted, drinking and talking, and then, after you'd had enough of both, to stop off for one more, over the zinc, on the way home.

Ultimately, though, it could be viewed as a swigs-and-roundabouts thing. After decades of suffering, partly because there was nothing worth doing in England after eleven, along came rave. Suddenly there was no better place to be than London after eleven o'clock. You could stay out as late as you liked, till the tubes started the next morning. In Paris, rave culture never quite took off in the same way because cafés were open till two in the morning and the talk was there to be talked. Gradually, the historic trend of young Brits dreaming of living in the Paris of Hemingway, Godard, and Binoche was reversed as the Eurostar filled up with French hurtling through the Channel tunnel to be in London rather than in the seductive bistro-mausoleum of Paris. Eventually—to conclude this crucial postscript to Judt's *Postwar*—everyone piled back onto trains and planes heading farther east to Berlin, for the best of both worlds. If you failed to get into Berghain or the KitKat it didn't matter—it did matter, obviously, it was devastating (or so I'm told; amazingly, I was never turned away) but you could still go and drink and talk in (horribly smoky) bars till four in the morning.

48.

'No more of that.'

No line of Shakespeare's better sums up the present moment, the interminable Covid accidie, than Othello's stark realisation of the way everything that was memorable and glorious in his life has come to a catastrophic end. Living a life that involves going out to a café and being back home by twelve at the latest—twelve noon, that is, after coffee for elevenses*—I find myself turning to Byron and lightly rewriting the contented melancholy of his famous lines:

> *So we'll go no more a raving so late into the night,*
> *though the heart be still as loved-up*
> *and the full moon still as bright.*

Jeez, but I'm glad I'm old, old enough to not mind staying in, sitting round here revising this book, remembering all this old poetry, watching the latest compilations of Roger's best dropshots or ultra-slo-mo footage of his backhand on YouTube, feeling clear-headed, not getting stoned and not drinking (we're back on it, back on the wagon, that is).

49.

Returning to Amis for the last—i.e., second-to-last—time, does it make sense to regard *Inside Story* as a return to form? Somewhat, though in discussions of literature and writers it always sounds more appropriate if 'form' is used to refer not to quality but to genre, as when a novelist forsakes their usual area of skill and success, ventures

---

* I look back on even *that* nostalgically. With cases surging in L.A. we're in full lockdown again.

into unfamiliar terrain with diminished commercial results, and then comes either skulking or bounding back to the arena in which they made their name. (In such cases I'm always drawn to the generically exceptional work, the one that lies outside the catchment area of a given authorial brand: the non-fiction account of the 'three short lives' of Christopher Wood, Richard Hillary, and Jeremy Wolfenden, for example, by the novelist Sebastian Faulks in *The Fatal Englishman*.) If we revert to the use of form as a gauge of quality, DeLillo was on a fine run with *The Names*, *White Noise*, and *Libra*. Then came the disappointment of the eagerly anticipated *Mao II*. What followed was not a return to form but a raising of the bar with *Underworld*. That was too early in his career—or insufficiently late—to be properly termed a comeback but it was a great book after a pretty bad one. After the great one came a *really* bad one, *Cosmopolis*, an ingenuous exercise in self-karaoke,* but even after that it was not appropriate to expect a comeback since it's not as if DeLillo went anywhere to come back *from*; he didn't retire, he kept writing short books until he faded into the sublime and slight vibration—the disembodied, self-extinguishing shimmer—of *The Silence*.

To stage a real literary comeback you need to have disappeared almost without trace, as happened when a planned radio adaption of *Good Morning, Midnight* prompted the BBC in 1956 to place an advertisement for information regarding the whereabouts of Jean Rhys. Missing, presumed dead, Rhys duly got in touch and, in response to another query from the publisher André Deutsch, said she was working on a new book. Eventually published in 1966, a full twenty-seven years after her previous novel, *Wide Sargasso Sea* was an immense and immediate success. 'It's come too late,' said Rhys.

The problem with the earlier books, it is often said, is that they had come too soon, but *After Leaving Mr. Mackenzie* (1931), *Voyage in the Dark* (1934), and *Good Morning, Midnight* (1939) were not just ahead

---

* It would be disingenuous not to mention that I've used this description of *Cosmopolis* before: an example of critical- or commentary-oke.

of their time; they were insufficiently rooted in the past. Owing no debts, as Al Alvarez put it, 'to the great—or even to the not-so-great—tradition,' they were, for a long time, almost ineligible for consideration as part of its extension. Rhys, characteristically, makes a similar point in more personal terms. On arrival in England from the West Indies she had hated the cold. 'There were fires, but they were always blocked by people trying to get warm. And I'd never get into the sacred circle. I was always outside, shivering.' It was not until *Wide Sargasso Sea*—an outsider's retelling of the story of the first Mrs. Rochester from *Jane Eyre*—that critics stood aside to welcome her as warmly and glowingly as possible. But even in 1976 there was no mention of her in *The Auden Generation*, Samuel Hynes's study of 'Literature and Politics in England in the 1930s.' In a sense, the omission is entirely appropriate. Rhys was an invisible genius.* Interviewed late in life by *The Paris Review*, she is asked to consider the opinion that she had 'been fighting oblivion since the twenties.' ('I'm not fighting oblivion now,' the aged writer responds hesitantly. 'I'm fighting . . . eternity?') She was not part of any literary generation or movement and, for a very long time, as Leavis said of Defoe (in a footnote in *The Great Tradition*), 'matter[ed] little as an influence.' Books about uprooted and downtrodden women who could not fit in, by a woman born in Dominica, who had a pathological inability to fit in *anywhere*, their stylistic freedom makes them seem unburdened by the claims of the past: the most contemporary of all the novels from Auden's low, dishonest decade.

Rhys's comeback was self-enabled—not something often said about someone utterly incapable of helping herself—in that a new book generated a revival of interest in the old ones. Sometimes the comeback is entirely passive or reputational without any participation from a writer who is rediscovered by a new generation of grateful readers. This is what happened with Eve Babitz, all of whose books were out of print and who was living as a virtual recluse after suffering a

---

* The full extent of the wreckage of Rhys's life became visible only after the publication of Carole Angier's biography in 1990.

terrible accident in 1997. The accident occurred, as accidents always do in L.A., while she was driving—driving and trying to light a cigar, which set her highly inflammable skirt on fire, leaving her with third-degree burns over half of her body. The journalist Lili Anolik tracked her down and published a piece in *Vanity Fair* about the books and her eventual meeting with their author. The books were reissued, Anolik expanded the original piece into a book of her own, and, to concentrate on one highly specific result of all this, my life was massively enhanced by the experience of reading Eve Babitz.*

The greatest 'passive' or reputational comebacks of all are, of course, from beyond the grave, as happened, to an almost mythic degree with J. S. Bach, Nietzsche (even if his resurrection began while he was physically still alive), and van Gogh.

50.

The comeback is more properly and commonly associated with sports and performance than literature or art. In sport, comebacks are a standard part of the experience of any athlete or team who comes from behind in the course of a match. Some sports are more conducive to this than others; a few seem designed to maximise opportunities for doing so. Almost every top tennis player will at some stage come back from a set—two in the men's Slams—and match point down. Win that point and the moment of maximum danger has passed and you can go on to grab the game and, with steadily diminishing drama, take the set and the match.

---

* *Slow Days, Fast Company*, the best of the reissued books, comes with an introduction by Matthew Specktor, who once said to me, 'No one in their right mind would seriously suggest that Hank Mobley is greater than Coltrane.' By contrast, the pantheon of literary reputation seems both obdurate and vulnerable to right-minded critical questioning. A number of second-tier writers, often women, are better than those for whom the front-row seats are habitually, even unquestioningly, reserved. With her rehabilitation ongoing, Rhys's standing is likely to rise still further in the course of a larger reconsideration of the literature of the 1930s and '40s. If such a survey permits a curriculum of expanded eligibility then *Black Lamb and Grey Falcon* by Rebecca West—an unexceptional novelist—will emerge as the single greatest prose work of the period.

Behind on points, bleeding from a cut over the eye, knocked to the canvas, a boxer can struggle to his feet at the count of eight and go on to knock out his opponent before the end of the round. The protagonist of the story 'Rocket Man' in Thom Jones's *The Pugilist at Rest* (1993) is talking with one of his cornermen about a terrible fight. The cornerman 'used two bottles of adrenaline' to try to close the cuts and when that didn't work he 'burned them shut with ferric chloride.' The fighter reminds the cornerman of what he said next as he slumped, exhausted, on his stool: 'You said, "There's a third wind." You said, "Kid, there's a third wind. It's between here and death."' He finds that third wind and fights on until he has a chance to throw the first clear punch that he's had all night: 'Blam! He went down like he was shot between the eyes with a .45. Two minutes into the tenth round.' He's done it but the price is terrible: 'I realized I had a fever and when I went to piss, I was pissing blood. I was too sick to drive myself to the hospital and I had no phone. I just lay for three days, delirious. I thought I was going to die. But gradually I did come out of it. He was a terrific body puncher. That fight, that beating was the beginning of the end for me. I was twenty-four years old and that's how I celebrated winning my title.'

Jones himself published three volumes of short stories but never completed a novel.

51.

Ben Okri once joked that being at a party with other writers was like being in a room full of boxers—who hadn't fought each other. And he's right, writers are notoriously competitive but while a writer is writing—as opposed to waiting to see how the product of that writing fares critically and commercially—the competitive instinct tends to be either sublimated or ignored. A writer might be trying to outdo someone who has tackled a similar subject before but these versions or verbal remixes tend to take the form of tribute or homage rather than assault. It's unlikely that a writer would be usefully motivated by

Alex Ferguson's famous determination 'to knock Liverpool off their fucking perch.' For a simple reason. Just trying to stay on your own little perch is so difficult there's no concentration or energy left over to worry about anyone else's.

It's not even that you're in competition with yourself. You're just trying to keep going, to keep at it. The opponent is a sly, shapeshifting mixture of laziness, tiredness, exhaustion, depression, and all-round is-it-worth-it-ness. You can say 'no mas' any time you want. Then, having said that, after spitting out the gum-shield and watching the gloves being cut off, you can put the gum-shield back in, tape up the hands, and go at it again for as long as you feel like it. And no one will be any the wiser. The great thing about this kind of comeback is that it takes place invisibly, ahead of quitting and retirement. It can happen, in fact, several times in the course of a normal and productive working week.

52.

With the comeback stitched into the fabric of sport it's no surprise that coming back after retirement is so common that hanging up the gloves—or racquet or boots—can seem like preparation for putting them right back on again. 'Only someone with the *genuine* arrogance of a Rimbaud or a Cantona could declare their retirement and actually mean it,' writes Don Paterson. 'To make a single return to the stage is to reveal oneself a mere applause-monkey.'

In the 2017 film *Borg vs McEnroe*, John McEnroe (played by Shia LaBeouf) suspects that the reason Borg sleeps in a hotel room with the AC turned to arctic frigidity is not that he's an ice-borg; he's really a volcano about to erupt. The volcano opted for its own extinction when, at the precocious age of twenty-six, Borg retired, turning his back on everything that had given his life meaning or had kept the lack of meaning at bay. Losses to McEnroe in the finals of Wimbledon and the U.S. Open in 1981 were crucial in hastening him towards the exit, as was losing his position as number one in the

world (also to McEnroe) at the end of the year. In a high-stakes erup-
tion of zero-sum mathematics and nihilistic calculation he explained
to McEnroe that either you were number one in the world or you
were nothing. (Tim Henman opted for a far simpler English arith-
metic when he pointed out that one of the people who had criticised
his performance as a tennis player when he was consistently ranked
number four in the world was not even number four in the bank or
whichever institution it was that employed him.) Borg couldn't take
the stress, the pressure, and was exhausted by the constant scrum of
reporters, photographers, and adoring girls. Most importantly, he no
longer enjoyed the tennis, but he hadn't fully grasped the nettle—had
barely even touched it—of what to do instead, what he might do afterwards. One of the things he did was to judge a wet T-shirt contest
that, with a bit of schedule-rejigging, could surely have been accom-
modated between important tennis contests while he was still on the
Tour. If the wet T-shirt is a metaphor for sexual profligacy—which is
reasonable since he had a child with one of the contestants—then retirement had its advantages in that he now had more time to indulge
in that (i.e., could spend slightly less time fighting women off and
more time inviting them in). But however much one likes sleeping
with new partners or partying or taking drugs (routinely compatible,
back then, with playing elite-level tennis) it's not something to give
one's life a sense of purpose, even at the age twenty-six.

I had come to an understanding of this, courtesy of Borg, soon
after leaving school. I loved watching Wimbledon on TV. It was all
I wanted to do—especially and gallingly on days when it rained and
there was nothing to watch. Even on cloudless afternoons I couldn't
watch nearly as much Wimbledon as I wanted to because there were
always clouds louring over me in the form of either exams or having to
revise for them. And then, in 1977, in the year between A levels and
going to Oxford, there were no impediments, I could gorge myself on
Wimbledon—and, as a result, watching it wasn't nearly as much fun.
The obligations and restrictions imposed by exams had enhanced the
pleasure of watching Wimbledon.

For Borg we might reverse this. The metonymic obligations of Wimbledon and all the other tournaments enhanced the pleasure of all the things he could do off-court even as it cut down on the time and freedom to pursue them. After retirement there were parties, failed business ventures, bankruptcies, failed relationships, custody battles (pursuant to the wet T-shirt contest), and various other lets (of a non-tennis nature) and hindrances. That left two things: comeback (with a wooden racquet) and a rumoured suicide attempt. If it happened, it didn't work. And neither did the comeback. So he had effectively come back to where he started—i.e., when he finished playing: wondering what to do next. (Unlike me, the one thing he surely didn't want to do was *watch* tennis on TV.) Even if he did next to nothing, that still required a degree of doing and so he got on with doing that. Existence itself requires a minimum amount of effort. Ironically, the less other stuff you have going on the *more* time and effort is taken up by just existing. After a point it fills every waking moment of the day and after that, when you're not even able to wake up, it takes up the rest of the day too.

Over the years, albeit with no apparent relish, Borg could occasionally be spotted taking a televised amble down memory lane with his old rival John McEnroe, who, alongside everything else—music, art, tennis commentary, and punditry—maintained a busy life reminiscing about his earlier life. Sometimes it seemed as if the lucrative business of reminiscing was not just a full-time job but a full-time life as McEnroe rehearsed the key moments and told and retold the old stories, in his autobiography, *Serious*, in numerous documentaries, in the course of his match commentary and punditry for TV (hopping profitably between the BBC and an American channel in the course of the same day), and, most actively, as his own tribute act on the seniors tour during which, one suspects, he was contractually obliged to throw at least one pseudo-tantrum irrespective of whether there were even the slightest grounds for dispute (which, logically, could thereby generate cause for complaint since there must have been days when he felt perfectly in accord with line judges and opponents). This life

THE LAST DAYS OF ROGER FEDERER

eventually caught up with him in the follow-up installment of his autobiography, *But Seriously*—a book even well-disposed reviewers had trouble taking seriously—focusing on the years he'd spent reminiscing about the period covered by the previous volume.

Something similar happened to the surviving members of the Doors. Introducing a story about the Lizard King for yet another documentary one of them would say something along the lines of 'I remember an afternoon in 1969. I was talking to Jim when . . .' What they really should have said was: 'I remember one day in 1985. I was reminiscing about Jim with Ray when . . .'

This tightening of the Eternal Recurrence, the media feedback loop whereby telling (and retelling) gets folded into the original experience, was a refinement Nietzsche could not have foreseen. Or perhaps he could. One of the most joyous entries in *Human, All Too Human* asks, 'How in a book for free spirits should there be no mention of Laurence Sterne, whom Goethe honoured as the most liberated spirit of his century! Let us content ourselves here simply with calling him the most liberated spirit of all time.' Nietzsche, as suggested earlier, might have revised this opinion if he'd had a chance to read Eve Babitz; in *Human, All Too Human*, unable to content himself with a mere mention of Sterne, he goes on to devote a further page and a half to extolling the virtues of *Tristram Shandy*, a book that 'resembles a play within a play, an audience observed by another audience.'

During end-changes the cameras at Wimbledon sometimes shift to people watching from the Royal Box, a group of notables that regularly includes former champions. I don't know if a perk of winning is that they can show up at the All England club whenever they get the urge, but it seems this was an urge that Pete Sampras never felt. The one time he was there he looked as if he was fulfilling an all-expenses-paid obligation with a possible appearance fee thrown in. The occasion was the 2009 final against Andy Roddick when Roger had the chance to overtake his record of fourteen Gram Slam titles. When that duly happened the cameras sneaked a glance at Sampras who looked like he couldn't care less as long as whatever further commitments lay in store wouldn't delay his getting a flight back to California. Sampras seems to be a champion who was entirely unfazed by life after tennis. Borg, in his untutored way, was heir to some non-specific Scandinavian malaise: an all-court jumble of Hamlet, Kierkegaard, Ibsen, and Strindberg, held in check during the course of his career by a sweaty headband (or, conceivably, *caused* by the headband?). In his playing career and retirement Sampras was a product of—and marvelous advert for—a kind of pure Californian brainlessness. I don't mean he's stupid—I've no idea of his mental capacities—I mean that the brain, except as the receptor and conveyor of match strategy, was an irrelevance. If Sterne was the most liberated spirit of all time Sampras *was* one of the most competitive spirits—dragging himself to victory in the 1996 quarter final of the U.S. Open after becoming so dehydrated that he threw up at the back of the court—and *is* one of the most contented spirits in sport. He played a lot of tennis and then stopped playing tennis. He was the most successful male player of all time and then he was the second most successful. Then Rafa overtook him. When Djokovic passed by him as well he was relegated to *fourth* in the list of all-time greats. And? So?

Those questions are inappropriate. As much a part of the history of Wimbledon as the grass on Centre Court, Sampras seems to share with it a similar incapacity for epistemological enquiry. He necessarily lacks the wit of McEnroe, who, in *Serious*, observed that he 'chose world-class mediocrity' for the last five or six years of his career. But McEnroe himself lacks the propensity for self-examination—for self-examination that is not an interior form of self-advertisement—of an athlete whose achievements were of comparable magnitude. 'I realize that my whole life is just a fucking waste,' Mike Tyson announced at the age of forty-four. With a ghetto-forged ability to situate himself within a context larger than the arena of his ferocious victories he had 'this uncanny ability to look at myself in the mirror and say, "This is a pig. You are a fucking piece of shit."' Norman Mailer wrote that when great boxers become champions they can 'begin to have inner lives like Hemingway or Dostoyevsky, Tolstoy or Faulkner.' After his fighting life was over this champion began to have an inner life like Larkin in his later years: 'What an absurd, empty life!'; 'I suddenly see myself as a freak and a failure, & my way of life as a farce.'

Tyson's brutal appraisal of his too sullied flesh is, it goes without saying, utterly at odds with the core lessons of the psychology of sporting success. Stay in the moment. The easy smash at set point that, in contravention of multiple laws of physics and biomechanics, you somehow managed to belt into the net? Put it behind you. Never think beyond the present match, the current game, the unfolding point. Play the ball not the point. And—by implication—don't start worrying about the point of that point because from there it's a very short step to thinking about the point of existence, losing the game and the plot, and deciding that, ultimately, tennis, like life itself, is just a wet T-shirt contest in the pouring rain, signifying nothing.

53.

Enoch Powell said that all political careers end in failure, as do many sporting comebacks. Andre Agassi's second act or reincarnation—from someone David Foster Wallace considered 'cute as a Port Authority whore' to beloved duck-waddle Buddha who claimed a further five Slams after his ranking had plummeted to 110 in the world—has the force of a parable because it is so unusual. Boxers who retire undefeated find themselves entirely defeated by life outside the ring. Hence the decision to make a comeback—which serves up the defeat they had previously avoided. So athletes come out of retirement as a way of reconciling themselves to the fact that there is no coming back. Armed with his wooden racquet Borg was doomed, like Fitzgerald's Gatsby, to fail in several attempts to repeat the past. George Best, as we have seen, came back multiple times, with consistently diminishing returns. Even the most spectacular or unlikely of comebacks can lead to ignominious defeat. 'Oh my God,' exclaimed the commentator Harry Carpenter when Muhammad Ali floored George Foreman after spending much of the fight on the ropes in Zaire, and after being banned from boxing for almost four years following his refusal to be drafted into the army. 'He's won the title back at thirty-two!' Ali was king of the world again. This victory led eventually to the titanic battle with Joe Frazier in Manila in 1975, which served, in turn, as prologue not to the imperial theme but a long dribble of pantomime and irreparable hurt.

54.

What is the difference between failure and defeat? Failure always feels like our own fault, not just to live up to earlier promise but when we fail to make the grade. We fail an exam, are not defeated by it. We are always defeated *by* something, even by bad luck. Failure—to convert break points—leads to eventual defeat, which can in turn give way to a lasting sense of failure. Because it is internalised, failure ultimately trumps defeat. To feel like a failure is to *be* a failure.

Hemingway's story 'The Undefeated' is about an ageing bullfighter coming back from injury who returns prematurely to the ring where, inevitably, he is gored. He gets up off the sand, 'coughing and feeling broken and gone.' For a writer the stakes are both lowered and doubled. You can be defeated—by the empty page, by the inability to find the words to fill it—and be a failure. You can be undefeated—and still be a failure.

We should also acknowledge the *lure* of defeat compared with the steady drip of discouragement: the knowledge gained by the defeated compared to the slow erosion and eventual withdrawal of the terminally discouraged.

55.

For several months a line of Jean-Luc Godard's, imprecisely remembered—I've been unable to track it down—has hovered around my consciousness. Something like: a film is, among other things, a diary of what the actors were doing during the time of its production. Is it pointless to add that this book is also a diary of what the writer was up to during the period of its composition?

56.

It wasn't just suspension of the Tour, the cancellation of Wimbledon, and the postponement of the French. Less widely lamented, the literary tour—the festivals that enliven the life of the writer—also came to an end as Covid took hold. Everything came to an end, including time itself as every day became a Sunday.

By June life and time had resumed sufficiently to allow my wife and I to return to England and Europe for four months. The abandoned football season picked up where it had left off, the Tour started up again, and the U.S. Open went ahead as scheduled, without spectators and without Roger or Rafa. Andy Murray, coming back from another round of hip surgery, came from two sets down to beat Yoshihito Nishioka in the first round. It lasted four hours and forty minutes and Murray looked done in by the end (more done in, in a way, than the person he'd done in). The good news was that his hip was OK. What hurt most, he said, were his big toes. It was an absorbing match, sort of, but mainly it was a grind and, as expected, Murray had nothing left in the next round when he received a comprehensive thumping at the youthful hands of Felix Auger Aliassime.

By then I'd been back in action for a while, sitting at my desk with no toe pain, grinding out results in the form of thousands and thousands of words. Thank God—how strange that this form of words still holds sway—that I'd had something to be getting on with during this universal off-season, something to do with my time in the expanse of non-time. A benefit of writing is that it makes one less susceptible to the numerous irritations and calamities of the world beyond the desk. It insulates from bad weather; it's a shield against Covid and Trump (against thinking about them all the time); it protects from injury (from being injured and not being able to play tennis), from boredom, depression, and fear of dementia. The best thing of all is that it saves you from not being able to write—though as Hemingway discovered in the course of banging out two hundred thousand words of *The Garden of Eden*, *keeping* writing can be a way of protecting yourself against the fear that you're no longer able to.

57.

'Every moment lived without a writing project resembles the last.'

I am so much happier writing this book, each day adding to—while simultaneously trying to resolve—the complicating difficulties of its structure, than I would have been if I were not working on it. Part of me is tempted to keep going, continuing to expand the book till Alexander Zverev, Stefanos Tsitsipas, or another representative of the Next Gen is contemplating retirement. It occurs to me, in fact, that I could keep writing this till I die, till I collapse with a big thump.

But I'm not going to do that and I'm not going to think about what to do when I finish it. Because I already know. I'll fall into idleness, boredom, and depression before eventually and reluctantly embarking on the gruelling rehab of trying to start another—trying 'to get my sound back,' as Miles rasped after a long lay-off.

58.

The first days of the delayed 2020 French Open were so cold that the few spectators allowed to attend—including the players' coaches and friends—were bundled up like extras on the set of *Ice Station Zebra*. The players themselves were kitted out in leggings and multiple layers of shirts. Normally there is a visible and audible desire to win but here the greatest wish seemed to be to get back inside, in the warm, irrespective of the result. Murray, who normally chunters away to himself and his box like a mumble-core Hamlet, was entirely muted in the course of a straight-sets tonking by Stan Wawrinka. After Murray hit a couple of winners the commentators on ITV4 reminded us that, on his day, Murray could still beat anyone. What they didn't say was that it seemed increasingly unlikely that such a day might occur twice in the same week, let alone seven times in a fortnight. Mats Wilander on Eurosport took a harsher view. 'I worry about Andy Murray,' he said. 'I would love to hear him say why he is out there, giving us a false sense of hope that he is going to come back one day. Is it his right to be out there doing that? Why? I did it and I shouldn't have. It was the biggest mistake I [made] in my career.'

59.

I fear I wasn't being completely honest or, more accurately, *accurate* when I wrote earlier about enjoying Wimbledon less when there were no obligations (exams) to ration my watching. It may have been true then but in the last five years I have watched more tennis—more tournaments, for bigger chunks of the day—with more enjoyment than ever. Part of the reason for this is because a writer-tennis friend shared his password for the Tennis Channel, an act of ostensible generosity that, I suspect, might also have been a subtly poisoned chalice, designed to undermine and gradually destroy my writing life. Yesterday, a Tuesday, I watched six hours of the French Open. That was hot on the heels of a major binge on Sunday when I was at it all day from lunchtime onwards. The only way I could watch more tennis is if I retired completely, which I have not done—because I define retirement as the phase of life in which I will do nothing but watch tennis (a transition marked by an upgrade to Tennis Channel Plus).* To think

---

* *Is* watching tennis on TV primarily an old person's game? I began to suspect it might be when I was watching one of the Masters 1000 tournaments—I forget which—on TV and all the ads were for erectile dysfunction or cataract removal. 'Or' not 'and': none of the featured

that I am approaching the age where I might no longer be physically capable of playing tennis, that it might no longer be something I do but exclusively something I *watch*, mainly on TV. Everything eventually ends as TV. There is a poignant moment in *Heaven's Coast* when the poet Mark Doty writes of his partner, Wally, sick with AIDS: TV *is* what he can do.

60.

For a long while I wasn't sure if I was having such trouble getting on with this book because I'd started it prematurely (too far from the end of my writing life) or because I'd left it too late (and had already come to the end).

---

medical institutions offered a buy-one-get-the-other-free package. Understandably, the cataract ads didn't mention Turner or cite Berger but I was surprised they didn't stress the primary benefit as the ability to watch tennis (or porn) on TV as you haven't seen it in ages.

The time that lies ahead of me grows shorter. There will inevitably be a last book, as there is always a last lover, a last spring, but no sign by which to know them.

—Annie Ernaux

01.

Pundits have been speculating about when Roger might retire for more years than Borg spent on the Tour, from the moment his aura of invincibility was dented. Retirement chatter increased in volume and intensity after he was beaten in the second round of Wimbledon in 2013 by Sergiy Stakhovsky, ranked 116. An ongoing back injury that was a factor in that defeat added to speculation about how long he might keep going. Between 2013 and 2016 he failed to win a single Slam. Knee surgery in February 2016 was followed by re-injury in July and subsequent withdrawal from all competitions for the rest of the year. During these years he batted away all questions of retirement as if doing a drill on the practice court, with variations but no apparent lack of conviction. It wasn't just the tennis, he said. He also liked being on the Tour. He liked the splendid hotels, the travel (by private plane), the adoration. He liked inviting Grigor Dimitrov and Tommy Haas back to his suite for a sing-along. He liked going to all the different cities even if, like most players, he didn't get to see much of any city, partly because turning up anywhere had the potential to create a love-riot.

In post-final speeches, whether as runner-up or victor, he said he'd be back next year. To be precise, he said he *hoped* to be back next year and even if he wasn't back then he always turned up the year after that (except at the French, which he tacitly admitted he had no chance of winning for a second time, until 2019 when he played Nadal in a semi-final rendered meaningless by hurricane-force winds). After losing to Nadal in the Australian Open final of 2009 he'd been reduced to tears ('God, it's killing me') but in the following years he came to terms with the pattern whereby he sailed through the calm waters of the early rounds before coming up against either the swirling menace of Nadal's left hand or the Balkan wall of Djokovic's implacable defence.

So even when it looked as if he would never win another Slam we were glad he kept playing, glad he didn't subscribe to Borg's zero-sum ideal of number one or bust, because it gave us a chance to see him. It may have been impossible to beat Djokovic or Nadal but against almost everyone else it looked like he was playing the most perfect tennis possible. It was an illusion that we could believe in.

And then came the annus mirabilis of 2017 when he bounced straight back from knee surgery to win the Australian Open, Indian Wells, Miami, and Wimbledon. We weren't able just to see him play; we were possibly seeing him at a new peak, when he was playing better than ever and when our ability to appreciate what we were seeing—what we had previously taken for granted—had itself been greatly enhanced. The backhand had long been vulnerable, constantly battered by Nadal's top-spin forehand. Now he was hitting shoulder-height backhand winners in rally after rally. His haul of Slams was nineteen, to be followed, in 2018, by his twentieth (at Wimbledon) and a couple of flickering returns to the number-one spot. But the real triumph was beyond statistics and calculation. He had again demonstrated that the most efficient way to play tennis was also the most beautiful—and vice versa. Aesthetics and victory could go hand in hand.

Plenty of top male players have gorgeous one-handed backhands (all but extinct in the women's game since the abdication of the majestic Justine Henin) but with Roger's fading the *reign* of beauty is coming to an end.

02.

One of the reasons we love watching Roger is because of the way—like Dennis Bergkamp—he looks like he is moving within a different, more accommodating dimension of time. The reason for this, in turn, is because he's taking away his *opponents'* time until, eventually, they have no time left to do anything about it. He does this by standing close to the baseline, by taking the ball early, and, increasingly, by trying to shorten the points. He even does it *between* points on his serve. Since he never gets close to the thirty seconds permitted the umpire may as well turn off the serve clock. Nadal, meanwhile, wants to take away Roger's ability to take away *his* time, barging right up against the allowed limit and almost always going over it at some stage and incurring a warning. While Roger reduces the amount of time his opponents have to prepare before his next serve comes spinning their way, the long seconds spent waiting for Rafa to twitch his way through his interminable pre-serve ritual gradually gnaw away at his opponents' reserves of concentration. (Djokovic might be even more infuriating; while Rafa's routine is unchanging you never quite know when Novak will stop bouncing the ball and deign to hit it.) Several times in their matches, Roger has complained to the umpire about how long Rafa was taking to serve. And whereas the server is supposed to be able to dictate the pace of play, Rafa is always trying to force Roger or anyone else (especially the volatile Nick Kyrgios) to wait till *he's* ready to receive. So some kind of match is in progress even when nothing is happening, when the ball is not in play: a subtle and invisible tug of temporal war.*

---

* In the second round of the 2021 French Open, Roger did get a time violation for keeping Marin Čilić waiting when he was ready to serve. This led to an extended dispute with the umpire as Roger argued that, since ball boys were no longer allowed to bring players their towels (because of Covid rules) more time was needed to make the long walk to the towel box and back.

03.

On the wall outside court eighteen a little plaque commemorates the longest match ever played at Wimbledon, over several days, in June 2010, when John Isner and Nicolas Mahut went toe to toe for eleven hours and five minutes. Since the introduction of a fifth-set tie-break in 2019 no match will ever again last as long. Isner and Mahut dug so deep they might reasonably have expected to find themselves playing in the Australian Open. In an era when it is often claimed that advances in technology have microchipped away at what it means to be human, two representatives of our resilient species comprehensively outlasted the electronic scoreboard, which found itself unable to cope with the scale of computations required to keep track of things long before one of them—Isner—finally prevailed at 70–68 in the fifth. Anyone watching felt similarly incapable of processing what was happening. It made no sense—actually made nonsense of any previously held notion of what might constitute a tennis match. In military terms it was the epic stalemate of the southwestern front. Both combatants entrenched themselves on the baseline, relying on heavy artillery and only occasionally going over the top to venture into the risky no man's land of the net. As in 1914–18 so in SW19 all attempts to bring the conflict to an end served only to extend it further. The source of the deadlock on the western front was that the means of defence were mechanised, whereas the means of attack were not. Here the serve, the attack, was mechanised, but for long periods neither man was capable of defending himself against it.

Recalling the fourteenth round of the 1975 fight in Manila between Ali and Frazier, Ali's doctor, Ferdie Pacheco, said, 'That's what gets people killed in boxing, when the fight becomes more important than life and death.' It's never that extreme in tennis and this particular match could never become more important than life itself for the simple reason that it *was* life itself. They kept toiling away not for any ultimate meaning or purpose but because, within those white lines, an inexorable logic held sway: he hits a ball and you try to hit it back. And so, through some perverse compatibility—those marriages that, unlike the ones mentioned by Larkin at the end of 'MCMXIV,' last for ages because of an insatiable and shared appetite for bickering—Mahut and Isner settled into a tranced deadlock, a check that could never quite mate. Normally, a player would be under immense pressure when serving to stay in the tournament but there were no nerves because, after a while—after the first three or four hours—there was no expectation that anything unusual might happen.

Understandably, the standard of tennis was not that high. Both players could still hit the ball but, for extended periods, neither seemed capable of doing so if that involved moving more than a foot—neither the unit of measurement nor the body part from which it derives. Not that this made the match any less compelling. It was unmissable and, oddly, for a match that notched up more points than ever before (or since), almost pointless. While the tennis equivalent of *They Shoot Horses, Don't They?* unfolded, important football games in the World Cup in South Africa flashed by like time-lapse summaries of the passing seasons. Except for a few knowledgeable loyalists, most of us, at the time, were ignorant of the players' identities and indifferent as to which of them emerged victorious. We didn't care who won but we were curious to see how they responded to each other when one of them did.

In tennis, it is often said, only one point ultimately matters—the last one. Normally, this point decides who wins and who loses but, in the case of Mahut–Isner, that was almost irrelevant, forgotten. (After a set-to like this, McEnroe pointed out, neither of them had a hope in hell of surviving their next-round match.) All that last point could do was bring the match to an end. After a while the idea was not to win, nor even to avoid defeat, but simply to ward off the end. Usually different parts of the crowd chant the names of one or the other player; on this occasion, as darkness fell on Wednesday night, everyone in the audience chorused, 'We want more! We want more,' even if, by any rational calculation, everyone had already had more than enough. But more *what* (given that much of it was rather boring)? What kept people watching was the fact that the whole thing was never more than a few minutes—and often only a few seconds, just one more point—from being over, done, and dusted. The lifelike peculiarities of the tennis-scoring system mean—or *meant* now that there is the fifth-set tie-break—that sudden death and perpetual extension are inextricably paired.

04.

It's tormenting at any stage if you lose having failed to convert a match point but although it's better in every way to get beaten in a final than to be on the plane home (which, for tennis players, translates into 'next stop on the tour') after the first round the incremental torment is exacerbated as the competition proceeds. You blow your chances in the third round—that's frustrating, to put it mildly, but you'd still have to rack up hundreds more points in each of the subsequent rounds if you were to win the championship. There is still an awful long way to go. But what if you are just a single point away from becoming champion?

Will there ever be a more agonising example than Roger serving in the 2019 Wimbledon final against Djokovic at 8–7 in the fifth? Two aces have taken him to 40–15. On the next point he hits a loose forehand into the right tramline. At 40–30 he comes to the net behind a so-so approach and is passed easily. Deuce. Djoko wins the next two points and it's 8–8. The match rolls on to a final-set tie-break—the first ever at Wimbledon—but from that point on one sensed that Roger's chance had gone. Perhaps he did too, especially given how Djoko had made a famous return from a perfect serve while two match points down in the semi-final of the U.S. Open in 2011, going on to win both the match and the championship.

To have those two Wimbledon points again, to have done things differently, to have stayed back rather than rushing to the net at 40–30 . . . It's the exact opposite of the passage in *The Gay Science* when Nietzsche asks us to imagine a moment so perfect you would live your whole life again, with all its manifold unhappiness and disappointments, in order to relive it through all eternity. Or is it?

There were so many ways in which those two points, those two moments, could have turned out differently but for that to have happened *everything* else, not just in that match but in Roger's career and life, would have to have been different, including beating big-serving Roddick in what became—in Roger's own words—a serving contest in the fifth. And maybe the other nineteen Slams as well.

It was an especially hard or heavy loss to bear because that one point—one from a total of thousands won and lost at that tournament alone—had, within an hour, been transformed into two more significant figures: twenty and sixteen, rather than twenty-one and fifteen—the number of Slams, that is, won by Roger and Djokovic respectively. That one point might have made the difference between his record remaining intact for all time and his being overtaken by both Djokovic and Nadal (who drew level at the French).*

05.

A lovely tradition: at Wimbledon the first match on Centre Court always features the winner of the last singles match from the previous year, the defending men's champion. And the two electronic scoreboards on Centre Court continue to show the results of the men's and women's singles finals until shortly before the start of the following year's tournament. Like this it seems as if there is no tennis or time outside the tournament: nothing but an endless loop of Wimbledon

---

* As I fiddled around, making last-minute changes to this manuscript, Roger, Nadal, and Djokovic were tied at twenty Slams apiece: a symmetrical triangle of shared and almost inconceivable greatness—until Nadal won his twenty-first in the 2022 Australian Open.

fortnights. Covid broke the loop so that both scoreboards—stuck in 2019 until 2021—were left displaying Wimbledon's equivalent of the last syllables of recorded time.

06.

Towards the end of his five-hour match against Diego Schwartzman in the quarters of the 2020 French Open, Dominic Thiem had nothing left. He was having to resort, without success, to the dropshots that Hugo Gaston had tormented him with in the previous round. There can come a time in a tennis match when, although you continue to chase after every ball and fight for every point—and sometimes, as a result, go on to win not just points but games too—you know that you don't have it in you to win the match. After that point it's impossible to win (unless something even more catastrophic afflicts your opponent). It's different to running out of energy or gradually becoming weak or tired or deciding to give up (no longer running down balls, sulking). You are resigned to losing though this resignation is only felt internally, is not manifested externally. On the surface nothing has changed except some slight alteration in that overused indicator, body language. So it's possible that Thiem gave way internally before his eventual physical undoing. 'Something in me wilted,' McEnroe said of the fifth set against Borg in the Wimbledon final of 1980. But perhaps even this is too corporeal, too suggestive of a physical failing or falling off. I'm thinking of something subtler and altogether less tangible even than wilting: almost like succumbing to a prophecy that is powerless to assert itself until one assents to its fulfillment.

07.

Outside of competition, a similar feeling of resignation—variations of *I'm not going to make it, It's not going to work out*—can take hold in life. You continue to chase down the relevant balls—you take out the trash, load and unload the dishwasher, enjoy surges of booze-induced well-being at parties, even occasionally discover a new piece of music—but at some level you know there's no coming back, that you're going through the motions, actively waiting for it all to be over with.

And yet you continue to believe that if things had gone differently at a few key points everything could have turned out quite differently.

08.

In November 2020 Tyson was back in the ring for an exhibition match against Ray Jones. The result was a draw so they both came out ahead. No second acts in American lives? There are third, fourth, and even fifth acts too. There's always another act, another gig, another shot at redemption, ideally on *Oprah*. For the returning and ostensibly contrite sinner on the way back like this, on the trail of TV tears, America is a far more forgiving—or maybe just forgetful—place than it is for anyone unlucky enough to be on the receiving end of a ten-year sentence for selling marijuana (which Tyson smoked before the fight).

A friend told me that Fitzgerald's famous line refers to a three-act drama so that what is missing is not the comeback but the interstitial period. You go straight from having everything (hero) in act 1 to nothing (zero) in act 3. Even if this is right, if that's what Fitzgerald intended, it's still wrong—as his own protracted decline demonstrates.

09.

It doesn't matter how deep the wounds or how rancorous the split, at some point band members will be persuaded to get back on the road or, failing that, back on stage for a gig or two. The only thing that prevents a band's re-forming—far stronger than mutual hatred or fidelity to an amicably shared belief that the band are finished artistically—is the knowledge that the longer the get-together is postponed the greater the clamour for tickets (and the attendant windfall) will be. So bands such as the Sex Pistols can re-form and become their own tribute acts.

Comebacks like this need to be distinguished from those of musicians who, for whatever reasons, have fallen out of favour and been unable to recapture their earlier success—until they achieve something that redefines or even surpasses that earlier success. Johnny Cash's late *American Recordings* were among the best things he ever did, even if he ended up turning in a few too many of these growl-in-the-gloaming covers. 'Bridge over Troubled Water' was the song that threatened the whole enterprise: simultaneously stripped-bare and weighed down by emotional overload, it sounded negatively contrived, as if it might at any moment collapse into the waters that—a foundational problem with the source material—have never sounded even slightly troubled in any extant recording. If Cash had lived a bit longer then, to adapt Lawrence's idea of Turner's last painting, he might have got round to covering 'Hotel California,' or, expanding beyond the vast empire of the American songbook, 'Wonderwall.' A residency of duets with Rod Stewart in Las Vegas may not have been out of the question.

10.

It's not only an author's or artist's work or life; historical periods also come to an end, as do certain art forms. Genres that have been dominant during a particular and sometimes prolonged period lose their vitality and fall into disuse. Sometimes this coincides with a larger historical era—the Edwardian, the Age of Revolution, or whatever—coming to an end; other times an art form can decline in the midst of what is more generally defined as an ongoing historical period. Consider, then, an artist who produces his or her last works, in a form that is widely perceived as past its best—potentially even dying off—

during the deep twilight of an age. Would the result be necessarily elegiac? Or, by hammering a final nail into its own coffin, would it be seen as ushering in a new era—even giving the dying form a new lease of life (and thereby dissolving the terms of the situation described)?

11.

For a musical equivalent of the boxer's or tennis player's comeback we can go back to the night of 7 July 1956 when the Duke Ellington Orchestra took to the stage to play the closing set at the Newport Jazz Festival. The festival was outdoors, there had been a thunderstorm, it was close to midnight, a lot of people had decided to leave early. It was late in a wider sense too. The era of the big band and swing had passed. So Ellington's orchestra was playing to a thinning, less-than-enthusiastic crowd whose interests, clearly, had moved on to newer forms of jazz.

In the middle of a set that seemed to be demonstrating that his time had passed Ellington announced 'Diminuendo and Crescendo in Blue,' an arrangement of a piece from the late 1930s featuring the tenor player Paul Gonsalves, who, after some hesitancy, embarked on an R&B solo. The audience liked it. Gonsalves gathered momentum, depth, and intensity, swung harder and harder with each chorus. The crowd, now fully engaged, became ecstatic. People were dancing, going crazy, so Gonsalves and the band kept going. He blew through twenty-seven raucous choruses that left the audience and himself exhausted and in rapture. (On record the fourteen-minute piece is followed by a 'track' designated 'Announcements, pandemonium.') It was a triumph. Ellington appeared on the cover of *Time* magazine shortly after, his popularity, reputation, and relevance secured, enhanced, and extended for almost another two decades.

12.

That reputation-reviving solo by Gonsalves is reminiscent of another R&B solo of similar length by Albert Ayler. Almost the polar opposite of Ellington, Ayler never reached a wide audience. Reviled and worshipped—later derided by former admirers—as an extreme embodiment of the New Thing, his music was too far out (this was something everyone *could* agree on) ever to achieve commercial success; within a small circle of admirers, however, his influence—on Coltrane among others—was profound. The striking thing about Ayler is that his pieces are among the catchiest ever composed and performed by any jazz musician—*and* the most nightmarish. 'Ghosts,' his best-known piece, from *Spiritual Unity*, is beautiful, joyous, haunted, atrocious (haunted by atrocity). His music is ecstatic but the ecstasy consumes itself in a delirium tremens of shrieks. He loved the ragged-at-the-edges regimentation of marching bands and the conventional splendour of national anthems, turning 'The Marseillaise' ('The Mayonnaise,' as he liked to call it) into the reeling and uplifting chaos of 'Spirits Rejoice.' Albert's brother Donald, a technically limited trumpeter, brought something else to an already intoxicating cacophony: the once-disciplined bugle call of a cavalry charge trampled underfoot by a *stampede* of bungled orders.

However extreme the Ayler sound it's easy to extrapolate backwards to hear his formation as an R&B player. So, when his producer suggested a short piece during the recording of a live gig at Judson Hall in New York in 1965, the band instantly conjured up a couple of minutes of brisk and relatively un-demented R&B in the form of 'Holy Family.'

There are several other versions of 'Holy Family,' the last recorded at Fondation Maeght in Vence (where Lawrence had died) in the South of France on 27 July 1970. Lasting for almost twelve minutes with Ayler blowing his way through multiple choruses, it sounds retrogressive compared to his form-shattering earlier work—and fabulous. The crowd loved it, as they would the wild, honking solos from Rahsaan Roland Kirk when he appeared there with Sun Ra a week later—and as the crowd at Newport loved the Gonsalves solo that had revived Ellington's fortunes. Only one other Ayler performance—from a concert the following day—was recorded after this.

Of the numerous troubles afflicting Ayler in his final years—including the derision heaped on the album *New Grass*, an ill-conceived attempt to move into the mainstream—none weighed more heavily than the fate of Donald, who had left the band in 1968 after a debilitating nervous breakdown. Back in New York, Albert, who appeared increasingly disoriented, was last seen on 5 November 1970. His body was found in the East River twenty days later. Rumours swirled about what may have happened but the truth was the simplest and most bitter: he had killed himself.

13.

In Austin during the 2015 South by Southwest festival my friend Steph added me to the guest list for a private gig at Willie Nelson's recording studio. There was room for about fifty people in the studio. I had no interest in the first band—rockers from L.A.—but the sound was amazing: not particularly loud but so powerful and clear as to be completely enveloping. For the headline act, because of Steph's VIP status, we were invited into the control booth where, we were told, the sound was even better. I'd not heard of the person we were waiting to see, a soul singer called Charles Bradley who, until recently, had had almost no success. He'd spent time living on the street, had been employed as a James Brown impersonator, and had released his debut album, *No Time for Dreaming*, only four years previously, when he was sixty-three, in 2011. But hearing the record, another friend said, was nothing compared to seeing him live. The band came on—young white guys—set up a tight groove, and we waited for Bradley to join them. He looked, when he appeared, like someone from another, rougher age. His face was deeply lined; he was wearing a dark sequined shirt, open to reveal a totemic belly. He opened his mouth and cried out, a moan of deep spiritual need and epic lust. It lasted a couple of seconds but tracing its genealogy would require hundreds of pages covering a history extending back more than a century. From that moment on it was obvious that, for the first time in my life, I was at a great soul gig. Except I wasn't quite. I was in the control booth, hearing the music but separated from the experience by glass. As is often the case the VIP area was the worst place to be. We made our grateful excuses and got out of the booth and into the studio, to share the experience with everyone else. It was wonderful, overpowering, immense.

Bradley was on the road, gigging as busily as Dylan during this phase of his life. I caught him again at a free, open-air festival at Flushing Meadows, New York, a few months later. He died in 2017, having achieved recognition and happiness right at the end of his life. Something similar happened with R. L. Burnside (1926–2005) and Junior Kimbrough (1930–98), the hypnotic Mississippi guitarists who, in the 1990s, in their sixties, were 'discovered' doing what they'd been doing for thirty years: playing a hill-country blues that sounded like a pre- and post-history of trance.* Jeannette Haien, a concert pianist, did not make her debut on the page, as a novelist, until she was in her sixties. Published in 1986 *The All of It* addresses, in Haien's own words, 'all the multifarious wonders of impossibility.'

These are not comebacks, of course, but belated arrivals—in Bradley's case an arrival that only narrowly predated his departure.

---

* What I said earlier about my belated discovery of *Colonel Blimp* applies even more strongly to Burnside and Kimbrough. So far they have been the greatest entirely *new* musical experience of my sixties (I'd dabbled in Beethoven's late quartets before), closely followed by Fred Eaglesmith (whose appearance at McCabe's Guitar Shop in Santa Monica on 7 February 2020 was the last gig I went to, pre-lockdown).

14.

The greatest musical comeback, after prolonged absence, is Art Pepper's. From the stage of the Village Vanguard on 30 July 1977 he announces 'Las Cuevas de Mario': 'the first five-four tune ever·written. I wrote it in 1950, way, way before "Take Five" came on the scene. Unfortunately I went to the federal penitentiary right after that and Paul Desmond and what's-his-name went on ahead playing in the clubs and all that, became big names, and I just sunk to the depths of zero.'

Pepper's was the life of a true artist who made use of everything that had happened to him. All the waste and futility, frustration and megalomaniacal self-belief can be heard in his playing from 1975 (with the comeback album *Living Legend*) to 1982, when he died, aged fifty-six, on 15 June, two weeks after his last gig. He didn't put the decades of incarceration and addiction behind him; he carried them with him every night he played. In properly Nietzschean fashion the final seven years were his best, *because* of everything he had gone through so that, ultimately, nothing was wasted.

15.

Listening to jazz solos—right now to Pepper's 'Make a List, Make a Wish,' recorded at a concert in Japan on 13 November 1981—I often ask myself when the climactic moment occurs. Does there even need to be *a* climactic moment—must one climax always surpass the others in intensity? In Pepper's case the peak moments occur when he strains towards an eloquence beyond his reach. Throttled by an intensity it is unable to express, the music gives vent to both that intensity *and* its own frustration. It's like the moment—those moments—when, during a performance of Coltrane's 'Olé' at the Keystone Korner in 1982, Pharoah Sanders takes the horn out of his mouth and screams. On 'The Night Has a Thousand Eyes' from the album *Moon Child*, on the other hand, my favourite passage occurs during the prolonged aftermath of the ecstatic shrieking, honking, and overblowing as Pharoah takes his foot off the pedal in a long glide back to the lyrical that, it becomes evident in retrospect, had never been left entirely behind.

Not as rare as one might think, this phenomenon whereby the climactic phase occurs, as it were, post-climactically. There's a track called 'The Windup' on Keith Jarrett's *Belonging* (1974) but many great Jarrett sequences occur during what might be called the wind-*down*. Actually, it's often difficult to be sure exactly when the peak has been reached (just as opinions differ as to when Jarrett himself was at his peak). The music is always capable of rousing itself again after repeated climaxes. (The unfortunately and inevitably sexualised vocabulary that has crept in here permits us to address the subject of Jarrett's writhing and groaning. Sometimes the groans occur at moments of bliss. On other occasions it can seem not that he's faking it, exactly, but that rather than being the unstoppable expression of rapture, the cries might be self-urging attempts to achieve a transcendence that has proved elusive.)

On 'Somewhere/Everywhere' from the album *Somewhere*, recorded at a concert in Luzern, Jarrett, Jack DeJohnette, and Gary Peacock start with the tune from *West Side Story* and then slide into the collective trance of a Jarrett original. It builds and builds and then, having achieved maximum intensity and complexity, begins its final descent around the fifteen-minute mark. But the best is still to come, in the remaining four minutes, which could happily have been extended to fourteen or forty. I feel the same about numerous Jarrett performances. If only the trio had kept grooving through the clear 'Caribbean Sky' in Tokyo, 1996, or if they'd continued 'Dancing' on *Changeless* (1989). Recorded in 2009 though not released until 2013, 'Somewhere/Everywhere' filled one with hope about the extended moments in store during the wind-down of Jarrett's life and art.

On 20 March 2015, during a solo performance at Carnegie Hall, Jarrett mentioned, almost as a joke or an aside, that he had lost a trio. No official announcement had been made but with those few words—and subsequent confirmation, in passing, during an interview—a subtle but definitive change of perception and fact was gradually registered. *The trio had not played for a while* became *The trio will never play again*. There had been no announcement, let alone a farewell tour or final appearance. There was just a gig—at the New Jersey Performing Arts Center on 30 November 2014—after which it would no longer be possible to go to hear them. Will not only the status of what might have been a fairly routine performance but its content—what we hear—be changed if a recording is released with the title *The Last Concert?*

16.

In the late spring and summer of 2020—and again, in December, when he announced his withdrawal from the 2021 Australian Open—it seemed possible that Roger might not get round to playing his last tournament, his last match. Possible, I mean, that instead of a *last* match with all the emotion and fanfare that would entail, his semifinal against Djokovic in Australia 2019—a match he never looked like winning, that had no epochal significance, that merely brought to an end his participation in that tournament—might turn out to be the last of his career. After that there were a few exhibition matches, followed by the news that he would take the rest of the year off in order to recover from a second installment of his second round of knee surgery (making a total of three operations), followed by the tour being suspended due to Covid. On the one hand, this came at a good time since he was going to be out of action anyway while his ranking would be preserved in a state of suspended animation; on the other, he was getting older. As was everyone else on the Tour, but whereas Zverev (who came as tormentingly close to beating Thiem in the final of the 2020 U.S. Open as Thiem had to beating Djokovic a year earlier) could lose a whole year and still look forward to ten seasons or more, the lost year was probably costing Roger 50 per cent of the playing time left to him.

This is one of the few ways in which the corona cancellations and shutdowns—as opposed to the actual physical risks posed by the disease itself—have impacted the young less than the old. Glück, in her poem 'Labor Day,' looks at her sister's daughter riding her bike:

> *What she wants is*
> *to make time pass.*
>
> *While to the rest of us*
> *a whole lifetime is nothing.*
> *One day you're a blond boy with a tooth missing;*
> *the next, an old man gasping for air.*

There are other positive sides to this acceleration. It's irritating if a flight is delayed by three hours but, at the same time, those three hours are nothing like as tormenting as they were thirty years ago. The last time this happened to me it seemed there was barely time to get a coffee, let alone the sandwich to which I was entitled, after I'd spent half an hour wresting the voucher from airline staff. It's not just that time passes more quickly as you get older; life becomes progressively less eventful until, by the end, all that happens is that it stops happening at all. For the young a year lasts for ages, and a night in—a night spent not getting wasted—feels like a wasted life. Without Covid the life I would have led in 2020 would have been broadly the same as the one I led in 2019, whereas the life you lead in any year of your late teens or early twenties is utterly transformative, especially if you're a student. So although I decry the civic irresponsibility of kids in England going to quarantine raves (I seem to have adopted the tone of someone who spends the long evenings of Covid composing indignant letters to newspapers), risking sending seniors like me to an early grave, I think of how awful it is to be twenty-five, to be stuck at home, and that accidental rhyme of 'rave' and 'grave' reminds me to enlist an unlikely source in their support:

> *Let them rave.*
> *Rain makes music in the tree*
> *O'er the green that folds thy grave.*
> *Let them rave.*

17.

'So sad, so strange . . .'

Amis, in *Inside Story*, is convinced that there is such a thing as a destination mood. This destination is usually arrived at in middle age. Tennyson's mood, a perpetual lingering on things coming to an end, descended on him early. From 1833 when his friend Arthur Henry Hallam died aged twenty-two, Tennyson, at twenty-four, found that morning was entirely taken over by its homonym, mourning. 'Calm is the morn, without a sound,' he writes in *In Memoriam*, 'calm as to suit a calmer grief.' No sooner has a new day dawned in *Maud* than it becomes a source of regret: 'Morning arises stormy and pale / No sun, but a wannish glare / . . . I had fancied it would be fair.' I've not made an exhaustive study, and there are exceptions—an obvious one being his youthful endorsement of progress as symbolised by the misunderstood technology of railways with their 'ringing *grooves* of change' in 'Locksley Hall'—but the general point stands: it's always late, both in Tennyson's daily life and in the context of the larger waning of his age. With the end of the day a constantly recurring idea or image it's appropriate that Hallam identified the effects of rhyme—'the recurrence of termination'—in a way that also sums up the atmosphere of the numerous poems, the multiple rhymes, in which his passing is remembered, rehearsed, and reimagined. As Tennyson contemplates the coming dusk—which he starts doing early in his life but then, like a worsening alcoholic, comes to earlier and earlier in the day— his mood resembles Dylan's in his late phase: it's not dark yet but it's getting there.*

Tennyson is so different to Housman, who writes elegies for lost youth that are brimming with the sap of youth, of youth cut down in spring. Tennyson is always looking back from the autumn of declining age. To Housman's Shropshire Lad he was the brooding aged bard, stumping along past those young girls on the Isle of Wight. In *Maud*—that strange, proto-modernist streak of dawn appearing in the depths of the Victorian evening—even youthful ecstasy is darkened by the obsession that engenders it:

> Birds in the high hall garden
> When twilight was falling,
> Maud, Maud, Maud, Maud,
> They were crying and calling.

Tennyson's afternoons are long, stretching to even longer dusks in which the day's light is absorbed by the lakes, plants, trees on which it has shone. The source of light has gone but the darkness continues to glow. He can keep this up for ages, sometimes to the point of parody: 'Low-flowing breezes are roaming the broad valley dimm'd in

---

* In the three years I spent as a student at Oxford I went to about a dozen lectures. Nine were deadly dull—rote stuff by faculty—and one, a special guest appearance by Raymond Williams, was incomprehensible. The other three were also guest lectures, by David Lodge, who cleverly subjected Hemingway's story 'Cat in the Rain' to cool new forms of narrative analysis (was this my first little glimpse into the arcane rites of structuralism?), and by Christopher Ricks, who not only was brilliant, twice, but was brilliant, both times, about Dylan. One of the lectures was on Dylan and cliché, the other was on how his songs end, how these endings are achieved technically, a style of analysis I was familiar with through Ricks's book on Tennyson. 'All Along the Watchtower' ends, explicitly, with things about to happen, about to begin: 'Two riders were approaching, the wind began to howl.' But the inevitability of the *aabb* rhyme scheme—imprinted on our consciousness by the two preceding verses—means that the narrative opening up signalled by the wind beginning to 'howl' is halted in its tracks by 'a wildcat did growl' in the previous line. The expectation of what's about to happen is held in check by the expectation of the rhymes that have already happened, that anticipate and tacitly insist on the song turning back into itself and coming to an end. This still seems to me an exemplary and unobtrusive bit of listening and reading on the part of Ricks.

the gloaming.' That seems just a string of words, but at its best the mood saturates a poem so thoroughly as to envelop the reader in what seems like the expression of the deep consciousness of an era.

I'm assuming that the young Joyce endorsed the opinion of Dedalus in *A Portrait of the Artist*—'Tennyson a poet! Why, he's only a rhymester!'—but the astonishment seems adolescent. Calling him 'Lawn Tennyson' was fun, the work of a punster of genius—even if the gag had been circulating before Joyce saw it into print in *Ulysses* (twice!)—but that backfires too since the phrase brings to mind one match in particular: the 2008 Wimbledon final between Roger and Rafa, which went on and on into the evening, everything growing blurry in the gloaming except the players' white shirts. It had become almost unplayably dark, the title likely to be decided not by who could hit the ball best but who could still *see* it.

18.

Tennis aside and despite the jibes, was the author of *Ulysses* really able to resist the immense tidal pull of 'Ulysses'?:

> *The long day wanes; the slow moon climbs; the deep*
> *Moans round with many voices.*

Read those lines aloud and your body is engulfed by their gathering darkness. As Ricks has pointed out, Ulysses's manifesto of reiterated affirmation can easily be read as an acknowledgement of its opposite: surrender to and acceptance of the coming dark. He implores us to do these things while all around the evidence mounts that there is no time, that it's the enumeration of all the adventurous things still to be done that reconciles him to not doing them—partly because so much time is spent preparing this rich itinerary of intention, coaxing the ghosts of unachieved ambitions back to life. Ulysses is burning daylight, letting the last dregs fade while he continues pondering the multiple ways in which this might be prevented. At the end of the day, as football pundits like to say, his position, despite and as a result of all his proud declamations to the contrary, is a way of reconciling himself to the 'idle' life that he railed against in the first line of the poem. Ultimately he's not that different to the Larkin of 'Aubade' who works all day, gets half-drunk at night, and is constantly being drawn back to 'The sure extinction that we travel to.' The dying light of Ulysses's evening—a dying that begins with the passing of Tennyson's friend Hallam—merges into and becomes all but indistinguishable from Larkin's morning when 'Slowly light strengthens, and the room takes shape.'

By the time he was my age Larkin had been staring death in the face for years. I scarcely give it a second thought, barely give it the time of day, as they say. What I do think about is how to occupy myself, how to make the most of the time left—shrinking by the day, obviously, but still in need of filling.

19.

'There is a major but very difficult realization that needs to be reached,' begins David Thomson's entry about Cary Grant in his *Biographical Dictionary of Film*. 'Difficult, that is, for many people who like to think they take the art of film seriously.' Thomson goes on to list some of Grant's accomplishments and qualities before the realisation is revealed: 'he was the best and most important actor in the history of the cinema.'

Yes, that might be more hotly contested than the claim that Roger is the greatest player in the history of tennis, but it is less contentious than one I'd make on Thomson's behalf: that his *Dictionary* is the great literary achievement of our time. From the start it was a highly eccentric reference book. 'Over the years, the making of this book has brought me so much pleasure,' he writes. 'In attempting to see shape in the history of motion pictures there is a steady battle between scholarship and partiality, enough to suggest that learning is often more warped than it realizes while daft enthusiasms do lead to quantities of obscure knowledge.' That's from the entry on Shirley MacLaine in the first edition. Part of the joy of subsequent editions is seeing Thomson revise his opinions, apologise for previous omissions, and correct some of his more egregious errors, even if this means compounding them (as when he overturns the 'accurate' information of an earlier edition in favour of the 'spiritual truth' that Chris Marker was born in Ulaanbaatar, Mongolia). Over time, the *Biographical Dictionary* has become an autobiography in the form of a reference book, a guide to its own composition and revision (not surprising given that it first appeared in 1975, three years after Thomson had published a critical biography of Laurence Sterne). 'I have always known that for me, this book is in part a way of staying loyal to writing in face of the nearly total seduction the movies had made of me.' That's from the entry on Raúl Ruiz, which appeared for the first time in the fourth edition. Each edition is updated but the single most important addition was to the third, in 1994, when he included an entry about a friend whose name I won't reveal because I want you to come across it, not to be directed to it. Thomson begins by writing about his life in the 1950s, how he met this friend on the steps of the National Film Theatre in London. He lists the fourteen films he saw in one week in 1961, how he discussed movies with his new friend, and, as a result of these talks, began to emerge 'slowly from a life of stammering.' That increasing eloquence and confidence gradually began to express itself in the form of the book in which, several editions later, we read about its gestation. And then, in the last paragraph, he writes of how his friend became ill and died. 'He was the best friend I'll ever have, and in a way I feel the movies are over now that he's gone.' I know of no more moving moment in literature. And it takes place in a reference book.

More editions were to follow, some of them with good entries added (as in the fifth when he realises that 'even with the book's famed reticence toward beautiful young actresses,' Scarlett Johansson should have been in the fourth) but, by and large, he was simply updating it, including an entry on Jennifer Lopez, say, because he felt he should. But he rarely—how could he?—recaptured the moment when he confessed, mid-*D*s, to being 'torn between his duty to everyone from Thorold Dickinson to Zinnemann and the plain fact that Angie [Dickinson] is his favorite actress.' There appeared a respectful, mildly interested entry on Ralph Fiennes, right next to one on W. C. Fields, which takes the form of a letter to Wilkie Collins from Dickens (whom Fiennes had played in a film he also directed) that had been there right from the start. Sometimes Thomson simply lists the films a newcomer has starred in or made. I'm reluctant to say that the later iterations mean the book was being made worse with each new edition but the greatness was becoming slightly diluted, by the dutiful. And how could this not have been the case given that crucial, heartbreaking entry in the third?

20.

Gary Peacock died today (4 September 2020) aged eighty-five. For more than thirty years he played bass with Jack DeJohnette and Jarrett in the Standards trio. On 10 July 1964, he and the drummer Sonny Murray were part of the trio led by Albert Ayler that recorded the era-defining *Spiritual Unity*, with its two deathless versions of 'Ghosts.'

21.

'. . . *in this dark world and wide.*'

Recorded at a concert in Dallas in 1987, 'Endless' is one of many tracks showing Jarrett's Standards trio at their matchless best. On later occasions their playing could sometimes sound a bit standardised, marked by high-quality predictability. Meanwhile, in the course of rummaging through his archival larder Jarrett kept finding old recordings—solo, trio, and quartet—which left him amazed at the exceptional, transcendent, or godlike quality of this concert or that session. All of this suggested that, contrary to the title of a collection of solo recordings from 1986, *No End* (released in 2013), the end was making itself felt in the form of deepening retrospection. But *No End*—on which he plays electric guitars, Fender bass, drums, tablas, percussion recorder, and piano—is a *double* CD: a sign of how abundant that creative life had been and how robust the self-belief continued to be.

And then, in late October 2020, came the devastating news. Jarrett had suffered two strokes, in February and May 2018. After spending two years in a nursing facility his left side was, he said, 'still partially paralyzed.' *The New York Times* reported: 'It is unlikely he will ever perform in public again.' There was, after all, to be no extended wind-down.

The announcement of Jarrett's stroke coincided with the release of a recording of a solo concert in Budapest, from his last tour, in 2016, a performance he considered 'the gold standard.'*

22.

'A moment later, we found ourselves
standing suddenly in the kitchen
where you suddenly opened a can of cat food
and I just as suddenly watched you doing that.'

Jarrett's life as a performing pianist could not have come to an end more suddenly. I had suffered a minor stroke myself—loss of vision

---

* In 1975 Roland Kirk, who had been blind from the age of two, suffered a stroke that left his right side partially paralysed. Having taught himself to play multiple instruments *at once* he was still able to play a single saxophone with one hand. He continued touring to the end, dying from a second stroke the morning after a gig in Bloomington, Indiana, on 5 December 1977.

on my left side for about thirty-six hours—in 2014 and then gradually forgot about the way that life can change in an instant. Novels are often billed as focusing on a day or night that will 'change the characters' lives forever.' Such claims always dissuade me from reading the book in question. The real interest is how things change neither dramatically nor suddenly but *gradually*. So gradually as to be imperceptible. No one has put this better than George Oppen who said (to Paul Auster) about growing old, 'What a strange thing to happen to a little boy.'

23.

In my late twenties and early thirties I played squash for an hour or an hour and a half four days a week. I'd come home, take a bath (there was no shower in my flat), gobble some Mr. Kipling Manor House cake, nap, wake up refreshed, continue working, and then go out (for dinner, gigs, drinking, parties, drugs). On a very few occasions I'd get a call from a friend who had a court booked in the evening, whose opponent had cancelled, whereupon I'd get changed and cycle back to the courts I'd left only a few hours earlier. In my mid-thirties I remember playing ninety minutes of football, three sets of tennis, and a game of ping-pong before going out to the pub.

I am *still* that person.

24.

I came home from tennis today as I always do: absolutely shattered. I just about had the strength, after carrying my bike up the stairs, to shower (if I'd got in the bath I might still be in it), put ice packs on my arm and shoulder, rinse out my stinky shirt, boil some pasta, and scoff it down before falling into a deep sleep. The tennis involved seventy minutes of continuous hitting without scoring, with quick gulps of Gatorade every fifteen minutes or so when we changed ends. After chasing down a lob and successfully belting the ball back the rotation left me feeling giddy; it was almost as if the blood or some kind of brain fluid were sloshing around in my skull. That sensation was new and troubling since my game has always been about running—that's why I hate doubles, because I love running. The essence of my character—my idea of myself—is that I am a dog. If you keep throwing the ball for me I'll chase after it and while I am chasing my tail will be wagging and I'll be happy. There were a couple of long rallies I had trouble recovering from. One of them ended with me hitting a winner but I was toast for the next two or three.

Back home I emerged from my death-nap fully revived in the sense that I could get out of bed, slump down on the sofa, put my feet up, and watch TV for the rest of the evening before crawling into bed. There was no question of doing any work.

I have *gradually* become this person.

25.

Accidents and injuries aside, our faces and bodies change so slowly that it's impossible to notice the transformations that occur, as it were, in real time. Or perhaps it's more accurate to say that the experience of these transformations *is* time itself. Once we get outside the realm of bodily time we are in the impersonal dimension not of time but of history. 1958, for me, is a date in history; time only began a few years later, in the 1960s, as I emerged, gradually, into consciousness.

Gradually one becomes stronger, taller (with a few sudden adolescent growth spurts), and more articulate. And then, much later, still more gradually, one becomes conscious of growing weaker, slower, more injury prone, less keen to go out. But it is impossible to locate the moment that this pivot occurs, *precisely*—and paradoxically—because there is no pivotal moment. There is only the gradually emerging feeling that things are not as they were even though they are, in some ways, exactly as they have always been. And it's not as if there is a single peak moment before which everything is improving, becoming stronger, after which everything is deteriorating. No, parts of one's body and brain go from strength to strength while others are already in decline. And since the pace of that decline, even after there has been an all-round cessation of improvement, does not occur at a uniform rate, it can feel as if some parts, relatively speaking, are getting stronger when really they're declining in a more leisurely way.

Over the last couple of years, if I've lain in a hot bath too long—which I do every time I have a bath—I feel giddy when I get out, sometimes have to sit on the toilet seat with my head between my knees. It's like fainting while still remaining conscious. Nothing unusual or worrying about that—it's the price to be paid for these prolonged soaks, which are somehow reviving even if the main symptom of that revival is complete enervation.

I've also started to feel occasional, milder versions of the same dizziness when I get up after lying on the sofa. And sometimes I feel briefly dizzy when I stand up from my desk. Conscious that Larkin celebrated his sixty-second birthday (his second-to-last) by writing to Kingsley about his 'dizzy spells,' it's the kind of thing, at sixty-two, that merits mentioning to my doctor but I'll wait till Covid stops raging—by which time I may have started to feel dizzy before I get up, *while* sitting or lying. In other words I might start to feel dizzy all the time—but since this would become my default mode I would, in a sense, no longer be conscious of a feeling of dizziness; rather, dizziness would have gradually become the hum of consciousness itself.

And yet the experience of the gradual contains within it an element of the sudden. On the last page of Salter's *All That Is* Bowman becomes suddenly conscious of something that has happened so gradually as to have escaped his attention until now. Weeding in the garden, he looks down 'to see, beneath his tennis shorts, a pair of legs that seemed to belong to an older man.'

26.

I felt like Bowman when I returned to tennis after a month off with the latest round of knee problems. Late afternoon. The sky as blue as it is has ever been anywhere on earth. After much agonising I had bought two knee supports. They were so tight that from the first few steps it felt like I was the beneficiary of a double leg transplant from an athletic donor who was half my age and half-gazelle. My knees felt like the new Vaporfly running shoes, spongy and supple, springy and strong, as if they had been sheathed in new layers of reinforced muscle. I don't think I have ever been happier on a tennis court. The sky turned pink as the sun began to sag over the ocean but I showed no sign of sagging.

'The support was incredible,' I said in an emotional speech afterwards.

I was so delighted with these supports that I spent the following morning doing further research. There are loads of braces and supports, for every part of the body—even the hip flexor. The one thing that doesn't exist is a total body support, something that would resemble a wet suit, supporting every joint and point of stress. How life-enhancing that would be. There *is* such a suit, I suppose, and it's called yoga or Pilates, covering the injury-prone skeleton with a thin layer of shapely, stretchy muscle and glowing, sexually alluring skin. Widely, almost universally available in California this form of corporeal attire is not eligible for instant or one-click purchase but must be patiently acquired and attained over several years.

These knee supports are part of a larger project. It's not just that I hope to keep playing tennis; I *invest* in it by stockpiling equipment and accessories: balls, overgrip, shoes (Asics), socks (Falke), racquets. The rationale for this is that since a major part of my genetic inheritance is made up of my dad's boundless skinflintery the thought of all this clobber going unused will goad the poor corpus into eking

out some kind of on-court existence even as it announces a daily increasing reluctance to do so.

27.

Few pieces of music change more gradually or subtly than *The Disintegration Loops* by William Basinski. In the first of these a very simple
melody, lasting perhaps six seconds, is looped over and over. It sounds
like a recording of a melancholy brass band, with parts of the past
from which it was exhumed still clinging to it. With some reverb and
other small, very subtle treatments the loop continues to unfold but,
as it does so, the sound quality slowly and imperceptibly deteriorates.
After about fifty minutes the melody is struggling to make itself heard
at all but hangs on tenaciously as we cling to its residual beauty. By
the end there is so little left that what we hear is almost indistinguishable from the memory of what had been imprinting itself on our
consciousness over the previous fifty minutes.

The loops were created partly by accident while Basinski had been
digitalising some old taped loops of Muzak. As the tape was playing
bits of metal began to flake off so that each time it passed through
the tape head it physically deteriorated still further. The loops are the
audible recollections or documentary records of this process. 'It was
almost like the core of this melody was trying to hold on till the very
end,' he has said. The deterioration or shrinking in quality of the few
endlessly repeated seconds of melody is countered by the way they are
allowed to expand in time so that the closed loop acquires the quality of
narrative in the process of that narrative passively and actively consuming itself. Adorno noticed something similar in Beethoven's late style: 'a
tendency towards dissociation, decay, dissolution, but not in the sense
of a process of composition which no longer holds things together: the
dissociation and disintegration themselves become artistic means.'

Every added moment of the tape's survival is also an additional
increment of self-destruction. The last instants of the piece are latent

in the first and the residue of that first moment is still there, even in its almost total extinction. Towards the end there is, unless I am mistaken, a gradual acceleration of decay as pieces of the tape fell off more quickly. This corresponds to the way that a toilet roll runs out more quickly towards the end (because a full loop consists of less and less paper—barely half a sheet by the end compared with two at the outset—as the roll shrinks and gets closer to the narrow circumference of the empty cardboard core).* Or, to avoid lowering the tone like this, it's similar to the experience of time accelerating as we get older, with each year consisting of a smaller and smaller percentage of one's life. The pace of decay accelerates in *The Disintegration Loops* while time—the almost imperceptible beat of the music, the duration of the loop—remains constant. What *increases* is the space between what remains recognisable as music.

The loops gained an extra narrative significance soon after they were made, as Basinski and friends sat on his rooftop in Brooklyn, watching and filming the towers burning and falling as the music played. A still of the burning towers is used on the cover of the album, and a version of the piece was played by an orchestra on the tenth anniversary of 9/11.

28.

We were in London for the hottest day—and night—of the year, sitting on our terrace listening to the first *Disintegration Loop*. The sky still glowed with the twilight that—the nights being so short—looked like it might hang around till the first hint of dawn. To the east Trellick Tower was bright with lights, starkly beautiful though not as lovely

---

* It's inordinately dispiriting to enter a bathroom and see the cardboard tube, exposed and bare except for a few bit of tissue dangling from it. Of course there's the practical problem—there's no toilet paper!—but the sight alone, even when we know that there's a packet of rolls in the bathroom cupboard (along with all the hoarded shampoo), is awful. It's like an augur of life itself running out, of this being what life ultimately will be reduced to. Maybe it has to do with the contrast of soft white paper and hard brown cardboard: a domestic vision of extinction and exhaustion. I don't want to make too much of this, just enough to emphasise that the jolt is way in excess of any practical and aesthetic reality.

as it had been a few weeks earlier when the service tower had been bathed in green light as a memorial to Grenfell (also visible, across the roofs, slightly west and south of us). Planes left the residue of vapour trails in the almost-darkness. There was a sickle of moon with a faint halation. On the chimney stack we had hung red fairy lights: magical and hazy. Years ago I had painted the chimney stack a hippy-ish purple; under the influence of the lights, it was wine-dark. The whole scene was like a nightclub or bar, very low key, with no al-coholic drinks and just two customers who were also the staff. As the night darkened, the red of the fairy lights glowed more brightly—but always gently. The music looped and continued—all the time deteriorating—in the process of consuming itself. I was in my early sixties, wearing a T-shirt and shorts.

In the past this is exactly the kind of scene I have written about, created, or recreated with lyricism and romance. Over time, that has diminished, disintegrated—both the actual experience and my ability to render it. What remains are the facts. There were no stars.

29.

Lying on my back on a bench in a field in Tuscany, looking up at the stars, listening to Beethoven's String Quartet in A Minor, op. 132 . . .

We'd come here on the sleeper train from Vienna, where, perhaps still under the residual influence of that conversation between Gins-berg and Dylan about graves, we had taken a tram to Beethoven's grave in the Zentralfriedhof cemetery. The grave was marked by a big obelisk or something and it was obvious, immediately, that there was no point in having come to see it. Even with the added proximity of Schubert snuggled up next door the place had zero power. In the past I'd made a point of visiting graves—Joseph Brodsky in Venice, Jim Morrison in Père Lachaise, Jean Rhys in Devon—and if I happen to be in the vicinity of the grave of someone whose life or work has meant a lot to me then of course I'll take a look and pay my respects, but this was absolutely the last time I'd make a special effort to do so. We stayed less than five minutes, got back on the tram and, a few days later, onto a sleeper train to Chiusi where we failed to get off in time. We had lots of bags, the attendant looking after passengers in our carriage was nowhere to be seen and I couldn't work out how to open the door. The train barely stopped, just paused for a few seconds before starting off again so we had to stay on till Orvieto, which was only twenty minutes away but there was no train back to Chiusi for two and a half hours. It was eight o'clock on a Sunday morning, there were no taxis, and I was in such a rage, filled with such hatred of the world, I said to my wife, that I was going to smash my head through the window of the wretched station café and tear my throat to shreds on the shards of glass. I meant it, too, but the time passed (quite quickly) and we got back on the train to Chiusi, lugging all our luggage. At Chiusi there were plenty of taxis and in half an hour we were eating the breakfast we should have been eating three hours earlier at the boutique hotel in the Tuscan countryside where we had stayed once before, twelve years earlier, and where, this time around, I ended up lying in a field, listening to the slow movement of op. 132.

30.

The String Quartet in A Minor was composed between February and July 1825, with a month-long interruption in April when Beethoven was suffering from a severe abdominal illness. In a Nietzschean way this was a blessing since it led to the slow movement with its lengthy explanatory subtitle: 'Heiliger Dankgesang eines Genesenen an die Gottheit, in der lydischen Tonart.' ('Holy song of thanksgiving from a convalescent to the Deity, in the Lydian mode.') That may be what it says on the packet but it's not what I hear. 'Inwards, as if into the distance,' was the phrase Lou Salomé used to evoke Nietzsche's peculiar gaze and what I hear is a valediction like that, at once inward and cosmically vast.

31.

Another slow movement from a quartet written in the second half of 1825—the cavatina from op. 130—was among the pieces of music included on the Golden Records when the Voyager space probes were launched in 1977. I remember how moved I was in 2012, when it was confirmed that *Voyager 1* had passed into interstellar space. In *The Farthest*, a documentary about the mission, one of the team members at NASA recounts how she cried when this man-made object passed beyond the heliosphere. My friend John Wray couldn't see what all the fuss was about since it meant that nothing interesting would ever happen to *Voyager* again. Which may be why many of us felt so strongly.

32.

What does this image of *Voyager* leaving everything behind have to do with Beethoven's offering the slow movement of op.132 as the experience of a convalescent?

Overwhelmingly conscious of a *return* to health, the convalescent rejoices in gradually returning strength, is full 'of a reawakened faith in a tomorrow and the day after tomorrow, of a sudden sense and anticipation of a future, of impending adventures, of seas that are open again.' The words are Nietzsche's, whose frequent bouts of ill health meant that his life, like Lawrence's, was spent in a state of constantly renewed convalescence—and relapse.* If the return to health is seen as a prelude to impending adventure, why does this song of thanks

---

* Naturally Larkin takes the slightly stale biscuit for least enviable recovery. 'My convalescence at home is currently being enlivened by re-re-reading *The Music of Time*. I am simply racing through it, and my only regret is that it is so short.' Or so he told Powell on 7 August

sound so *elegiac*? Assuming that the composer can't be looking back fondly on the experience of sickness it becomes an elegy in advance of eventual release and departure from the myriad vexations—which Beethoven itemised and moaned about so frequently—of being alive, of being on earth. Could it be that Beethoven's thanks are offered in anticipation of—and longing for—nothing interesting ever happening again? The music struggles to free itself from the laws of its own gravity—a force created, in part, by these very exertions—to achieve a condition of weightlessness.

There are two alternating elements to the 'Heiliger': the slow hymn or chorale and a jaunty dance tune marked *'Neue Kraft fühlend'* ('feeling new strength'). We hear the return of the chorale, more and more faintly, but also more and more insistently. It is, by the end, almost a memory of how it originated, where it came from. The alternating dance is also heard repeatedly but its claims on our attention diminish with each recurrence; its purported strength *weakens*. In the chorale the memories—of *all* the things that have happened—prove increasingly difficult to let go, even as they fade. The song of thanks is for all that *has been*.

33.

It's not just me (to repeat a phrase from the shampoo and towels movement of the present work) who hears the music this way, not just a deficiency on my part. 'Beethoven's thanking is always related to leave-taking,' notes Adorno in his unfinished book on Beethoven. Rebecca West wrote that Beethoven 'recorded what happens after a thing has happened, what life amounts to after it has been lived.' And in *Beethoven for a Later Age*, Edward Dusinberre, first violinist with the Takács Quartet, mentions how the *'Neue Kraft'* or dance sections

---

1985. Three days later he wrote to John Wain that this re-read had 'confirmed my earlier conviction that it loses its way after the war volumes, and goes quite mad at the end.'

of the 'Heiliger' undermine themselves because, by virtue of repetition, 'the strength is no longer newly found.' As the piece proceeds the character of each of the sections seems 'increasingly provisional, the rhetoric of recovery and new strength open to question.'

Happy to enlist the support of a musician, I was glad to find Dusinberre, a few pages later, calling in the support of a writer, Aldous Huxley. In Huxley's 1928 novel *Point Counter Point* Maurice Spandrell invites Mark Rampion (a character modelled closely on Lawrence) and his wife to listen to a recording of op. 132. With typical Lawrentian stubbornness Rampion is determined to resist the lure and consolation of the music but Spandrell, who has planned this episode as a prelude to final moments of his life, hears

> the serenity of the convalescent who wakes from fever and finds himself born again into a realm of beauty. But the fever was 'the fever of the living' and the rebirth was not into this world; the beauty was unearthly, the convalescent serenity was the peace of God. The interweaving of Lydian melodies was heaven.

In the repeated fading and return—so insistent that even the final fading of the hymn carries within it the possibility of further return—I find myself returning, again, to Lawrence's 'The Ship of Death':

> *And everything is gone, the body is gone*
> *completely under, gone, entirely gone.*
> *The upper darkness is heavy on the lower,*
> *between them the little ship*
> *is gone*
> *she is gone.*

> *It is the end, it is oblivion.*

The poem, we remember, doesn't end there but continues with 'the cruel dawn of coming back to life / out of oblivion.'

All of these tensions are felt in the serenity of the adagio. What, after all, could be more Beethovenian than tension in serenity, serenity in tension?

34.

This is background to the experience of listening to the adagio on my headphones, lying on the bench in Tuscany, gazing up into the star-sprayed sky, conscious of the slight impairment of light pollution, of a slight haze of cloud, of the slight discomfort of lying here like this, slightly chilly, of the distracting temptation to go back into the house to retrieve a hoodie and a pillow so that I could remove the obstacle of self—of corporeal consciousness—from the vision of stars. I was conscious also of some other lines by Lawrence, from *Twilight in Italy*, about how 'we conceive the stars. We are told that they are other worlds. But the stars are the clustered and single gleaming lights in the night-sky of our world.'

Could it be that the stars still seem like that—not as dead memories of themselves, but living memories of our world—even when seen from above, from space itself?

35.

There can be no gods, Nietzsche joked in *Zarathustra*. If there were then how could he endure not to be one? Beethoven, a believer, 'treated God as an equal.' In 1798 he asserted, with the proto-Nietzschean swagger of a man who has yet to turn thirty: 'Strength is the morality of those who distinguish themselves from the rest.'

Given these signs of kinship it seems strange that Nietzsche wrote so little about Beethoven, that the composer didn't occupy a greater part of his consciousness. Part of the explanation may be that Nietzsche was, for a long while, so besotted by Wagner that there was no room for any other composer. By 'for a long while' we could reasonably mean the whole of his adult life since even after their acrimonious break Nietzsche had no doubt that his happiest days had occurred when he had been welcomed into the composer's inner circle in Tribschen and then, far more briefly, in Bayreuth. Those days were gone, but Nietzsche was able to keep their memory alive, even if only negatively, by revisiting, in many different forms, the reasons for the split (without ever mentioning what might have been the most important point of all, what he privately called 'the mortal insult' of Wagner's conviction that the philosopher's chronic problems with his eyes were a result of compulsive masturbation). It's reminiscent of the song in which Dylan lists, time and time again, the numerous ways in which he's over the split with an unnamed woman, so much so that he doesn't even think about her—'most of the time.' Nietzsche had to regard his life as a process of overcoming—his philosophy depended on it. As he put it in the preface to *The Case of Wagner*: 'To turn my back on Wagner was for me a fate; to like anything at all after that, a triumph.' What he came to like was Bizet, especially *Carmen*. This, he concedes, was 'not merely pure malice'—though there was a suggestion of a joke—at Wagner's expense. He had to go forwards, to show that there was music and life after the heady days of his obsessive Wagnerising came to an end. He had to leave not only Wagner behind but the part of himself that had been so susceptible to Wagner. This required a special self-discipline—'to take sides against everything sick in me'—that was part of the larger project required of any philosopher: 'To overcome his time in himself, to become timeless.' Wagner, in this light, was 'merely one of my sicknesses,' a prelude to Nietzsche's 'greatest experience' of recovery.*

Here we have, fleetingly expressed, something of the recovery and leave-taking of Beethoven's 'Heiliger,' with the force of vanished happiness all the more powerfully felt for being so insistently abjured.

---

* Stefan Zweig, while utterly sympathetic to Nietzsche's cause, undermines this claim, seeing Wagner as inflicting an 'almost fatal . . . wound that will never properly heal.'

But whereas Beethoven offered his thanks to god, for Nietzsche that would only have been a sign of further sickness: not of release but of more insidious bondage. Nietzsche was left with himself, with a debt of gratitude not to the creator but to every part of his life, *including* the part played by Wagner, since, if listened to with sufficient attention—even devotion—the music could be heard to contain within it that which pointed to the need for it to be left behind. And there is more—more of the *same*.

Nothing is more crucial to Nietzsche's thought than his rejection of any possibility of relief and release. Paradoxically, his idea of the Eternal Recurrence might best be understood as the opposite of endless repetition. It stresses that we will live this *one* life over and over, without variation, as a way of removing any possibility of parole, alleviation, or change. In practical terms this meant long years of wandering and of almost total loneliness. Chronic ill-health, disappointed hopes of love, tensions and quarrels with his family would constitute the foundation of his life. Much of this also holds true for Beethoven, whose troublesome relationship with his nephew, Karl, bore down on him with a greater weight of day-to-day anxiety than Nietzsche's with his sister. (The apparent cosmological vastness of the Eternal Recurrence, it needs emphasising, is a test of one's daily life and little habits.) There were differences, of course. Beethoven enjoyed the rough and tumble of crude and boozy banter with friends—lopsided, admittedly, because his deafness meant their parts had to be written down. Nietzsche, who objected to all signs of beery German boorishness, had cut rather an awkward figure even during those happy days at Tribschen. 'God Nietzsche!' Cosima told Richard Strauss in 1901, five years after he had composed *Also Sprach Zarathustra* in homage. 'If only you had known him. He never laughed and always seemed taken aback by our jokes. He was shortsighted, too, to the point of weaksightedness; a poor nightbird, blundering into things right and left—one whom it is strangely touching to encounter as an advocate of laughter.'

Nietzsche's near-sightedness was as nothing compared to the

affliction of Beethoven's hearing loss. The inability to read was, he claimed in *Ecce Homo*, one of the things that made possible his transition from academic philologist to writer and, as such, was a cause not for regret but gratitude: 'For years at a time I read nothing—the *greatest* favour I have ever done myself!' For Beethoven the only solace or redemption lay in the possibility that his deafness enabled him to conceive music more complex than any he might have been capable of hearing.

Still, there was one all-important way in which Nietzsche's circumstances were much harder to bear than Beethoven's. Beethoven was feted, acknowledged, and venerated as the greatest composer in Vienna and, by extension, Europe and the world. Until right at the end of his sane life Nietzsche's critical and commercial failure as a writer and thinker was complete. He understood so much, about the world, his times, and himself—Freud said he had 'a more penetrating knowledge of himself than any other man who ever lived or was ever likely to live'—but the way each book after the *Untimely Meditations* failed not only to sell but even to make a stir was incomprehensible. Wagner, the subject of the last of these four meditations, was not inaccurate in his snide claim that 'people read Nietzsche only in so far as he upholds our cause.' (Even, Wagner might have added later, when he seeks to *undermine* it, for it was not until *The Case of Wagner*—'a panegyric in reverse' as Thomas Mann called it—that a book of Nietzsche's finally attracted a fraction of the attention he craved.) Considering that with *Zarathustra* he had 'given mankind the greatest gift that has ever been given it' the silence that greeted its publication was, he wrote, 'a devastating experience which can destroy the strongest man; it has freed me from all ties with the living.' In a moment of self-awareness Beethoven admitted that everything outside music he did badly and stupidly. But the music was all-redeeming.

Every new installment of Nietzsche's works increased the gap between himself and the world. He was offering to remake that world but he was also, it seemed, reduced to writing solely for himself. 'This book,' he wrote in a preface to *The Antichrist*, 'belongs to the very few.

Perhaps not a single one of them is alive yet.' Asked by the violinist Felix Radicati if he really thought the op. 59 quartets were music, Beethoven responded breezily, 'Oh, they are not for you, but for a later age!' This seems an entirely plausible and reasonable claim. By 1888 Nietzsche had become aware 'that one of the main ideas of life has been extinguished in me, the idea of the future.' And yet he 'walk[ed] among men as among fragments of the future: of that future which I scan.' On that score he was as accurate as Beethoven but to anyone listening he would have sounded deluded. Not that anyone was listening. If Beethoven had written an autobiography with a chapter called 'Why I Write Such Excellent Symphonies' this would have seemed an entirely fair—and eagerly anticipated—explanation. For Nietzsche, who went still further ('Why I Am a Destiny'), it was sort of a joke—the joke of a maniac. Even without the physical causes of insanity—for a long time assumed to be syphilis, more recently, meningioma of the right optic nerve—everything about Nietzsche's circumstances was conspiring to drive him mad. He was horribly conscious of the discrepancy between the value he put on his work and the sense of it—the almost complete *lack* of sense—registered by the world at large. A writer or artist of any stripe needs to retain a degree of confidence in order to keep working but you worry also that, given the value-gap, you might be a megalomaniac, a lunatic. In Nietzsche's case the solution was to inflate still further his notion of the unprecedented importance of his books in order to explain their lack of appeal. Indifference to his work was another symptom of how pathological the need for it had become: a sane strategy that seemed a further manifestation of insanity.

36.

Several years ago I had an idea for a book about three people, something along the lines of one of Zweig's trios in his *Master Builders* trilogy (the second of which featured Nietzsche). Two of the three would be Turner and Beethoven. Chronologically they were near-contemporaries whose careers overlapped (Beethoven died at the age of fifty-six in 1827 when Turner was fifty-one) and I was struck by the way that accounts of the artist could be applied without change to the composer, and vice versa. 'All that is called life shall be sacrificed to sublime Art!' Beethoven decided in 1815. 'And so he made a simple choice,' writes Franny Moyle in her biography of Turner. 'He chose his Art as the sole purpose of his life. Domestic life was no longer allowed to impinge on what from now on would define him.' More generally, I was drawn to the idea of the dawn of the uncouth genius, of how a larger socio-economic history might be embodied in their lives. Their belief in themselves was absolute, unqualified. They sought out and moved easily in the company of aristocratic patrons—to whom they considered themselves superior—without ever acquiring the social refinements of that class. 'Prince!' wrote Beethoven to his long-time supporter Prince Lichnowsky. 'What you are, you are by circumstance and by birth. What I am, I am through myself. Of princes there have been and will be thousands. Of Beethoven there is only one.' Described as 'a mean-looking little man' by one of his contemporaries, as an 'odd little mortal,' and 'miserly and miserable' (by Thomas Cole), Turner was compared to a coachman, a sailor, and, by Eugène Delacroix, 'an English farmer.' If he and Beethoven were both physically unprepossessing neither made much effort to cultivate the manners that might counter any unfavourable first impressions. They remained, even in the eyes of many who revered, indulged, and funded them, coarse, ill-mannered, and frequently ungrateful. For anyone less persuaded of their genius it was an easy business to shift qualities associated with the person across to the work so that Turner's *Fall of the Rhine*, for example, was 'marked by negligence and coarseness.' But this traffic went both ways. Faith in their own abilities, their undoubted success, and what Updike (in reference to Turner) called 'uncouth ambition' combined to place on established calibrations of social status the same strain that their later work imposed on the conventions of their respective arts. As a contemporary said of Beethoven, 'there was something about him overall that did not fit into any classification.' In numerous accounts contradictory impressions are yoked together. Constable, on meeting Turner, found him to be exactly as expected: 'He is uncouth but has a wonderful range of mind.'* Goethe considered Beethoven 'more concentrated, more energetic' than any other artist. 'His talent amazes me; but his personality is unfortunately quite untamed.' Again, accounts of artist and composer sometimes read as mirror images of each other. An Austrian diplomat and writer who 'made the acquaintance of Beethoven' in 1811 'found this reputedly savage and unsociable man to be the most magnificent artist with a heart of gold, a glorious spirit and a friendly disposition. What he has refused to princes he granted to us at first sight: he played on the fortepiano.' Prior to meeting 'the man who beyond all doubt is the greatest of the age,' Ruskin wrote in his diary that 'everybody had described him to me as coarse, boorish, unintellectual, vulgar.' Convinced this was impossible, Ruskin was delighted to find Turner 'a somewhat eccentric, keen-mannered, matter-of-fact, English-minded gentleman: good-natured evidently, bad-tempered evidently, hating humbug of all sorts, shrewd, perhaps a little selfish, highly intellectual, the powers of the mind not brought out with any delight in their manifestation, or intention of display, but flashing out occasionally in a word or a look.'

Even as their works brought in sizeable sums of money their habits remained frugal, austere. Increasing recognition of the value of their talents proceeded in tandem with suspicions about who might profit from it. Sir Walter Scott was displeased to discover that Turner would 'do nothing without cash and anything for it. He is almost the only man of genius I ever knew who is sordid in these matters.' Scott never met Beethoven, obviously! For every swooning account of the composer's nobility and generosity of spirit—and there are many— there is a story of his double-dealing or outright dishonesty. Turner,

---

* Cf. the friend of Jean Rhys who said she was 'almost without education—but with a wonderful mind.'

an acquaintance recalls, 'was by nature suspicious'; Beethoven was remembered as 'avaricious and always mistrustful.'* In both, shabbiness and the sublime, epic pettiness and poetic grandeur thrived in troubled intimacy. A printseller was struck by Turner's 'coarse, stout person, heavy look, and homely manners contrasting strangely with the marvellous beauty and grace of the . . . creations of his pencil.' A visitor to Beethoven's lodgings recalls the door being opened by 'a very ugly man of ill-humoured mien.' Invited in, he was naturally delighted to see the composer's piano, less so—but equally naturally—by the 'unemptied chamber pot' beneath it. The juxtaposition was a stark expression of what made Beethoven incomparable and what he had in common with everyone else on the planet. ('My shit is better than anything you thought,' was Beethoven's famous response to a critic's poor opinion of the orchestral piece *Wellington's Victory*.) Turner, one suspects, would have been happy with Peter Ackroyd's terming him 'a Cockney visionary.' In this regard he is a direct descendant of Blake but the speed with which his talent was recognised—and the rapid change of social horizons that opened up for him—looks ahead to those archetypal figures of London in the 1960s, David Bailey and Michael Caine. Needless to say, Turner was not unchanged by all these changes; 'M'lord Turner,' as the joke ran, could be imperious, self-important, grand.

Beethoven is still more complex and contradictory. The diplomat who had been so charmed by him in 1811, was, by 1814, struck by the way he had grown 'uncouth' and 'was particularly averse to our notables and gave expression to his repugnance with angry violence.' Revolutionary sympathies and expressions of contempt for the birthright of princes notwithstanding, Beethoven was keen to articulate his status in the kind of aristocratic terms later adopted by Nietzsche.

* This account of Turner's suspiciousness also includes a partial explanation: 'Oh! what a different man would Turner have been if all the good and kindly feelings of his great mind had been called into action; but they lay dormant and were known to so very few.' Adorno notes that 'what we know about Beethoven as a private person suggests that the grim, unfriendly aspect of his character had to do with shame and rejected love . . . Associated with the boorishness is an open-handed generosity, but also mistrust.'

It suited Beethoven to believe in what the biographer Jan Swafford calls 'an aristocracy of mind and talent and spirit' but that counted for nothing when, in the course of the legal battle for custody of his nephew, Karl, he conceded that 'van,' the Dutch prefix to his name, conferred nothing of the noble standing of the German 'von.'

Wagner had heralded Beethoven's music as a 'Germanic deed, a Germanic art, a Germanic effort towards a Germanic goal.' On several occasions Nietzsche remarked on Beethoven's nobility and majesty of spirit but 'German,' for him, was synonymous with the boorishness and coarseness that Beethoven so often displayed in his daily life— qualities incompatible with Nietzsche's regrettable belief in a pan-European aristocratic ideal of excellence.* Certainly he compared Beethoven unfavorably with Goethe for his behaviour during their famous encounter with the Empress and her court in Teplitz in 1812. Notwithstanding Beethoven's injunction—'They have to step aside, not we'—Goethe did just that, stepping aside and taking off his hat while Beethoven strode right through the centre of the group of dukes and royals. For Nietzsche their two different responses represented 'semi-barbarism [Beethoven] beside culture [Goethe].' This incident is paired in my mind with the later one in Turin when Nietzsche throws his arm around the horse. Similarly lacking in corroborating evidence that things occurred as related (in this case by a young and thoroughly besotted Bettina Brentano) it has similarly mythic, even epochal reverberations.

There is something else too—tenuous and associative but, to me, strangely appropriate. I joked earlier, as part of my pitch for the statue in the Piazza Carlo Alberto, that although Nietzsche sought to comfort the horse it was the philosopher who needed comforting. The semi-barbarism/culture comparison is the first in a list of antinomies distinguishing Beethoven from Goethe in Nietzsche's eyes.

---

* 'Hugo von Hofmannsthal said about Napoleon somewhere that he knew he couldn't walk like a king. The same could be said about Nietzsche,' writes Zagajewski in *A Defense of Ardor*. 'His endless praise of aristocratic behavior, power, and elegance betray him as someone who is more a Napoleon than a hereditary monarch.'

Coincidentally—though remember Nietzsche's claim, from shortly before the incident with the horse, that there are 'no more coincidences'—Beethoven in Teplitz is seen as 'the man in need of comfort next to the man who *is* comforted.' In the process of compiling the minor charges by which Beethoven might be indicted, Nietzsche offers evidence—hearsay, highly conjectural—of their kinship and shared need.

37.

To go alongside the English painter and the German composer I needed a writer, French ideally, or possibly American, who demonstrated some of the same qualities and whose career—or part of it at least—chronologically overlapped with theirs. Walt Whitman came too late (he would have been seven when Beethoven died) and, in spite of his famous and, for my purposes, perfect self-description—'one of the roughs'—didn't fit the bill, was, in some ways, the *opposite* of Beethoven and Turner.*

I could have just concentrated on the pair of them, on Beethoven and Turner, but I felt a trio or triangle would lend stability to a structure that might otherwise be flimsy. The lack of a third party wasn't the only problem. There was also the fact that I was really only interested in the final phases of Beethoven's and Turner's work (from 1814 and 1835 respectively), which, in numerous accounts, are described in almost identical terms as one or the other would 'throw all caution to the wind' and 'embark upon a final quest for freedom' or—in Adorno's severe formulation—spurn 'sensuous charm under the dictates of the imperiously emancipated mind.' This is in keeping with the expected trajectory of the ageing artist who, in the words of de Kooning's biographers Mark Stevens and Annalyn Swan, 'begins

---

* After meeting Whitman, whose work had earlier displeased him, W. D. Howells discovered that 'the apostle of the rough, the uncouth, was the gentlest person; his barbaric yawp, translated into the terms of social encounter, was an address of singular quiet, delivered in a voice of winning and endearing friendliness.'

to give himself away with a kind of fearless abandon,' who 'exchanges substance for light.'

Once I accepted this more limited field of interest the search for a third person (a writer who, in addition to the advertised requirements, also had a distinct final phase—another reason why Whitman wouldn't work) was called off.

Now that *was* part of something else that interested me: books you can't and won't write; the way a working life comes to an end not because of any feelings about what you *have* done, what has already been accomplished (Philip Roth having written god-knows how many books, Wittgenstein having solved all the problems of philosophy after just one, are extreme cases), but because of the impossibility of moving beyond whatever obstacles lie in your path. (Often the two go together, as they did for Borg, who, having won eleven majors, lost to McEnroe at Wimbledon and the U.S. Open in 1981.) That interested me a lot, and, as a result, an alternative way ahead did become clear. The obstacle *became* the path.

Those unwritten and unwriteable books become part of—get folded into—a book one *can* write. *This* one.

38.

There was another difficulty with Beethoven. Not knowing anything about music or musical terminology, having no access to the language of music—the language of another world that I never learned—I'm particularly vulnerable to Barthes's barbed claim that in music criticism 'a work (or its performance) is only ever translated into the poorest of linguistic categories: the adjective.' But what else is there?

Well, there's C-sharp minor, A minor, B-flat major . . . *

---

* One of the reasons the world of classical music seems inaccessible and intimidating is the simple business of how to refer to the compositions and the various parts of a given piece. Say 'opus 132' and you sound like a bit of a ponce; add further clarification with 'A minor' and you sound even more of a ponce; throw in what Beethoven deemed 'absurd terms' such as

I have no idea what anything in the previous line means. That's why—much as I appreciate Mingus's reassuring admission, on *Blues and Roots*, that 'E's Flat Ah's Flat Too'—I had to call for the distant help of *Voyager*.

But when *listening* to music can I understand that which I will never learn? To any musicians who say that I can't I nod along in agreement. The best I can do is give myself to it, to the music. And I may be able to illustrate the extent of that unprovable, impossible-to-articulate capacity with the help of a film.

39.

'In what does the expression of the human manifest itself in Beethoven? I would say, in the fact that his music has the gift of sight.'

Ron Fricke's *Baraka* (1992) opens with shots of Nepal, the Himalayas, covered in snow. High up in the mountain—or so we are led to believe—a snow monkey is shivering, twitching calmly in a pool of frosty water. The monkey is actually in the Nagano springs in Japan, but the film relies on our highly evolved habit of reading film to suggest and sustain the illusion of narrative continuity. Pensive-looking, the pink-faced monkey is recognisably a relative of ours, albeit a distant one, with no interest in listening to string quartets let alone understanding their structure and opus numbers, or the grammar of film construction. For we humans who are articulate in the language of film editing, however, the suggestion is irresistible: after watching the monkey blink its eyes, turn its head away, and then turn its gaze back towards us the next thing we see—jump-cut to a star-filled cosmos,

---

'andante' or 'adagio'—to say nothing of the added provocation of 'Tuscany'—and the needle of that unfailing and enduring feat of chippy English engineering, the trusty old ponce-ometer, dives into the red. And since the brain is not configured to remember numbers, the combination of op. 132 with the incomprehensible code of A minor or D major means that I have trouble identifying and remembering which quartet is which, whereas if you say the *Moonlight* piano sonata or the *Archduke Trio* then I know instantly what you're talking about.

which then becomes suddenly illuminated—is a point-of-view shot: an ultimate exterior that is also an X-ray of the monkey's inner life or consciousness as he looks 'questioningly, longingly, into the infinite expanse.' That's how the violinist Karl Holz recalled Beethoven when the idea for the adagio of the second of the Razumovsky quartets came to him, on a night when 'the clear stars illuminated the heavens.' It is also a shot of what I was seeing as the sound of op. 132 filled my head, lying on the hard and slightly chilly bench in Tuscany.

40.

Amid the overall paucity of Nietzsche's writing on Beethoven, a comment in *Human, All Too Human* becomes crucial to this discussion. Nietzsche has in mind a passage in the Ninth Symphony, but he anticipates not only the feelings evoked by the adagio of op.132 but also the adjectives and imagery I've relied on to express those feelings:

> He is hovering above the earth in a dome of stars, with the dream of *immortality* in his heart: all the stars seem to glitter around him and the earth seems to sink farther and farther away. If he becomes aware of being in this condition he feels a profound stab in the heart and sighs for the man who will lead him back to his lost love, whether she be called religion or metaphysics.

The relevance of this goes beyond Beethoven. Written while relations between Nietzsche and Wagner were becoming strained, *Human, All Too Human* was instrumental in their break. Wagner had sent Nietzsche an autographed copy of the outline of *Parsifal* in January 1878; Nietzsche reciprocated by sending two copies of *Human, All Too Human*, which Wagner and Cosima received in April. Nietzsche claimed later, in *Ecce Homo,* that each accepted the other's gift with silence, though he had his sister send an admiring letter, restricting his adverse impressions of *Parsifal* to himself and to private correspondence with others. For his part the composer read only a few lines of *Human, All Too Human* before putting it aside so that—as he politely told a friend—it would not spoil the impression made by Nietzsche's earlier books. The relationship deteriorated beyond repair, for multiple additional reasons—Nietzsche's praising of Brahms, Wagner's anti-Semitism, the 'grave insult,' and so on—but not, for Nietzsche, without a massive sense of loss.

If we substitute Wagner for 'lost love' the passage from *Human, All Too Human* doubles as a prophetic description of how powerfully Nietzsche felt the tug of those giddy days amid friends in Tribschen and during the first visit to Bayreuth in May of 1872. The Bayreuth festival became tainted but he wrote of the first visit, when the foundation stone was laid, as 'the happiest days I have had. There was something in the air that I have never experienced anywhere else, something quite inexpressible but full of hope.' Alone in Turin, with his scorn focused on Wagner, Nietzsche was able to declare that the composer had been 'the great benefactor of my life.'

One of Wagner's biographers, Martin Gregor-Dellin, emphasises that while the relationship with Wagner was, for Nietzsche, life-defining, for Wagner 'the Nietzsche affair was only an episode.' This is undoubtedly correct but when we recall that Nietzsche considered Wagner a master of 'what is smallest, in spinning out the details,' certain details jump out from the overall narrative. Wagner claimed to have done his friend a favour by not reading his book, but Roger Hollinrake, in a detailed chronology, writes that 'despite this Cosima's diary shows that W devoted most of May and June to [its] study.'

When Nietzsche heard of the death of Wagner—'by far the *fullest* human being I have known'—he admitted that it brought 'the greatest relief': 'It was hard to be for six years the opponent of a man whom one has admired above all others, and I am not built coarsely enough for *that*,' he wrote. 'I shall be in good measure his heir.' While Wagner did not brood on Nietzsche the way that Nietzsche did on Wagner, the philosopher was in his thoughts, gallingly, at the end—without, it seems, either the beneficence that underwrote the younger man's vehement repudiation or his eventual understanding: 'We—Wagner and I—basically experienced a tragedy together.' In Venice on 3 February 1883, ten days before her husband's death, Cosima noted in her diary Wagner's comment that 'everything about the man [Nietzsche] disgusted him.' And the following day: 'Finally R said to me: Nietzsche had no ideas of his own, no blood of his own. What flowed in to him was other people's blood.'

That combination of rancour and dismissal—exactly the kind of knot that Nietzsche, as a psychologist, was so adept at disentangling—suggests that Wagner had some inkling that the opposite might be the case, that the short-sighted professor might create works to rival or even surpass his own. The eventual truth would have been still more intolerable: that Nietzsche's ideas would become part of the lifeblood of twentieth-century thought. By then, they would also be tragically associated with the flow of real blood, 'with the recollection of something frightful,' as Nietzsche himself had written, 'of a crisis like no other before on earth.'

41.

In *Friends and Heroes*, the final volume of Olivia Manning's *Balkan Trilogy*, the heroine Harriet and her friend Alan are walking in Athens in 1941 when the German propaganda bureau is wrecked by Greeks. A portrait of Hitler is thrown from an upper window and a scattered heap of books is about to be set on fire—'a bonfire of anti-culture.' One of the books, its cover gone, falls at Harriet's feet:

> 'Let me see!' Alan looked at it and laughed: '*Herrenmoral und Sklavenmoral*. Poor old Nietzsche! I wonder if he knew which was which?' He put the book into his hip pocket. 'A souvenir,' he said.
> 'Of what?'
> 'Man's hatred of himself.'

In *Alamein to Zem Zem* Keith Douglas, who was killed, aged twenty-four, in Normandy on 9 June 1944, writes: 'I had one or two German novels and magazines which I had picked up out of enemy vehicles and positions, and a copy of *Also sprach Zarathustra*, the owner of which had pencil-marked most of the quotations in it applicable to Nazi ideas.'

42.

Zarathustra became Nietzsche's best-known book. It was also his most Wagnerian—in the worst way. He had claimed that *Parsifal* would be undermined by its staging, by the acting and costumes (by the production problems that assailed the first Bayreuth festival); something similar could be said of the big-budget parable in monologue that was *Zarathustra*: a one-man orchestral suite, performed in fancy dress and delivered through a megaphone of mytho-prophetic rhetoric that was ill-suited to what, ironically, marks Nietzsche's work at its best: his human, utterly human vulnerability and psychological sensitivity. Nietzsche was a prophetic writer in the sense that he foresaw states of mind and being that were in the process of formation—that were brought into being partly by his writing. Whether in the form of invective, boasts, asides, confessions, commentary, or psycho-philosophical investigations, these were set out with lightness, brilliance, wit, subtlety, scorn, tenderness, playfulness, exuberance—qualities that become distorted when pronounced through the amplifying mask of Zarathustra. Think even of his most world-shaking lines and you never feel like appending 'also sprach Nietzsche.' Thomas Mann, in his *Last Essays*, is almost admiring when he writes of Nietzsche's 'audacious insults to his age'; he is also accurate when he says that *Zarathustra* verges on the 'ludicrous.' I never get tired of reading Nietzsche but *Zarathustra* is tiresome in the extreme. Despite his claims to be dynamite, to be hurling thunderbolts, to be accomplishing the work of millennia, Nietzsche was not suited to the big stage, to the philosopher's equivalent of stadium rock. Fantasising that *The Antichrist* would be 'translated into 7 languages; the first edition in each language c. one million copies,' he continued scribbling, unnoticed, in his room. If he speaks of his pride, that is a sign of how deeply it had been hurt. The psychic wounds that, Whitman-like, he sought to dress were also his own. His most earth-shattering passages tend also to be the most intimate. His ambitions are simultaneously modest, vast, and private. 'I would like to take away from human existence some of its heart-breaking and cruel character,' he wrote in a letter of 1882. 'Yet, to be able to continue here, I would have to reveal to you what I have never yet revealed to anyone—the task which confronts me, my life's task.'

43.

It's far more common for an artist, writer, or musician to leave behind unfinished works than it is for the body of work to be completed, wrapped up, and ready to be neatly shipped off to posterity. It's then up to the estate to decide what is fit to be published despite being unfinished. But consider briefly the distinction between something unfinished (a symphony by Schubert; Camus's *The First Man*; Rhys's autobiography, *Smile Please*; Adorno's book on Beethoven; Edward Said's work on *Late Style*) and the unfinishable, projects that, almost from inception, are destined never to be completed: what Vila-Matas calls 'impossible' books. Jane Austen's *Sanditon* was left incomplete at the time of her death; in *Middlemarch* George Eliot created the archetype of the work that would never be completed—the Reverend Casaubon's *Key to All Mythologies*—even if its author had all of eternity at his disposal in order to do so. 'The scope of the undertaking, the volume of materials collected, was assuming epic proportions,' write the English translators of Walter Benjamin's *Arcades Project*, 'and no less epic was the manifest interminability of the task.'

Turner explained how 'some fresh follerey comes across me and I begin what most probably never to be finish'd.' The anxiety was understandable since he was sixty-six at the time. Robert Caro, eighty-four as I type, is engaged in a diligent race against time in his attempt to complete the fifth and final volume of his life of Lyndon Johnson. If he stays healthy for long enough there is no doubt that he will manage it. James Turrell's Roden Crater is a more uncertain case. For many years he has seemed close to finishing this massive combination of installation and land art. Journalists and donors have been allowed to visit the site in northern Arizona but just when it looks like Turrell might be approaching the final straight, a new phase of construction is announced. In several ways there's no real incentive to bring things to a conclusion since the funding would then slow to the relative dribble required for maintenance. Or maybe that's too cynical, maybe achieving this apotheosis of land and light, of human perception and transcendence, was always destined to take far longer than envisaged—or that was envisage*able*.

And it's not as though Turrell's case is unique. Robert Harbison points out that while plenty of architects have drawn up plans for structures that have not yet been built but that have the *potential* to be realised (in the same way that Beethoven's twenty-ninth piano sonata—op. 106, or *Hammerklavier*—was considered unplayable*) others have contented themselves with fantasies that are not just technologically far-fetched but that fall into the third category of his title, *The Built, The Unbuilt, and the Unbuildable*.

44.

Relationships between the completed, the unfinished, and the un-finishable are crucial to Romanticism, most obviously in the lives cut

---

* Beethoven more modestly estimated that it would keep pianists busy for the next fifty years. And Kretzschmar, in Thomas Mann's *Doctor Faustus*, notes that Beethoven's late sonatas convey a sense of being unfinished, especially the very last, op. 111, which comprises only two movements. Kretzschmar's brilliant lecture on op. 111, on why there is no third movement, is almost certainly derived from Adorno, who served as Mann's 'musical advisor' on the novel.

short before the body of work could be fully realised: Shelley, Keats, Chatterton ('the marvellous boy,' as Wordsworth called him). Within a poet's body of work the unfinished or the fragmentary—Coleridge's famously interrupted *Kubla Khan*—came to be valued more highly than the finished and complete. As subject matter, few sights were more inspirational than that which had fallen into ruin. Completed at variously distant points in the past, the sites of 'The Ruined Cottage,' 'Michael,' or, most spectacularly, 'Ozymandias,' achieved fuller realisation in decay, completed meaning in dereliction. The ideal, naturally, was that which fell into ruin before it could be completed. The poetic manifestation of this was the inherently unfinishable work that thereby achieved ideal form by virtue of being incomplete or abandoned.

45.

Nietzsche had a mania for writing prefaces and forewords, could not resist adding introductions to new editions of old books—old books that he regarded as introductions to the ones that were still to be written. Notwithstanding that it was the greatest gift ever offered to mankind, even *Zarathustra* itself was variously described as 'porch, preparation, preface,' as 'only the gateway to a coherent philosophical work.' At one point that work was to be called *The Will to Power*, itself abandoned in favour of a task that was to take the form of a four-part *Revaluation of All Values*. On 3 September 1888 he wrote a foreword to this *Revaluation* that he considered 'the most impressive foreword that has perhaps ever been written.' Only the first installment, *The Antichrist*, was completed but, as Nietzsche's grand plans dissolved and speedily re-formed in favour of self-contained—yet overlapping—increments, a reversal took place whereby the *Revaluation* was deemed to have been completed with this single volume. *Ecce Homo*, a survey of how his earlier books came into existence, was also intended to be 'a preparatory work in the highest degree' and a 'prelude to the *Revaluation of All Values.*' Starting on his forty-fourth birthday, on 15 October 1888, Nietzsche surged through the story of 'how one becomes what one is' in three weeks; it was published posthumously, by his sister, in 1908.

Intended initially as part of a very long poem *The Recluse*—which would also incorporate the long poem *The Excursion* (book 1 of which included a version of 'The Ruined Cottage')—Wordsworth's *The Prelude* grew around and in keeping with its theme: 'Growth of a Poet's Mind.' The poem was 'completed' in May 1805, but rather than publish it Wordsworth continued, at intervals, to revise it until 1839. Even in that final revision the title was 'not fixed upon.' Coleridge, in October 1799, presumably in response to a suggestion of Wordsworth's, liked the idea of it being 'the tail-piece of *The Recluse.*' The poet's sister, Dorothy, in 1804, termed it 'an appendix to *The Recluse,*' but the expanded poem eventually acquired the title—at the suggestion of Wordsworth's widow—that is precisely the opposite of an appendix or tail-piece, and was published after the poet's death in 1850.

So, the story of how Wordsworth became a poet ends up in a state of perpetual becoming, incapable of achieving definitive or fixed form, partly because the process was ongoing and partly because the story involved—this, after all, was what *The Prelude* was a prelude *to*—his inability to articulate it to his satisfaction, to bring it to a conclusion. The introduction to the selections from the poem included in *The Oxford Anthology of English Literature: Romantic Poetry and Prose* puts it starkly: 'perhaps he just did not want to be reminded, or have others reminded, of how much he had lost.' While Wordsworth was still occasionally working on it—or at least while he had not published it—he was still a poet. When it was done—to use the word my friend had applied to Dylan after the gig in Texas—he would be done.

As with Dylan's constant revisions of his songs so, to a degree, with Wordsworth's *Preludes*. At college we studied the two versions of *The Prelude* in the Penguin Parallel Text edition (with Caspar David Friedrich's *Mountain Landscape with Rainbow* on the cover). The Oxford anthology deems the 1850 version 'rhetorically superior'; others argued that the 1805 version had more immediacy, that in the 1850 Wordsworth was straining for effects that had come more easily in the earlier version. Easily swayed, I didn't feel strongly one way or the other. Still don't. Some bits are slightly better in one version, some in the other, and a lot is pretty much the same in both.

In book 11 of 1805 or book 12 of 1850 a key passage is different in only a couple of small ways. Here's the 1805:

> *The days gone by,*
> *Come back upon me from the dawn almost*
> *Of life; the hiding-places of my power*
> *Seem open, I approach, and then they close;*
> *I see by glimpses now, when age comes on*
> *May scarcely see at all; and I would give*
> *While yet we may, as far as words can give,*
> *A substance and a life to what I feel:*
> *I would enshrine the spirit of the past*
> *For future restoration.*

In 1850 'my power' has become 'man's power,' which turns it from a personal observation—with all the attendant anxiety on the poet's part—to a pronouncement (with all the attendant aversion that pronouncements induce in the reader). Despite the subtitle—*Growth of a Poet's Mind*—*The Prelude* is also about that mind's anticipated, then gradual and, taken as a whole, demonstrable diminution. If Wordsworth tacitly concedes the fading of the very powers whose growth he intended to celebrate then the poem achieves the double feat of simultaneously fulfilling *and* indefinitely postponing the anticipated decline. In 1839, at the time of his last revisions, he can still see 'by glimpses' despite the earlier fear that, by this point, he might not be able to see at all. So the restoration has been achieved by the line in which this project or intention is declared: 'I would enshrine the spirit of the past / For future restoration.' While it might have been more accurate to talk of future 'exhumation' the connotations of that were too dreadful to contemplate. And yet exactly such an unwelcome suggestion does creep in a few lines later. Resuming the narration of events from his childhood, 'these to me affecting incidents' of 1805 have, by 1850, become 'these memorials.' The poem has become a memorial—to itself. Wordsworth would never again get close to the original, unmediated experience. That experience could be verbally rearranged—expressed with sometimes more felicity, sometimes with less rhythmic power—but not comprehensively reconsidered or reconstituted because, as he had written in 1805, it had already been 'enshrined.' The earlier version had become not just a barrier between him and the experiences; it had *become* those experiences.

It's a version or prelude to something that has become common since the advent of photography and the technological creation, preservation, and reproduction of moments in time: the way that one's memories of childhood consist of memories of photographs of experiences rather than the experiences themselves. This is in keeping with the one of the key elements of the 'spots of time' described and enumerated by Wordsworth: those moments that retain a 'vivifying virtue' throughout the course of one's life. The 'spot'—that's how Wordsworth refers to the location in 1805, but in the 1850 version the pun has been removed—where a murderer was hanged is memorable not just because of what occurred there but because the murderer's name had been carved in 'monumental writing,' which, by superstition of the neighbourhood, is cleared of grass so that 'to this hour / The letters are all fresh and visible.' Contemplating words preinscribed by an 'unknown hand' in 'times long past,' then inscribed by his own hand (in 1805), Wordsworth is left with the possibility of re-inscribing or revising them.

I'm conscious, naturally, that something akin to that process is being repeated here, that I've quoted those lines before, in *The Ongoing Moment*. I keep coming back to them because the story—a prelude that is ongoing, that is also an accompaniment, appendix, or postscript—of any writer's mind always concerns the growth (to be followed, if one is not careful, by shrinkage) of his or her life as a *reader*. For me *The Prelude* is itself a spot of time but when I say that I 'keep coming back' to it that is not quite accurate. I learned chunks of it by heart when I was eighteen. I don't need to come back to it (except, on occasions like this, to check for accuracy) because it never went away.

46.

These readerly spots of time are also inextricably bound up with my awakening appreciation of visual art. Appreciation of words brought with it a fascination with and curiosity about the paintings featured on the covers of Penguin editions. Friedrich was one of the first artists I was able to recognise in the sense that I noticed that his paintings were on the cover of not only *The Prelude* but also Herman Hesse's *Narcissus and Goldmund* (ravaged trees and spectral ruins in the mist of *Abbey in an Oak Forest*), *A Nietzsche Reader* (bare tree on a hillside), and *Ecce Homo* (the solitary figure of *Wanderer over the Sea of Fog*).

47.

To get a first inkling of the Eternal Recurrence, poised like Friedrich's wanderer at a spot '6,000 feet beyond man and time,' might reasonably be described as a peak experience; attempting a revaluation of all values is a hefty undertaking by any standards, with ample potential to be left uncompleted. But bear in mind the modesty of the proposals Nietzsche made along the way. Famous for proclaiming the death of God, the self-appointed anti-Christ recommends that instead of the religious practice of praying in the morning, we 'think on awakening whether one cannot this day give pleasure to at any rate *one* person.'

What a lovely idea! An advocate of what he called 'the courtesy of the heart,' Nietzsche extolled what would later become the easily mocked virtues of the Californian culture of habitual niceness:

> Amongst the small, but countlessly frequent and therefore very effective, things to which science should pay more attention than to the great, rare things, is to be reckoned goodwill; I mean that exhibition of a friendly disposition in intercourse, that smiling eye, that clasp of the hand, that cheerfulness with which almost all human actions are usually accompanied . . . Thus one finds much more happiness in the world than sad eyes see, if one only reckons rightly, and does not forget all those moments of comfort in which every day is rich, even in the most harried of human lives.

48.

Nietzsche's time in Turin was brightened by small things, by the way that—or so it seemed to him—people's faces lit up when he entered a shop or by the old women in the market who kept their best grapes ('glorious' in one letter, 'sweetest' in another) for him. At the same time there attached to his name 'a quantity of doom that is beyond saying.'

After wrenching himself free of Wagner Nietzsche's idea of what music should be underwent a necessary change—he wanted it to move with light feet, to be 'cheerful and profound,' more 'southern,' with nothing German about it ('I shall never admit that a German *could* know what music is'). Wagner famously said of the opening slow movement of Beethoven's op. 131 string quartet that it was the saddest thing ever written in notes. The saddest thing, to me, is that Nietzsche in Turin did not have access to these notes, this music. Having finished *The Case of Wagner* he added a postscript, then another postscript, and then an epilogue—how reluctant he was to let go of Wagner! In the second postscript he stresses that his war on

Wagner does not mean that he wanted to celebrate 'any other musicians.' Beethoven didn't need celebrating but when I picture the exuberant, lonely, and ridiculous figure of Nietzsche in Turin—converting news of an occasional reader somewhere into the belief that he has readers everywhere, the grip of eventually vindicated delusion tightening daily around him—I can't help thinking of these late quartets and the *consolation* they might have brought him.

49.

Maybe that is sentimental and inappropriate in discussing works that, however beautiful their melodies, can never be played sentimentally. Was it Joyce who defined sentimentality as unearned emotion? To play the late quartets, however badly, is a guarantee that their emotions have been earned (writes the person who can neither play nor read a note of music). It is impossible even to *listen* to them sentimentally.

While we're on this note, this little note about sentimentality, mention should be made of a dinner in Palos Verdes where, as can happen in California, I found myself sitting next to an astrophysicist. We didn't talk about Beethoven but, naturally, I asked about *Voyager* and its having passed into interstellar space. She was not only unmoved but quite contemptuous of the idea. There's no transition, she insisted. There's just more of the same, which, if I understand things correctly, means less of the same.

50.

I'm not the only one to see a special connection between Nietzsche and Beethoven. *The Unbearable Lightness of Being* begins with a discussion of the Eternal Recurrence and how Nietzsche thought it 'the heaviest of burdens (*das schwerste Gewicht*).' A little later one of the characters backs up an important decision he has made with the words 'Es muss sein.' 'It was an allusion,' Milan Kundera explains, to the last movement of Beethoven's last quartet. To make clear what both Beethoven and he himself intended Kundera explains how the composer introduced the movement with a phrase, 'Der schwer gefasste Entschluss.' Commonly translated as 'the difficult resolution,' the phrase 'may also be construed as a "heavy" or "weighty resolution."'

Through some typically light-footed wordplay and thought (albeit without mentioning that Beethoven's solemn inscription might have been a joke at the expense, quite literally, of a rich admirer of his music), Kundera allows the last movement of Beethoven's last quartet and Nietzsche's idea of the Eternal Recurrence briefly to come close to each other, without their names ever sharing the same page. In *Testaments Betrayed*, however, the association becomes explicit as they are seen, in formal terms, to share the same *living space*. After describing the 'compositional' qualities of Nietzsche's books, Kundera points out that the thought contained in these books cannot be separated from their form and style. In music, by contrast, one of the reasons composers such as Haydn were so prolific is because they were filling out a form or a 'pre-existent matrix' with their inventions. Beethoven, in his piano sonatas, was content to rely on these established forms until the form itself became 'radically individual.' Thereafter each of the later sonatas was 'composed in a manner unique and unprecedented.' This has the wider implication, for all artists, that 'the composition should itself be an invention, an invention that engages all the author's originality.' So the philosopher of the future—the philosopher after Nietzsche—will be 'an *experimenter*.'

Another consequence of all this—distinctive stylistic signature, formal innovation, rejection of 'commonly accepted systems' of thought, refusal to accept the barriers between various philosophical disciplines—is a broadening of themes so extensive as to bring 'philosophy closer to the novel.' For the first time the philosopher, like the novelist—and the great composer—is able to ponder 'everything human.' The task for philosophy from Nietzsche onwards, Kundera concludes, will be to 'open rifts for venturing into the unknown.'

The irony is that Kundera set out these ingenious calculations and formulations in a work of non-fiction, opening up the possibility of venturing *beyond* the novel.

51.

John Coltrane's last studio recordings, made on 22 February 1967 with the drummer Rashied Ali, were released posthumously as *Interstellar Space*. Coltrane died less than five months later, on 17 July 1967, aged forty. In any other field of activity that would be a desperately short life. Only in jazz is it broadly in line with actuarial norms. And because he became ill and died so suddenly we can speak not of a late period in his work—it was too early for that—only of a *last* phase. Rather than a late period in the accepted sense in which Beethoven arrived at a late style, there was only a ceasing of the unceasing torrent of sound. In the same way, Garry Winogrand's sudden illness and death at the age of fifty-six in 1984 meant that he left an ocean of images—a third of a million exposures by some estimates—which he had barely glimpsed.

The interest of recordings from Coltrane's final phase lies partly in what they preserve and partly for any hints they contain as to where he might have headed next. Given the composition titles from that last session—'Mars,' 'Venus,' 'Jupiter,' 'Saturn'—the question might reasonably be asked, where was there *left* to go? The trumpeter Charles Tolliver's answer to that rhetorical question is hard to beat. Coltrane, he said, went 'cosmic.'

One of the recent discoveries—more exactly *re*coveries since parts of the concert have circulated as poorly produced bootlegs—in the ongoing archaeological dig of Coltrane's work was recorded at Temple University in Philadelphia, on 11 November 1966. There's a degree of irony about the date, Armistice Day, with its traditional Minute's Silence, given the shrieking, screaming, and wildness—the ferocious anti-silence—of the music. Things were happening so fast in jazz at the time—and with Coltrane in particular—that a mere fourteen months had passed since the last, partially great recording with the classic quartet (McCoy Tyner, Elvin Jones, Jimmy Garrison) on 2 September 1965.

Playing *First Meditations (for Quartet)* after listening to the Temple recording I found it, if such a thing is possible, even more overwhelming than I did when I listened to it regularly back in the 1980s.* I say 'partially great' because it still loses me after the first two pieces, 'Love' and 'Compassion.' Numerous times in the past the quartet had brought back a tune from the silence into which it had subsided (on 'Spiritual' from *Live at the Village Vanguard*, or 'Alabama' on *Live at Birdland*). The transition between 'Love' and 'Compassion' will be the last such resurrection, all the more miraculous because, in 'Love,' the yearning of Coltrane's cry is enhanced by resignation: by the acknowledgement (an advance on the section of that name on *A Love Supreme*) that it will not be answered. Coltrane might not have had a late phase but his quartet certainly did.

Tyner and Jones stayed on for a while, the latter's contributions diluted by Rashied Ali who appears, along with Pharoah Sanders, on the revised version of *Meditations* recorded on 23 November. That was the album playing at the Jazz Café at Burning Man when I made my unprompted and apparently unappreciated contribution to the seminar on free jazz, urging those present to listen to the original quartet version. After the departure of Jones and Tyner only the bassist Jimmy Garrison from the quartet remained in Coltrane's final band (though he happens to be missing at the Temple gig, replaced by Sonny Johnson) with Sanders, Ali, and Coltrane's wife Alice on piano.

On the one hand, it's an extraordinary idea, adding another drummer when he already had *Elvin* behind the traps. Coltrane, in this

---

* I listened to *First Meditations* for the first time in my friend Chris's room in Brixton in the mid-1980s, but it's the *second* time I heard it, a few months later, that sticks in my memory. I was in the hallway of a house party where, above the funk playing in the main rooms, I could make out what sounded like Coltrane. I followed the sound upstairs to a bedroom where three or four guys were listening to the album at high volume, with the tranced concentration of the deeply stoned.

regard, seems to have felt compelled to add musicians in the hope that doing so would better clarify the reason for having done so. On the other, you can hear, in *First Meditations*, that the quartet has become constricting, is in the process of generating ways to break out of itself—while also, inevitably and simultaneously, thwarting any such attempt. The extra musicians force the issue, taking the music beyond the immense gravitational tug generated by Tyner and Jones irrespective of cost or direction—even as that direction comes to seem, in retrospect, inevitable. Pharoah, a constant partner on tenor in this final phase, is briefly joined at Temple by a couple of young saxophonists, Steve Knoblauch and Arnold Joyner. Four additional percussionists also have a chance to sit in. One applauds the democratic inclusiveness while remaining unconvinced by the result. It must have been incredibly exciting to have been there that night (even if, for circumstantial reasons, the house was not full) but, as often happens with free jazz, that excitement fades after the event, on record. Or perhaps it makes evident what was harder to grasp in the intoxicating frenzy of the moment: that free jazz had run its course—come up against its limits—while the course was still being run and the limits breached. The fact that things fall apart does not mean that they can't keep going, especially given the huge freight of history that the music was, at this point, obliged to bear. On that note, one wonders about Yeats's claim that the best lack all conviction while the worst are full of passionate intensity. Coltrane is as passionately intense as ever. Did he lack conviction? Maybe the Yeatsian opposition is false and passionate intensity covers up or disguises a deeper lack of conviction.

The novelty or specific interest of the Temple gig is the way that Coltrane sort of sings, or vocalises, or makes noises and beats his chest in the midst of 'Leo' and 'My Favorite Things.' These eagerly anticipated moments actually sound a bit daft—which is not to say that they were without value. Perhaps they—or Ayler's doing something similar when he played at Coltrane's funeral—lodged in Pharoah's mind and provided inspiration for the occasion when, in the process of tearing up Coltrane's 'Olé' at the Keystone Korner on

23 January 1982, he takes the horn out of his mouth and screams. The scream is fuel thrown on a fire already blazing with the intensity of Pharoah's solo and the force of the rhythm section. That propulsive power—saturated with elements first harnessed by Coltrane's classic quartet—was diminished in the sonic shimmer of Coltrane's last phase: something he felt he no longer needed, that he may even have regarded as holding him back in his quest.

This quest is routinely characterised as spiritual but I would question whether there is something audibly 'spiritual' about music that doubled as both map (of where he might be headed) and record (of what was being left in his wake). If it's there I can't hear it and I don't experience this—as I do the inability to get through *The Sound and the Fury*—as a loss. What I do hear, in late Coltrane, is the momentum of what he'd done before—and a situation he'd helped to create—carrying him towards a terminus, a brick wall, a dead-end characterised by what Elvin, explaining his reasons for quitting, called 'a lot of noise.' Now that is something I would like to have heard my astrophysicist acquaintance from Palos Verde talk about. Is it possible that, in the fathomless and far-out paradoxes of theoretical physics, the limitless interstellar void is also a dead-end?

The sense of inevitability is tempered by the adjacent and scarcely less formidable figure of Miles Davis. It's hard to imagine that famously mean mother letting all those kids sit in—though he might have hired one of them after hearing them at someone else's gig—or of anyone describing his musical journey in 'spiritual' terms. For numerous reasons—musical, temperamental, and, crucially, commercial—he avoided the trap of free jazz while harnessing much of its swirling energy. At the time of Coltrane's Temple University concert Miles was leading his second great quintet (with Ron Carter, Herbie Hancock, Wayne Shorter, and Tony Williams) and would soon move into the sidereal minimalism of *In a Silent Way*, the electric maelstrom of *Bitches Brew*, and beyond (before almost wiping himself out in his green Lamborghini and a white-out blizzard of cocaine: an earth-bound instance of the void as dead-end).

Davis survived and after a prolonged retirement came back, diminished, but active to the end of his life. With Coltrane there's just no knowing. The rest, perhaps, was not bound to be noise. On the first quartet album for Impulse he recorded 'The Inch Worm' and perhaps, at the end, he was inching his way to a wormhole through which astonishing discoveries were possible. Had he lived, he might have found a way to multiple further phases. And even though, to return to that earlier distinction, Coltrane's was a last rather than late phase, bits of Adorno's defining analysis of late style flare into view while listening to his last recordings. The clichéd idea of Beethoven's late style, according to Adorno, is that he broke through to a realm of pure expression, free of conventions. In late works, the artist's personality 'breaks through the envelope of form to better express itself,' is Adorno's summary of this conventional assessment, 'disdaining sensual charms with the sovereign self-assurance of the spirit liberated.' Is that what happens here? And isn't that what free jazz is all about? Except, of course, Coltrane keeps coming back to old forms and old favourites—opening the Temple set with 'Naima' and ending it by gouging out all but the beating heart of 'My Favorite Things.' (By comparison with this performance the version recorded in Japan less than three months earlier is positively catchy.) Little is left of the original Rodgers and Hammerstein composition but amid all the wreckage, as Adorno said of late Beethoven, 'one finds formulas and phrases of convention scattered about.' Their loveliness is briefly enhanced by the ravaged landscape that is always threatening to engulf them.

52.

Adorno's 'Late Style in Beethoven' was an important early reference point for this book about *last* things, some of which *are* late, while some are precociously early. Not that this was ever intended to be a comprehensive study of last things, or of lastness generally. It's about a congeries of experiences, things, and cultural artefacts that, for various

reasons, have come to group themselves around me in a rough con-
stellation during a phase of my life. Though not my last, hopefully,
this phase is marked by a daily increasing consciousness that the next
may well be—so much so that I feel I'd better get this done now in
case it comes round sooner than I think, or that the last phase, whenever it comes, might be distinguished by an inability on my part to
identify or articulate it.

53.

On 5 July 2018 I took the tube from Wimbledon to Soho, just in time
to catch Pharoah Sanders at Ronnie Scott's. There was a fitting continuity: bearded Benoît Paire had been playing with one leg so heavily
bandaged that when he won after losing the first set 6–0 it seemed
less like a comeback than the return of an unusually athletic mummy.

I'd seen Pharoah many times before but this was surely going to
be the last. Although it was nominally his gig it was really a trio with
saxophone cameos. Pharoah was much diminished, playing with a
fraction of the power he'd had at his disposal twenty years ago. But
how immense that power had been! We want to believe that other
qualities—wisdom, depth, soulfulness—can take the place of lost
power and energy but in Pharoah's case that earlier energy and power
was fuelled by depth, soul, and anything else one can think of. So
there was only loss.

He spent much of the gig resting on his stool. He could not have
looked more Pharaonic as he perched there, eyes closed, white-
bearded, seemingly eternal, maybe even catatonic. The rhythm section played the melody from 'The Creator Has a Master Plan' but
its creator just sang stuff about it being a beautiful day in London.
It was, it had been. But now it was deep twilight on the banks of
the Nile. He talked into the bell of the horn as though it was an
enormous phone on which someone in Cairo had misdialled a barely
remembered number. The whole thing was a combination of buffoon-

ery and, barely, the fulfilment of contractual obligations (a seldom remarked-on aspect of the later life of legends). Seeing him get up from his stool was like witnessing the high point of an archaeological excavation; when he headed offstage to his dressing room it seemed as if he was tottering back to his tomb.

I was there with my friend Chris who had introduced me to jazz, on whose stereo I'd heard so many great tracks for the first time. Late one morning in November 1987 we met at Franco's pizzeria in Brixton. Then we bought an album each from a record stall at the market. I got *Fire Music* by Archie Shepp, he got *Tauhid* by Pharoah. We walked back up Effra Road to my flat in Crownstone Court to give them a listen but since it was such a lovely clear day we decided, in the omnivorous way of intellectuals at the tail-end of their twenties, to take some mushrooms and head out again. We ended up on Clapham Common, surrounded by huge bonfires of trees blown down by the recent hurricane. That became the closing scene for my first novel, *The Colour of Memory*.

54.

The recurrence of termination! On 12 October 2019 I went to see Pharoah again, in Santa Monica. He was, if anything, in even worse shape this time, his frailty more nakedly exposed because he was playing with just a piano-player (who had to do the lion's share of the work). He was also recovering from a fall and had to be helped onto the stage, shuffling along in his slides. He played a bit, did the same daft sing-along to 'The Creator Has a Master Plan.' From time to time you could hear the faint flicker and faded majesty of former glory but there was no escaping the truth: it was an evening of assisted-living jazz.

Pharoah came to prominence as a free player but his roots, like Ayler's, are in R&B. After Coltrane's death the frenzied shrieks and the deep rhythmic honk became mutually reinforcing. When 'Upper

Egypt and Lower Egypt' on *Tauhid* finally gets going he cries out and then responds to the cry by urging it to dance—which was why the cry had started and where it longed to go. And now it was almost gone.

It took everyone a while to see it, to hear it, but the tradition was there all the time, even in his name. King Oliver, Duke Ellington, Count Basie . . .

Ah Pharoah—where should your ashes be scattered? In Egypt or Arkansas? In Little Rock or Luxor? Wherever it is he has earned his right to rest forever in the Valley of Kings.

55.

In October 2019 my wife and I went to the Disney Hall to hear members of the L.A. Phil play op. 132. I put it like that because rather than an established quartet this was just four players from the orchestra. It was OK—which is to say it was also inadequate. They weren't able to generate enough resistance to the leaving-everything-behind soul of the 'Heiliger.' The regret at leaving—the reluctance—has to be immense in order to enhance the achieved leave-taking. So it ended up being just an amazing piece of music, finely played, when it has to become so much more. That, in a way, is what it's about; leaving even *music itself* behind . . . Certainly that's how these late quartets struck Beethoven's contemporaries. There's something there, one of them remarked, as if peering dimly at another world through an inadequate telescope, but we don't know what.

But the above formulation, about leaving music behind, was incomplete. The goal was to leave music behind while still being music. ('Nothing transcends,' Adorno reminds us, 'without that which it transcends.') For Beethoven what greater repose could there have been?

56.

All of this was in my mind during the concert—a sure sign of not being completely transported by it—because I'd spent the weekend at my friend Tao's place in Joshua Tree. I drove out there with Jamie, a laid-back, broad-shouldered surfer. Half the population of Southern California surfs but Jamie had been a pro. He's in his mid-fifties now: the Cliff Booth, we agreed, to my Rick Dalton. I didn't just like hanging out with him; I also felt a kind of pride at having such a dudely friend, as if I became cooler by association. We were dressed almost identically—skateboard shoes, jeans, plaid flannel shirts—and it was easy to forget, as we sat side by side in his clapped-out station wagon, that rather than making me seem cool, those wide, easy-going shoulders of his made me look even scrawnier and more uptight than usual.

On pre-Covid Friday afternoons it often felt as if California was so jammed with cars that it was impossible for anyone to get anywhere until Saturday morning. We were in the car for ages, stuck in traffic for hours in L.A. and then for hours more in Riverside. It was a relief to get to Tao's but it's intimidating turning up at a place where people are already lounging round the pool or soaking in the hot tub, especially when they are all naked, some are already tripping, and, on one of the loungers, there is a water-wrinkled copy of *Being-in-the-World*, Hubert Dreyfus's commentary on Heidegger.

I'd warned Jamie about this, about the initial intimidation factor, and I'd also told him that while every weekend at Tao's place was guaranteed to be wonderful, each weekend had its own distinctive and unpredictable character of wonderfulness. The previous time I was there I'd held a human brain in my hands (a visiting neuroscientist happened to have one in the trunk of his car). This weekend came to be defined by DMT, something I'd been very keen to try twenty years earlier during my last phase of psychedelic experimentation.

There was some doubt about how best to ingest it. All we had was a little pot pipe. Tao said we needed to mix the DMT with tobacco but

I knew, from the few times I'd attempted to smoke hash mixed with tobacco, that this would make me nauseous. In the end we settled for sage instead of tobacco. In every other respect our preparations were meticulous. A comfortable chair was set up facing a dull brown mandala from Bhutan in the living room—home to Tao's superb McIntosh sound system. One person would hold the pipe for whoever was doing the DMT and would then leave, rejoining the others waiting in the kitchen. On the Friday night I sat down comfortably in front of the mandala. The music on the stereo was by SUSS: ambient country, open-sky soundscapes. I took a scorching hit on the pipe, held the smoke in, and then took another, holding it in for only a short time before coughing. I felt a brief inner turbulence and then the mandala glowed a radiant gold and became infinitely three-dimensional. But I always knew exactly where I was and who I was and was fully conscious of the passage of time. Everyone else had similar experiences.

I had another go on Saturday morning and the effects were milder than the night before so three of us—Jamie, me, and our friend Danny—set out to buy the correct equipment. This meant, not to put too fine a point on it, buying a crack pipe—easy to do in Joshua Tree as long as you did the polite thing and asked for a glass pipe. After buying the glass pipe that was really a crack pipe that was really a DMT pipe we had an epic breakfast at the Crossroads Cafe, where, as we waited for a table, I received a text from a friend in Dublin. 'This is of the utmost importance: go all the way with a breakthrough dose. Otherwise you won't get what makes it unique.'

For some reason, in addition to a huge egg breakfast each, we had also ordered an enormous helping of pancakes which Danny proceeded to divide up with his fork. Because he had what looked, relatively speaking, like a pancake-sized cold sore on his lip neither Jamie nor I wanted our share of this shared item so Danny set about methodically scarfing the lot. It was such a massive undertaking that Jamie asked if he had 'ever eaten competitively?' This was probably the most unusual question I had ever heard anyone ask and although I had not included questions of any kind in my list of things that might make a weekend at Tao's wonderful this was one of the details that contributed to the wonderfulness of this particular weekend. It's also important to mention that we always refer to Danny as Crop-Top Danny because he wears these crop tops to show off his impressively muscled abdomen, which showed no signs of expansion even after he'd worked his way through both his own breakfast and the bonus pile of pancakes.

We drove back to Tao's in Danny's car, a Buick LeSabre from the 1980s, moving surprisingly fast over the ruts, craters, and boulders on the dirt road up to the compound. The car had amazing suspension—though by the time I returned a month later it was out of action, because of a problem with the suspension, which, for all we know, might have been put under additional strain by the quantity of food Danny had snaked away.

To make sure everything would be done properly we watched public-spirited instructional DMT videos on YouTube. There are a lot, some featuring teenagers in their bedrooms, most hosted by older, more experienced heads, at least one of whom looked like he was still recovering from the trauma of Jerry Garcia's passing. A scrupulous evangelist said we needed scales to measure out a fifty-milligram dose. We didn't have scales so we cleverly crushed a two-hundred-milligram ibuprofen pill and divided it into four piles so we'd know roughly what fifty milligrams looked like. The rest of the afternoon was spent hiking up a nearby hill, charging down it again—which I managed to do without twisting my ankle—and hanging out by the pool and hot tub. I was wearing shorts and a faded T-shirt from a bicycle café in Sedona. A new couple arrived, at the same time that we had the day before. I expected to be able to enjoy their slight self-consciousness but they felt immediately at ease and were naked in the hot tub within minutes of arriving, leaving me feeling so self-conscious in my T-shirt and shorts that I 'read' *Being-in-the-World*, conscious that I couldn't understand any of it, before getting up to fiddle with the sound system.

For the Saturday night DMT session the living room had been

even more beautifully prepared. To one side of the mandala there were lush plants, with a cuddly toy propped up beside them. In *The Celestial Hunter* Roberto Calasso writes of a time when you never knew if an animal you saw might be a god. Looking back it seems clear that this adorable cuddly toy was a god, even though I can't remember which animal it was supposed to be. A cool friend of Tao's who lived nearby had come for dinner: a musician in her mid-thirties, called Janie, confusingly. The identity borders built around these neighbourly consonants proved too porous to be effective; several times in the course of what turned into a long evening I said Janie when I meant Jamie, and Jamie when I meant Janie, as though, along with everything else going on, they were turning into each other. Janie took the first hit of the properly administered DMT and reported very mild effects. Then it was my turn. The experience was even more diluted than it had been in the morning (which had itself been a dim-inution of what had happened the night before). Surfer Jamie: ditto. Had the DMT gone off? Scab-face Danny went next, lighting the pipe himself. Having broken through multiple times before he was well-placed to deliver a definitive verdict. It works, he said when he came back into the kitchen, but not as powerfully as some he'd taken before. He'd had to breathe his way into it.

By now, after all these failures and false starts, there was only one dose left. I didn't want to do it and neither did Jamie, though our demurral had nothing to do with Danny's cold sore, which, we had learned, was not a cold sore. We had suddenly gone from shortage to surplus. Janie duly stepped up for her second attempt, with Tao lighting the pipe for her. Peeping round the kitchen door we saw her flop back into her seat, as is supposed to happen, watched over by the little cuddly toy-god. Then we heard her groaning.

'She's really far gone,' Tao said.

The groans and moans continued. We became a little concerned, then scared. I was in an entirely characteristic state of mind, balanced between relief ('Thank god it's not me') and regret ('That could have been me'), which encapsulates in miniature much of my experience of being-and-not-being in the world.

After twenty minutes Janie came floating back into the kitchen looking like she'd spent hours, maybe even years, having the best sex of her life, possibly of anyone's life. And she had not been scared at all—which was quite impressive since, by most accounts, DMT *is* scary. Even experienced users get scared because it's so far out. You may have been there before but the strangeness of the DMT world overwhelms you. Every time you get there it's as if for the first time—even if, as is commonly reported, it also feels as if you are returning home.

After returning home, having failed to break through to that other home, I spent many hours in the following days watching videos of Terence McKenna, who, in one of them, says the risk with DMT is that you might die of amazement. So it's insane not to try it. We spend a lot of time and money going to the Galápagos; we endure all sorts of inconvenience and discomfort travelling to Sossusvlei in Namibia—and here is a wholly other world you can get to in about fifteen seconds and back from in fifteen minutes, for about fifteen dollars, without leaving your armchair. In another of his videos McKenna says that if a flying saucer landed on the lawn of the White House, DMT would still be the most extraordinary thing in the universe. Even if it goes horribly wrong fifteen minutes is nothing—especially compared with the awful marathon of an acid trip with all its potential for unexpected hazards. The problem is that while, from the point of view of people waiting in the kitchen, you're only gone for as long as it takes to drink a cup of chamomile tea, for the person in the DMT world there is no time. You're stranded in eternity—and a little bit of eternity goes an awful long way. You're stuck you don't know where for fifteen minutes of forever—and you don't know who you are either. Tao forwarded an account by another friend of his, a Heidegger expert, who had tried DMT (under Tao's supervision) and had found it absolutely terrifying. The music he chose to accompany him on this journey into the unknown was not a soothing ambient composition but a late Beethoven quartet (he didn't specify which, unfortunately). That was asking for trouble in multiple ways. You don't want music that demands concentration. You want to create a nice environment not, as is the case with acid, in order to immerse yourself in it more completely, but in order to settle your nerves before leaving it behind.

So, as everyone says, it is natural to be apprehensive, anxious, afraid. The key thing is to keep breathing, to remain calm, to go with it. The worse thing is to try to resist because, after that second or third scalding intake of smoke, whatever is going to happen is going to happen anyway. If you're used to meditating, are familiar with breath control, then you can increase the chances of transforming a potential white-knuckle ride into a high-speed glide into this other world. They're all breathers, these Californians: breathers, polyamorous meditators, and doers of yoga, whereas I was just a breather in the normal, untutored English sense that I had managed to keep doing it, without thought or discipline, for more than sixty years, though there was a time, I remembered from my childhood, when my mother told relatives that I held my breath—it was a quite common thing among kids back then, a stripped-down and instinctive protest against the terms and municipal conditions of being in the world.

It's telling that the two most hesitant people were also the oldest, Jamie and me. At forty I'd have gone for it with abandon and that very abandonment would have increased the chances of everything working out ok. It's not just physical flexibility you lose as you get older, it's also mental. The friend who'd texted me with that message of 'the utmost importance' is thirty-five. Like someone who's listened to the ancient mariner droning on for forty years I'm wiser now than when I first took acid in my early twenties, but what is the point of wisdom, of having ploughed through eleven hundred pages of *Black Lamb and Grey Falcon*, twice, if it reduces the chances of having the breakthrough experience of DMT even once? Isn't that the opposite of wisdom, isn't it uniquely stupid? Especially since, as far as I can discover, DMT, unlike LSD, carries no risk of permanent mental damage or derangement (once you re-emerge from the ultimate permanence of eternity) aside from becoming a bit of a DMT bore. And I have less to lose, now that the brain has done the bulk of the work of which it was ever going to be capable. I expect to live beyond seventy but if we translate the old three-score-years and ten of life expectancy into days of the week then it's now early Sunday morning. Or, if eighty is the new seventy, it's Sunday with a bank holiday, Monday thrown in as a bonus day—one of those English bank holidays from the 1970s when everywhere was shut, there was nothing to do, and, for that reason, you'd treat the Sunday night as a Saturday and spend the extra Monday flopping around the house incapacitated by a thumping hangover.

In some ways then the DMT experience is a test. Of one's self. And the result depends on one's ability to lose that self, to leave it behind for ten minutes *and*—the echo of Nietzsche is inevitable—for all of eternity.

The DMT realm: to know it's waiting there, 'pre-formed,' as my Dublin friend explained in another text: 'an entirely robust and intact freestanding dimension.' It's reassuring, to know that it's not going anywhere any time soon, that there's still time. That's what enables one to put off going there, to wait for another chance to break on through.

57.

Since we've ended up—allusively at least—back where we started I confess that my first experience of a song called something like 'The End' came not from Jim Morrison in California but from Peter Hammill in England: the last track on *Chameleon in the Shadow of the Night*, his first solo album after the break-up of Van der Graaf Generator. The exact title is 'In the End,' written in 1972 when Hammill was twenty-three and released in May 1973 when I was fourteen. After a lengthy piano introduction he sings:

> I promise you, I won't leave a clue:
> No tell-tale remark, no print from my shoe.

Hmm, OK, though the song itself is both a clue and an extended series of remarks on giving up the life of touring Europe as a prog rock star—a star, admittedly, who was never seen to burn as brightly as the star-man David Bowie. And while the opening imagery suggests that he's leaving the scene of a potential crime, the life he's saying goodbye to is a tranquil one—'No more rushing around, no more travelling chess'—compared with the excesses of Keith Moon or Mötley Crüe. Still, he concludes, it's 'time to resign with equanimity and placidity / From the game' in favour of what the cover art suggests is a life of full-sized chess (wearing a torn-elbowed scoop neck in the water colour on the back) and walks in the long-haired, gatefold wilderness of rural England (inside photograph). In the 1970s, remember, the countryside was not a place of retirement but of regeneration and recreation. It's quite possible that one's house in the leafy depths of Albion could be within cycling distance of wild gatherings or recording sessions at the stately homes of rockers who had really hit the big time and spent half the year packing out the world's stadia.

I got into Van der Graaf too late to have seen them live, in their first incarnation, never caught them during their subsequent re-formations, and never saw Peter Hammill play solo. I would have gone to his three-night residency at the Cafe Oto in London in March 2017 but I was living in L.A. and, in any case, all three nights sold out as soon as tickets became available. I have seen him performing 'In the End' live, at the piano, in Amsterdam in January 2010 on YouTube when he was sixty-one—the age I am as I write this passage about him. Partly due to the Covid lockdown we've ended up with exactly the same haircut. When I started listening to Van der Graaf I was almost half his age; the figure now has risen to about six-sevenths.

58.

'My neck is incurable . . . *because there's nothing wrong with it. Ha ha.'*

A month ago I suffered an almost complete collapse of my left flank: left knee, left neck, left lower back, left elbow . . . Three years ago when I had terrible tennis elbow I went to see a Doctor Lyn in Korea-town. He was an old white guy who, shunning all New Age fluff, described himself as a mechanic. In his office were signed photos from various grateful clients, including Laurence Olivier (as Lear) and a member of Canned Heat. If those photos suggested that his best days lay in the past this suspicion was confirmed when, having been told that I was having trouble with my elbow, he mistakenly focused his waning powers on jiggling the bones in my *wrist*. Two days later I was ready to send him a signed photo of myself, back on court, as my tennis elbow magically evaporated (and stayed evaporated for a full three years). This time around Lyn was shuffling about his office on canes and his mechanical, no-nonsense magic failed to work—my elbow is still killing me. And it's not just tennis elbow, it's *elbow* elbow—right in the joint, horrible karmic payback for that joke about Becker's scrotum elbow.

It hurts like mad, wakes me up in the night when it becomes sort of locked. I spent ages trying to get into the habit of taking my racquet back with my non-playing hand (my right); now, half-asleep, I use my right arm to unlock my left. I worry that it's the first installment of a new phase of injury—the corporeal onset of late style—that gets *worse* with rest. With Covid surging—and warnings of 'surge upon surge' on the way—I don't want to go to a physio so the outlook is not good. It feels like the end but I take heart from something else I said earlier, something that wasn't a joke, about cavalry charges. I'm reassured by the way the last charge kept turning into the next-to-last, by the words of Dylan's lover in that early version of 'Tangled Up in Blue,' by the way that it's felt like the end so many times before due to multiple permutations of trouble: rotator cuff, hip flexor, wrist, cricked neck, lower back, and bad knees (both). You name it. And I'm still batting. I mean *was* still batting, before I had to stop batting because of this latest round of left-hand, west-side woe, and even when I was batting I wasn't batting in the sense of *serving*. Did I not mention that before? I had to stop serving years ago to preserve (maybe post-serve?) my shoulder. That was no loss since, in spite of my height, my serve was always more liability than weapon, a uniquely double-edged, dog's dinner of a sword that was actually blunt on both sides. I was happy to let that go even though, ten years ago, I would have thought that not being able to serve meant not being able to play tennis. Now it means not being able to play *serving* tennis (or 'tennis,' as it's more commonly known): a perfect expression of the simultaneous deterioration and stubborn resilience of life. From the point of view of students— students who are being denied what they call the 'uni experience' by Covid—the life I am living is so threadbare that I'm already reduced to a quality of tennis far lower than the care-home jazz of Pharoah (who people were willing to pay to see play). I'm just pleased that I can do everything except serve—or *could* do everything except serve if I were able to play at all—and even though at some level it feels like the end, at exactly the *same* level, the fact is that since the unimprovable, unqualified, and unfailing glory of three Grade-A A-levels, I've spent four decades, coming back from whatever life has either thrown at or taken away from me. The facts support this. The knee-supports support this. I retire hurt. I limp home. I lick my wounds. Undefeated even in defeat, I rest, I ice, I elevate, I take two hundred milligrams of ibuprofen twice a day. I do the unbelievably boring stretches and physical therapy until I am back out there again, until the next body part fails or the same part fails again. Put me back on the bike, as Tom Simpson said after his heart burst smilingly (he was loaded with amphetamines at the time) high in the mountains during the 1967 Tour de France. What is it about these Simpsons and mountains? Or John Simpson, for that matter, when the peloton of reporters got hit by friendly fire on the open road in Iraq. Did he lie in a ditch worrying what might have happened if he'd been wearing his famous white jacket instead of a flak jacket? Of course he did. But once he'd come to his senses he dusted himself down and filed an unscripted piece to a blood-spotted camera, spurred on by the thought of Jeremy Bowen and Kate Adie eating their livers out when they saw him on TV that night. And don't forget. Help is on the way in the form of the vaccine rollout. The cavalry are on their way but, as Anthony Fauci said on TV, just because the cavalry are on the way doesn't mean you stop shooting. Even if you can't hold a gun because your mangled elbow feels like it's got an arrow through it you keep shooting till you're out of ammo, and when you run out of shampoo you go and buy some more. This is stirring stuff, I know. As I move towards my peroration—'I'll read two more poems'—I'm conscious of sounding like Tennyson's Ulysses, like Larry Olivier at Agincourt, like the marathon runner whose leg was blown off by the Boston bomber. Maybe it was both legs but who's counting? Who cares? That's my point. No one gives a rat's arse whether they ever see my long limbs flailing away on the Ocean View courts again, but see them again they will, probably, even if it's getting dark, too dark to see; I'm not knocking on heaven's door any time soon. I'm not going anywhere but if I were I'd be going out on my shield even if the shield, in my case, is a desk. And the point would still apply if the desk were a bed. Though much is taken, much abides. The long day wanes, the slow moon climbs. Is it self-defeating to think that if I don't make it back to the tennis courts there is a fortune to be made as a motivational speaker?

59.

In retrospect it seems that I did achieve a kind of breakthrough at Tao's place out in Joshua Tree: a breakthrough to a state of the purest regret I've ever experienced. If only I were back there now, or if he and that cuddly toy-god of his were here in my apartment, with a fresh supply of DMT. I'd do it right away and properly go for it, sprawled anxiously on my space-craft sofa in the cone of sound from my speakers, listening to the latest Basinski album *Lamentations* (while steering clear of the penultimate track, 'Please, This Shit Has Got to Stop'). Éliane Radigue's *Trilogie de la Mort* might actually be a safer bet: music so devoid of time it's almost not even music. A friend likened it to hearing the blood move through your body, which seemed an apt comparison, but only for a moment, because that has a pulse, a rhythm. It's more like the sound of your brain, but it's not that either; it's the soul, 'the timid soul,' in Lawrence's lovely phrase, as it leaves the body.

60.

Last night's sleep featured the latest installment of my twice-yearly football dream. This time the ball was not really a ball, just a clump of green foliage that was hard to distinguish from the grass of the pitch. Unravelling in the process of being kicked, it became impossible to get over the line—oh, and there was no line. Was this a conceptual advance into the purity of a parable about the pointlessness of all goals, of human endeavour generally? If so it's easy to imagine what might come next. No vestige of a ball, or of anyone to kick it; nor of dream or anyone to dream it—just a death-expanse of empty grass.

Annoying! The same old story!
When one has finished one's
house one realises that while
doing so one has learnt unawares
something one absolutely *had* to
know before one—began to build.
The everlasting pitiful 'too late!'—
The melancholy of everything
finished! . . .

—Nietzsche

Postscript

Even after adding two postscripts and an epilogue to *The Case of Wagner*—and offering 'with all cheerfulness, a postscript' to an editor who had written about it—Nietzsche was still not done with his former idol.* Almost the last thing he did, only a few months after receiving copies of *The Case of Wagner*, was to assemble an anthology of passages about Wagner from his earlier works in *Nietzsche contra Wagner*. 'Read one after the other,' he explained in yet another preface, 'they will leave no doubt as to Richard Wagner, nor indeed myself: we are antipodes.' The earliest selection was from 1877 but with more time one suspects Nietzsche might have gone back still further to show how, even during the period of complete idolization, he was not uncritical, had actually begun to turn against Wagner before he had heard so much as a note of his music.

The semi-final against Djokovic in the 2019 Australian Open wasn't Roger's last match after all. He came back, falteringly, in 2021, beating Dan Evans in his first match at the Qatar Open before going out to Nikoloz Basilashvili, having surrendered a match point, in his second. (Among Roger's many records might he also claim the unwanted crown of having lost more matches, from match point up, than any other player?) At Roland-Garros he survived a draining third-round

---

* I wonder if Nietzsche's compulsion to add postscripts and epilogues is the formal manifestation of a deeper—and self-undermining—urge: to escape the hermetic loop of the Eternal Recurrence.

encounter with Dominik Koepfer only to withdraw ahead of his next match against Matteo Berrettini in order to protect his knee for the upcoming grass season—which got off to a start (and a stop) in the first round of Halle. That left Wimbledon, where time and score had stood still since the final against Djokovic in 2019. He could easily have gone out in the first round if Adrian Mannarino had not slipped and landed in a scary heap. Everyone was slipping on the slick and greasy grass, on all the courts; most managed to untangle their limbs, pick themselves up, and carry on. Mannarino (knee), like Serena Williams (ankle), was forced to retire. After that narrow escape Roger looked to be getting back to something approaching his best—whether his forgotten or remembered best was hard to tell—until, on a gusty second Wednesday, he put in a less than gutsy performance against Hubert Hurkacz and was gone, in three sets. Gone, it turned out, for another bout of knee surgery.

Andy Murray, meanwhile, persisted in coming back for more even if more meant less and less. As he succumbed to Denis Shapovalov, in three sets in the third round of Wimbledon, there was a perceptible feeling that, commendable though it is to rage against the dying of the light, we'd had almost enough of the on-court mutterings and rantings, the all-round gnarliness that helped fuel the rage to compete. Instead of soldiering on, maybe it was time for him to halt off into the twilight.

British attention, in any case, was already drifting. While the light thickened on Centre Court the sun was rising, at implausible speed, over at Court 1, on Emma Raducanu. Just eighteen—the same age as Geoffrey Wellum when he began flying fighters—she played with a high-kick smile rather than a Dunblane scowl: with 'light feet' and 'without a grimace,' as Nietzsche said of *Carmen*. Emmania flash-lit the land! Two months later, at the U.S. Open, it lit up the world. And something utterly unexpected happened, more unexpected, even, than Raducanu's taking the title: I was starting to forget about Roger.

———

I didn't experience a conversion to late Dylan but I have spent many hours surrendering to the tidal mysteries of 'Key West.' It's like hearing the confession of a drowning man whose life is passing before his eyes, haunted by the ghosts of his past (which is also, always, a shared past): history drifting slowly from the wreckage of chronology. Maybe that should be 'drowned' rather than drowning; the song floats in a liminal space of unmeasurable duration, infinitesimal and oceanic, between life ending and beginning over again, suspended between identified geography—'down in the flatlands, way down in Key West'—and the horizon line.

Nothing else on *Rough and Rowdy Ways* quite found its way through to me. Nor, unfortunately, did the simulated club performance of *Shadow Kingdom*, which many people said was 'a return to form,' not least because Dylan's voice had been rehabilitated by the long hiatus of Covid. I failed to stream the show before the deadline expired, but the astonishing fact remains: I know someone who has performed with Dylan. Last seen in the kitchen at Tao's place in Joshua Tree, his neighbour Janie can be seen playing bass—or could have been before the whole session became unseeable and unfindable. Contra Nietzsche, what goes around doesn't always come around again.

During an onstage discussion I once asked John Berger about his creative longevity, how he'd managed to write so many books, over such a long period of time. It was, he said (after a pause so extended it felt like the conversation might have come to an end), because he believed each book would be his last.

To encourage me my wife points out that I've been saying I'm finished as a writer ever since we met, more than twenty years ago. During this time I've written a lot of books. In a Berger-like way it's the belief that I'm finished that's kept me going, but since the gravitas he brought to my question sounds entirely inappropriate, my own preferred explanation is that each book has felt like getting in an extra round before time is called. But at some point time will be called and I'll be proved right. Keep saying 'this is the end' often enough, as I said on the first page of this book, among the first of its 86,400 words*—Nietzsche was right, 'there are no coincidences any more'—and you *will* have the last word. It's a reason to keep talking, to keep on keeping on.

'In my thirties I used to go to the gym even though I hated it. The purpose of going to the gym was to postpone the day when I would stop going. That's what writing is to me: a way of postponing the day when I won't do it any more, the day when I will sink into a depression so profound it will be indistinguishable from perfect bliss.'

    This was part of one of my ten tips on how to write, published in *The Guardian* ten years ago. I stand by it.

'I finished my book!' I wrote to a friend. Now, after six months of doing almost nothing, I wonder if I got that the wrong way round. Has *it* finished me?

It's often said that writers have only one or two themes they consistently return to, finding new ways of addressing them, new fictional situations in which they can be explored. My theme, I have no doubt, is giving up. That's what's kept me going.

    So, somewhat in the style of Nietzsche, I'm tempted to go through my old books in order to collect all the passages about quitting, ending, giving up, tapping out, calling it a day. I'll save that for the rainiest of

---

* Including all epigraphs, but excluding title, footnotes, endnotes, and section numbers.

days, so that I've got something to look forward to. For now I'll content myself with this, from *The Ongoing Moment*, about Edward Weston and his wife, Charis, chancing upon a dead man in the parched wilderness of the Colorado Desert in 1937:

> Charis had never seen a dead person before and expected it to be more dramatic. As she looked at the unmoving man he looked so peaceful 'it was hard to believe he was really dead' . . . Charis found a note in his pocket—he was from Tennessee—and she wondered what California symbolized to him. Maybe he still 'held the vision of better things to come, even as he wrote: "Please tell my people . . ."' Charis does not tell us what it was he wanted told. The only message we have is the photograph . . . This was a man who ran out of life-fuel, who couldn't take another step, or knew that even if he took one more he certainly couldn't take three or four or a hundred more, and unless he was able to take at least four or

five thousand more there was no sense taking even one. And at that point, as he sat down for the last time, he must have felt as peaceful as Charis believed him to be. The only thing he wished was that he still had a hat to keep the sun from squinting in his eyes. Other than that, where he was was as good as anywhere he was ever going to get. Once you've come to that conclusion the only pillow you need is the hard earth itself. So he just lay there, the sun boring into his eyes, the sound of insects in his ears and the tickle of a fly on his face, until there was not even that, just the stubble on his chin that didn't have the sense to know it was beat.

I think here I will leave you. It has come to seem
there is no perfect ending.
Indeed, there are infinite endings.
Or perhaps, once one begins,
there are only endings.

—Louise Glück

Notes

10 'I've always been a quitter': T. C. Boyle, *Budding Prospects* (London: Gollancz, 1984), 3.

14 'frying an egg onstage': Michael Gray, *The Bob Dylan Encyclopedia* (New York: Continuum, 2006), 248.

15 'the only place': quoted by Ian Bell, *Time Out of Mind* (New York: Pegasus, 2014), 336.

16 'eroded rock formation'; 'magnificent ruin': Bell, 528, 527.

17 'it is fairly': Clinton Heylin, *Behind the Shades* (London: Viking, 1991), 269.

20 'thoroughly incoherent'; 'On the Road *will be published*': Jack Kerouac, *Selected Letters: 1940–1956*, edited by Ann Charters (London: Viking, 1995), 376–77.

20 'What happened was': Jack Kerouac, *Selected Letters: 1957–1969*, edited by Ann Charters (London: Viking, 2000), 287.

20 'wild spontaneous yowks': Kerouac, *Letters: 1957–1969*, 45.

20 'fuckyou freedom': Kerouac, *Letters: 1957–1969*, 334.

20 'going back to': Kerouac, *Letters: 1957–1969*, 345.

20 'enormous overdoses': Kerouac, *Letters: 1957–1969*, 302.

20 'phenobarbital tablets': Kerouac, *Letters: 1957–1969*, 239.

20 'remained unmovably': Timothy Leary, quoted in Kerouac, *Letters: 1957–1969*, 280.

21 'being lifted by Jews': Kerouac, *Letters: 1957–1969*, 301.

21 'Free to do anything': Kerouac, *Letters: 1957–1969*, 323.

21 'endless rows of perfect': Kerouac, *Letters: 1957–1969*, 304.

21 'drinking and talking': Kerouac, *Letters: 1957–1969*, 332.

21 'all this lionized manure': Kerouac, *Letters: 1957–1969*, 209.

21 'the appalling monotony': Dorothy Parker, quoted in Kerouac, *Letters: 1957–1969*, 121.

21 'I cant type': Kerouac, *Letters: 1957–1969*, 438.

21 'most dreadful part': Kerouac, *Letters: 1957–1969*, 439.

21 'rapidly going to pot': Kerouac, *Letters: 1957–1969*, 180.

21 'a big glooby blob': Kerouac, *Letters: 1957–1969*, 303.

21 'thrown out of all poolhalls': Kerouac, *Letters: 1957–1969*, 438.

21 'maybe once I was': Kerouac, *Letters: 1957–1969*, 192.

22 'bought a copy': Ann Charters in Kerouac, *Letters: 1957–1969*, 64.

23 'And I, the last': Alfred, Lord Tennyson, *Morte d'Arthur*.

23   'You've come to the end': all quotes from Geoffrey Wellum, *First Light* (London: Penguin, 2020), 291–93.

26   'There is nothing': D. H. Lawrence, *Complete Poems*, edited by Vivian de Sola Pinto and F. Warren Roberts (Harmondsworth: Penguin, 1977), 658.

26   'I've tried A!': Tom Wolfe, *The Right Stuff* (London: Picador, 1991), 356.

28   'born bronchial': *The Letters of D. H. Lawrence*, vol. 6, *1927–28*, edited by James T. Boulton, Margaret H. Boulton, and Gerald M. Lacy (Cambridge: Cambridge University Press, 1991), 115.

29   'never felt so'; 'If I don't like': *The Letters of D. H. Lawrence*, vol. 4, *1921–24*, edited by Warren Roberts, James T. Boulton, and Elizabeth Mansfield (Cambridge: Cambridge University Press, 1987), 239, 224.

29   'Yet I'm not ill': *The Letters of D. H. Lawrence*, vol. 7, *1928–30*, edited by Keith Sagar and James T. Boulton (Cambridge: Cambridge University Press, 1993), 205.

29   'my health is': Lawrence, *Letters*, vol. 7, 591.

29   'Somewhere I am': Lawrence, *Letters*, vol. 7, 595.

29   'I feel so': Lawrence, *Letters*, vol. 7, 546.

29   'the malarial tremble': Lawrence, *Letters*, vol. 7, 263, 262.

30   'But I do believe': Lawrence, *Letters*, vol. 7, 574.

30   'it's Europe that': Lawrence, *Letters*, vol. 7, 574.

30   'Never did he': Earl Brewster, quoted in John Worthen, *D. H. Lawrence: The Life of an Outsider* (London: Allen Lane, 2005), 392.

30   'could go to': Lawrence, *Letters*, vol. 7, 591.

30   'desire has died': Lawrence, *Complete Poems*, 507.

30   'Neither writing nor': *Letters*, vol. 7, 395.

31   'the last two years': Aldous Huxley, quoted in Worthen, *Lawrence*, 395.

31   'never forgive': *The Letters of D. H. Lawrence*, vol. 3, *1916–21*, edited by James T. Boulton and Andrew Robertson (Cambridge: Cambridge University Press, 1984), 391.

31   'But I do want': Lawrence, *Letters*, vol. 7, 617.

31   'They want to': Lawrence, *Letters*, vol. 7, 626.

31   'in bed allowed': Lawrence, *Letters*, vol. 7, 638.

34   'And if, in': D. H. Lawrence, 'Shadows,' *Complete Poems*, 727.

35   'the last fumes of': Friedrich Nietzsche, *Twilight of the Idols*, in *The Complete Works of Friedrich Nietzsche*, vol. 9 (Stanford, CA: Stanford University Press, 2021), 59.

35   'Ever, he sought': D. H. Lawrence, *Study of Thomas Hardy*, in *Life with a Capital L*, edited by Geoff Dyer (London: Penguin, 2019), 68–70.

36   'under a certain': John Ruskin, quoted in Franny Moyle, *The Extraordinary Life and Momentous Times of J.M.W. Turner* (London: Viking, 2016), 443.

36   'evidence of the': Ruskin, quoted in Moyle, *Extraordinary Life*, 14.

36–37   'and hereby declare': Ruskin, quoted in Moyle, *Extraordinary Life*, 443.

37   'senile decrepitude': Philip Gilbert Hamerton, quoted in *Late Turner: Painting Set Free*, edited by David Blayney Brown, Amy Concannon, and Sam Smiles (London: Tate Publishing, 2014), 60.

37 'Turner's pictures always': Benjamin Robert Haydon, quoted in Moyle, *Extraordinary Life*, 354.

37–38 'a talent running'; 'Turner is hopelessly': quoted in James Hamilton, *Turner: A Life* (London: Sceptre, 1997), 283, 301.

38 'indolent and slovenly'; 'evidence of': Ruskin, quoted in Moyle, *Extraordinary Life*, 424.

38 'indicative of mental disease': Ruskin, quoted in *Late Turner*, 25.

38 'throw all caution': Moyle, *Extraordinary Life*, 356.

38 'Ain't they worth': Turner, quoted in Peter Ackroyd, *Turner* (London: Chatto & Windus, 2005), 60.

38–39 'Sky and water'; 'great last period': Adrian Stokes, *The Image in Form*, edited by Richard Wollheim (Harmondsworth: Pelican, 1972), 212, 228.

39 'very crude': quoted in Ackroyd, *Turner*, 39.

39 'the question of finish': Moyle, *Extraordinary Life*, 232.

39 'have been unable': *Late Turner*, 76.

39n 'in his old age': Johann Wolfgang von Goethe, quoted in Julius S. Held: 'Commentary,' *Art Journal* 46, no. 2 (Summer 1987), 127.

39n 'very late pictures': Francis Haskell, 'Titian and the Perils of International Exhibition,' *The New York Review of Books* 37, no. 13 (August 1990).

40 'have been vapourised': J. K. Huysmans, quoted in John Gage, *J.M.W. Turner: A Wonderful Range of Mind* (New Haven: Yale University Press, 1987), 15.

40 'only the faintest': Lawrence, *Study of Thomas Hardy*, in *Life with a Capital L*, 69.

40 'You never get': Lady Trevelyan, quoted in Moyle, *Extraordinary Life*, 412.

42 'been put out': quoted in *Late Turner*, 27.

42 'paints now as': William Beckford, quoted in *Late Turner*, 33.

43 'Consider some of': John Berger, *Selected Essays*, edited by Geoff Dyer (London: Bloomsbury, 2001), 337.

43 'clouding eyes': Walter Thornbury, quoted in *Late Turner*, 60.

44 'whiter than anything': John Berger, *Cataract* (London: Notting Hill Editions, 2011), 44.

44 'Red, blue, and': quoted in *Late Turner*, 186.

45 'the cattle had': George Eliot, *Middlemarch* (Harmondsworth: Penguin, 1965), 597.

46 'There comes a': William Makepeace Thackeray, quoted in John Gage, *Turner: Rain, Steam and Speed* (London: Allen Lane, 1972), 14.

46 'all sense / Of': Philip Larkin, *Collected Poems*, edited by Anthony Thwaite (London: Faber, 1990), 114.

48 'a period when': Stokes, *Image in Form*, 213.

49 'All the kiosks': Elizabeth Taylor, *A Game of Hide and Seek* (London: Virago, 1986), 254.

52 'In the train': E. M. Cioran, *The Trouble with Being Born* (London: Quartet, 1993), 210.

52 'Think it through': Raymond Williams, *The Country and the City* (London: Chatto & Windus, 1973), 105.

54 'well launched on': Martin Amis, *The Pregnant Widow* (London: Jonathan Cape, 2010), 115.

56 'Nietzsche's great luck': Cioran, *Trouble with Being Born*, 22.

56 'the reason for': Friedrich Nietzsche, *Selected Letters*, edited by Christopher Middleton (Indianapolis: Hackett, 1996), 220.

56 'Nietzsche was in many ways': Richard Wolin, *The Seduction of Unreason*, 2nd ed. (Princeton, NJ: Princeton University Press, 2019), 32.

57 'in a white': Curtis Cate, *Friedrich Nietzsche* (London: Hutchinson, 2003), 565.

57 'some people are': Nietzsche, *Selected Letters*, 308.

57 'One pays dearly': Friedrich Nietzsche, *Ecce Homo*, translated by R. J. Hollingdale (Harmondsworth: Penguin, 1979), 105. (All citations for *Ecce Homo* throughout the notes refer to this edition unless otherwise noted.)

57 'challenging humanity'; 'there attaches': Nietzsche, *Selected Letters*, 340.

57 'a buffoon'; 'merely a believer'; 'One day': Nietzsche, *Ecce Homo*, 126, 106, 126.

58 'I am every name': *The Portable Nietzsche*, edited by Walter Kaufmann (New York: Penguin, 1954), 686.

59 'abysmal': Nietzsche, *Ecce Homo*, in *The Complete Works of Friedrich Nietzsche*, vol. 9, 221. (This passage does not appear in Hollingdale's earlier translation of *Ecce Homo*.)

59 'perplexed': Milan Kundera, *The Unbearable Lightness of Being* (London: Faber, 1984), 3.

60 'a connoisseur and admirer': Wolin, *Seduction of Unreason*, 59.

63 'the sole witness': Stefan Zweig, *Nietzsche* (London: Pushkin Press, 2020), 3.

63 Cate on Nietzsche's poor sales: Cate, *Nietzsche*, 470.

63 'Suddenly Nietzsche's name': Wolin, *Seduction of Unreason*, 28.

64 'I have even': Nietzsche, *Ecce Homo* 73.

64 'increasingly, Germany counts': Nietzsche, *Twilight of the Idols*, in *Complete Works*, vol. 9, 83.

64 '6,000 feet beyond': Nietzsche, *Ecce Homo*, 99.

64 'Stay not where': Friedrich Nietzsche, *The Gay Science*, edited by Bernard Williams (Cambridge: Cambridge University Press, 2001), 12.

64 'The greatest weight.': Friedrich Nietzsche, *The Gay Science* (New York: Vintage, 1974), 273. (All other quotes are from this edition.)

65 'merely put up with life': Nietzsche, *Ecce Homo*, 103.

65 'the sunlit uplands': Sue Prideaux, *I Am Dynamite!: A Life of Friedrich Nietzsche* (London: Faber, 2018), 308.

65 'A fine wind is': Lawrence, 'Song of a Man Who Has Come Through,' *Complete Poems*, 250.

65 'a sudden sense': Nietzsche, *The Gay Science*, 32.

65 'Now and again': quoted in Lesley Chamberlain, *Nietzsche in Turin* (London: Quartet, 1996), 127.

66 'The only reason': Lawrence, *Complete Poems*, 522.

66 'Not only is health': quoted in Chamberlain, *Nietzsche in Turin*, 115.

66 'never believed': quoted in Chamberlain, *Nietzsche in Turin*, 24.

66 'day after day': Nietzsche, *Selected Letters*, 318.

66 'a Claude Lorrain': Nietzsche, *Ecce Homo*, in *Complete Works*, vol. 9, 297. (This translation sounded a little nicer than the version in Hollingdale's Penguin edition.)

66 'a real miracle': Nietzsche, *Selected Letters*, 322.

67 'In the metaphysical streets': Wallace Stevens, 'An Ordinary Evening in New Haven,' *The Collected Poems* (New York: Vintage, 1990), 472.

68 'I am the only': Giorgio de Chirico, quoted in Ara H. Merjian, *Giorgio de Chirico and the Metaphysical City* (New Haven: Yale University Press, 2014), 16.

68 'Silence and calm': de Chirico, quoted in *Theories of Modern Art*, edited by Herschel B. Chipp (Berkeley: University of California Press, 1968), 402.

68 'One must discover': de Chirico, quoted in *Theories of Modern Art*, 447.

68 'see everything': de Chirico, quoted in Elizabeth Cowling and Jennifer Mundy, *On Classic Ground* (London: Tate Gallery Publishing, 1990), 74.

68 'Everything near becomes far': the original German is in Goethe, *Selected Verse*, edited by David Luke (Harmondsworth: Penguin, 1986), 330 (translation changed slightly).

69 'which in spiritual power': de Chirico, in *Giorgio de Chirico: The Changing Face of Metaphysical Art*, edited by Victoria Noel-Johnson (Milan: Skira, 2019), 208.

69 'dimensions, lines, and forms': quoted in *On Classic Ground*, 72.

70 'The arcade is here': de Chirico, quoted in *Theories of Modern Art*, 400.

70 'The intense, mysterious feeling': de Chirico, quoted in James Thrall Soby, *Giorgio de Chirico* (New York: Museum of Modern Art, 1955), 32.

70 'the present alone': Arthur Schopenhauer, *The World as Will and Idea*, edited by David Berman (London: Dover, 1995), 180.

70 'occasional applied touch': all quotes from V. S. Naipaul, *The Enigma of Arrival* (London: Viking, 1987), 91–95.

72 'replica': de Chirico, quoted in Soby, *de Chirico*, 134.

72 'all done between': Robert Hughes, *Nothing If Not Critical* (London: Collins Harvill, 1990), 163.

73 'the idea of writing'; 'the friendship': V. S. Naipaul, *A Writer's People* (London: Picador, 2007), 36, 41.

73n The story of Powell and the plumber is told by Nigel Day in *I Once Met . . . Chance Encounters with the Famous and Infamous*, edited by Richard Ingrams (London: Oldie Publications, 2008), 9.

73n 'and his wife Violet': Naipaul, *A Writer's People*, 70.

76 'late *late James*': Frederick W. Dupee, introduction to Henry James, *Autobiography* (New York: Criterion, 1956), iv.

79 'Definitely not': Joy Williams, *The Visiting Privilege* (New York: Knopf, 2015), 76.

81 'politely through the': Nietzsche, *Selected Letters*, 338.

81 'one fulfilment, one': Henry Miller, *The Colossus of Maroussi* (London: Penguin, 2016), 172.

82 'would one day': Miller, *Colossus*, 170.

82 'To continue writing': Miller, *Colossus*, 171.

83   'times and habits': Cynthia Ozick, *What Henry James Knew and Other Essays on Writers* (London: Jonathan Cape, 1993), 2.

84   'Nobelese': Martin Amis, *The Second Plane* (London: Jonathan Cape, 2008), 70.

84   'deep melancholy': Adam Zagajewski, *Slight Exaggeration* (New York: Farrar, Straus and Giroux, 2017), 296.

84   'Do you think': Philip Larkin, *Selected Letters of Philip Larkin, 1940–85*, edited by Anthony Thwaite (London: Faber, 1988), 605.

84   'You'll never go mad': *The Letters of Kingsley Amis*, edited by Zachary Leader (New York: Talk Miramax Books, 2001), 875.

84   'not v. good': *Letters of Kingsley Amis*, 949.

84–85   'Albert, go that way': quoted in Herbert Lottman, *Albert Camus* (London: Axis, 1997), 675–76. (Lottman translates Camus's reply into English; I've translated it back into French.)

86   'unconquerable summer': Albert Camus, 'Return to Tipasa,' *Selected Essays and Notebooks* (Harmondsworth: Penguin, 1970), 152.

86   '"Dear Dr. Larkin': Larkin, *Selected Letters*, 636.

86   'the mortal hilarity': Martin Amis, *Time's Arrow* (London: Jonathan Cape, 1991), 93.

86   'the solving': Larkin, 'Ambulances,' *Collected Poems*, 132.

86   'a genuinely great poet': Zagajewski, *Slight Exaggeration*, 188.

86n 'grieved over': Vivian Gornick, *The Odd Woman and the City* (New York: Farrar, Straus and Giroux, 2015), 95.

87   'Yours is the': Larkin, *Selected Letters*, 29.

87   'like something inflated': Larkin, *Selected Letters*, 687.

87   'like the Cheshire': Larkin, *Selected Letters*, 570.

91   'There is a whirlwind': Michael Ondaatje, *The English Patient* (London: Bloomsbury, 1992), 16.

91   'the way Eskimos know': Eve Babitz, *Slow Days, Fast Company* (New York: NYRB Classics, 2016), 70.

92   'drying the hills': Joan Didion, *Slouching Towards Bethlehem* (New York: Touchstone, 1979), 217.

92   'The mistral is': Lawrence, *Letters*, vol. 7, 156.

92   'deep down inside': Babitz, *Slow Days*, 85.

92   'Janet and Shawn': Babitz, *Slow Days*, 120.

92   'hogwash': Eve Babitz, *I Used to Be Charming* (New York: NYRB, 2019), 225.

92   'a wet ball': Annie Dillard, *Teaching a Stone to Talk* (New York: Harper Perennial, 2008), 149.

93   'Now: let us': Don Paterson, *The White Lie* (Minneapolis: Graywolf, 2001), 41.

93n 'prayer really is': Don Paterson, *The Book of Shadows* (London: Picador, 2004), 118.

94   'practices courtesy': Theodor Adorno, *Introduction to the Sociology of Music* (New York: Continuum, 1988), 87.

102 'Beneath it all': Larkin, 'Wants,' *Collected Poems*, 42.

103 *'to appear in their present'*: Peter Reading, *Last Poems* (London: Chatto & Windus, 1994), no pagination.

103 *'the last summer of its kind'*: Alan Hollinghurst, *The Swimming-Pool Library* (London: Chatto & Windus, 1988), 3.

103 *'The glorious summer'*: Volker Weidermann, *Summer Before the Dark* (London: Pushkin Press, 2016), 19.

103 *'the cloudless, golden'*: Penelope Fitzgerald, introduction to J. L. Carr, *A Month in the Country* (London: Penguin, 2000), ix.

104 *'The last shepherd'*: Billy Collins, 'The Last Shepherd,' unpublished.

104 *'Since the days of'*: all quotes from Ulrich Raulff, *Farewell to the Horse* (London: Allen Lane, 2017), 98, 99, 111, 113.

105 *'a rout, a panic'*: Frederick Benteen, quoted in Nathaniel Philbrick, *The Last Stand* (New York: Penguin, 2011), 257.

105 *'concerted "last stand"'*: Philbrick, weighing up Richard Fox's claim that there was no last stand, *Last Stand*, 402.

105 *'The main body'*: S. C. Gwynne, *Empire of the Summer Moon* (New York: Scribner, 2010), 5.

106 *'I have endeavored'*: Albert Bierstadt, *Chicago Tribune*, 18 May 1889.

106 *'It shows no white hunters'*: Robert Hughes, *American Visions* (New York: Knopf, 1997), 201.

107 *'There is something corrupt'*: John Updike, *Still Looking* (New York: Knopf, 2005), 43.

108 *'owes its origins'*: Anne Hollander, *Moving Pictures* (Cambridge: Harvard University Press, 1991), 357.

108 *'a straggling band'*: Larry McMurtry, 'How the West Was Won or Lost,' *The New Republic*, 22 October 1990, 38.

108 *'a scraggly band'*: John Graves: *Goodbye to a River* (New York: Vintage, 2002), 62–63.

109 *'The repetition of'*: Roberto Calasso, *The Marriage of Cadmus and Harmony* (London: Jonathan Cape, 1993), 136

109 For the back story of the film of Goodnight's buffalo hunt, see Stephen Harrigan, *Big Wonderful Thing: A History of Texas* (Austin: Texas University Press, 2019), 458; and Alex Hunt, *Panhandle-Plains Historical Review* LXXVII (2004).

109 *'two beeves every other day'*: quoted in Gwynne, *Empire*, 295.

109 *'near the end'*: McMurtry, 'How the West,' *New Republic*, 38.

112 *'That the profoundest mind'*: quoted in Prideaux, *Dynamite*, 315.

112 *'to address what some called'*: Annie Dillard, *The Maytrees* (New York: HarperCollins, 2007), 201–2.

112 *'What in the Sam Hill'*: Annie Dillard, *Holy the Firm* (New York: Harper Perennial, 1988), 60; the same question is asked in Dillard, *The Abundance* (New York: Ecco, 2016), 189.

112 *'really a book about'*: Annie Dillard, quoted in Diana Saverin, 'The Thoreau of the Suburbs,' *The Atlantic*, 5 February 2015.

115 *'a sky ablaze'*: Milan Kundera, *Testaments Betrayed* (London: Faber, 1995), 77.

116 *'pisscuntment'*: Larkin, *Selected Letters*, 604.

117   'perpetual lack of': Nietzsche, *Selected Letters*, 282

117–18   'the only director'; 'was only an ashstick': Michael Powell, *A Life in Movies* (London: Faber, 2000), 62–63.

118   'The Old Man ceased': William Wordsworth, 'The Ruined Cottage.'

123   'they are houses': Nietzsche, *The Gay Science*, 227.

124   'mad metaphysical theories': Zagajewski, *Slight Exaggeration*, 26–27.

125   'It is like a prayer': Tomas Tranströmer, 'Vermeer,' in *The Half-Finished Heaven* (Minneapolis: Graywolf, 2001), 88.

133   'If he had known': Dillard, *The Maytrees*, 72.

133   'steeplechase hills': James Salter, *All That Is* (London: Picador, 2013), 35.

133   'everything he had': Salter, *All That Is*, 189.

134   'a life superior': Salter, *All That Is*, 140.

134   'of a tangible centre': Salter, *All That Is*, 152.

134   'He woke in the early light': Salter, *All That Is*, 180.

134   'I'm leaving.': Salter, *All That Is*, 258.

134   'the power of': Salter, *All That Is*, 261.

135   'Yes, this old man': quoted in Eric Griffiths, *The Printed Voice of Victorian Poetry* (Oxford: Clarendon Press, 1989), 134.

136   'I think it's all over': Edwin Reardon in George Gissing, *New Grub Street* (Harmondsworth: Penguin, 1985), 79.

137   'diary that is': Enrique Vila-Matas, *Bartleby & Co.* (New York: New Directions, 2004), 2–3.

138   'I wrote Bartleby': Vila-Matas, interview in *Tin House*, December 2018.

138   'I didn't exactly': Richard Ford, *The Sportswriter* (New York: Vintage 1995), 40.

139   'there are those': Ford, *The Sportswriter*, 42.

139   'real writing requires': Ford, *The Sportswriter*, 64.

139   'a no-frills voice': Ford, *The Sportswriter*, 11.

140   'pram in the hall'; 'Whom the gods': Cyril Connolly, *Enemies of Promise* (London: André Deutsch, 1973), 17, 121.

140   'all true artistic': Connolly, *Enemies of Promise*, 123.

141   'being unable to': Martin Amis, *Inside Story* (London: Jonathan Cape, 2020), 197.

141   'in the old': Larkin, *Selected Letters*, 600.

141   'a turned-off tap': Larkin, *Selected Letters*, 714.

141   'however sincere': Cioran, *The Trouble with Being Born*, 50.

142   'The work has burnt': Don DeLillo, *Mao II* (New York: Viking, 1991), 52.

142   'Finish. I'm finished': DeLillo, *Mao II*, 48.

142   'it would mean': DeLillo, *Mao II*, 52.

142   'That the withheld work': DeLillo, *Mao II*, 67.

142   'by the emergence': DeLillo, *Mao II*, 73.

143   '"latest," perhaps his last': Henry James, 'The Middle Years,' in *The Portable Henry James*, edited by John Auchard (London: Penguin, 2004), 108.

143   'of ebbing time'; 'pacified and reassured'; 'a glimpse of a possible': James, 'Middle Years,' *Portable Henry James*, 109.

143   'Ah for another go!': James, 'Middle Years,' *Portable Henry James*, 110.

144   'It is not only Hemingway's': Maxwell Geismar, quoted in Michael Reynolds, *Hemingway: The Final Years* (New York: Norton, 1999), 228.

144 'Everything that was': Don DeLillo, *The Silence* (London: Picador, 2020), 67.

144 'He might still': Mark Stevens and Annalyn Swan, *De Kooning: An American Master* (New York: Knopf, 2004), 602.

145 'I have a considerable': William Faulkner, *Selected Letters*, edited by Joseph Blotner (New York: Random House, 1977), 182.

145 'With ominous frequency': John Updike, *Higher Gossip* (New York: Knopf, 2011), 4.

145 'No amount of learned skills': Updike, *Higher Gossip*, 3.

145 'He had started': Ernest Hemingway, *The Garden of Eden* (London: Hamish Hamilton, 1987), 239.

146 'Apart from everything'; 'virtually packed up'; 'seem to write': Larkin, *Selected Letters*, 578, 548, 714.

146 'When the words': Carol Ann Duffy, 'Alphabet for Auden,' in *New Selected Poems: 1984–2004* (London: Picador, 2011), 6.

147 'I think you can': Rachel Cusk, *The Paris Review*, Spring 2020, 60.

150 'I pressed the': Amis, *Inside Story*, 448.

150 'eyes oystery with': Amis, *Inside Story*, 274.

151 'the year of living': Christopher Hitchens, *Mortality* (New York: Twelve, 2012), 54.

152 'I have been': William Hazlitt, 'A Farewell to Essay-Writing,' *Selected Writings*, edited by Ronald Blythe (Harmondsworth: Penguin, 1970), 487.

152 'personality change': Amis, *Inside Story*, 231.

163 'to the great': Al Alvarez, *Risky Business* (London: Bloomsbury, 2007), 341.

163 'There were fires': Jean Rhys, *The Paris Review Interviews*, vol. 3, edited by Philip Gourevitch (Edinburgh: Canongate, 2008), 198.

163 'been fighting oblivion': Rhys, *The Paris Review Interviews*, 209.

163 'matter[ed] little as': F. R. Leavis, *The Great Tradition* (Harmondsworth: Pelican, 1972), 10.

165 'used two bottles': Thom Jones, *The Pugilist at Rest* (London: Faber, 1994), 215.

166 'Only someone with': Don Paterson, *The Blind Eye* (London: Faber, 2007), 57.

169 'How in a book': Friedrich Nietzsche, *Human, All Too Human* (Cambridge: Cambridge University Press, 1986), 239.

170 'begin to have': Norman Mailer, 'Ego,' in *I'm a Little Special: A Muhammad Ali Reader*, edited by Gerald Early (London: Yellow Jersey, 1998), 105.

171 'What an absurd': Larkin, quoted in Andrew Motion, *Philip Larkin: A Writer's Life* (London: Faber, 1993), 446.

171 'I suddenly see myself': Larkin, *Selected Letters*, 329.

171 'cute as a': David Foster Wallace, *A Supposedly Fun Thing I'll Never Do Again* (New York: Little, Brown, 1997), 225.

172 'coughing and feeling': Ernest Hemingway, *Men Without Women* (London: Granada, 1977), 35.

174 'Every moment lived': Annie Ernaux, *A Girl's Story* (London: Fitzcarraldo Editions, 2020), 17.

192 'all the multifarious': Jeannette Haien, *The All of It* (London: Faber, 1987), 144.

196 'What she wants': Louise Glück, *Poems 1962–2012* (New York: Farrar, Straus and Giroux / Ecco, 2012), 206.

197   *'Let them rave'*: Tennyson, 'A Dirge.'

197   *'so sad, so strange'*: Tennyson, 'Tears, Idle Tears.'

197   *'the recurrence of termination'*: Arthur Hallam, quoted in Christopher Ricks, *Tennyson* (London: Macmillan, 1978), 314.

199   *'Tennyson a poet!'*: James Joyce, *A Portrait of the Artist as a Young Man*, in *The Essential James Joyce*, edited by Harry Levin (Harmondsworth: Penguin, 1963), 113.

199   *'Lawn Tennyson'*: James Joyce, *Ulysses* (Harmondsworth: Penguin, 1969), 56, 202.

200   *'Slowly light strengthens'*: Larkin, 'Aubade,' *Collected Poems*, 209.

200   *'There is a major but'*: David Thomson, *The New Biographical Dictionary of Film*, 6th ed. (New York; Knopf, 2014), 424.

200   *'Over the years'*: Thomson, *New Biographical Dictionary*, 653.

201   *'spiritual truth'*: Thomson, *New Biographical Dictionary*, 672.

201   *'I have always known'*: Thomson, *New Biographical Dictionary*, 911.

201   *'slowly from a'*: Uh-uh, no cheating! Like I said, I want you to come across this entry for yourself.

201   *'even with the'*: Thomson, *New Biographical Dictionary*, 531.

202   *'torn between his'*: Thomson, *New Biographical Dictionary*, 285.

202   *'in this dark'*: John Milton, Sonnet 19, 'On His Blindness.'

203   *'A moment later'*: Billy Collins, 'Tension,' *Aimless Love: New and Selected Poems* (New York: Random House, 2013), 102.

204   *'What a strange'*: George Oppen, quoted in Paul Auster, *The Paris Review Interviews*, vol. 4, edited by Philip Gourevitch (Edinburgh: Canongate, 2009), 328; Auster also quotes this line in *The Invention of Solitude* (London: Faber, 1988), 145.

206   *'dizzy spells'*: Larkin, *Selected Letters*, 714.

207   *'to see, beneath'*: Salter, *All That Is*, 290.

208   *'a tendency towards'*: Theodor Adorno, *Beethoven* (Stanford: Stanford University Press, 1998), 189.

211   *'Inwards, as if into'*: Lou Salomé, quoted in Ronald Hayman, *Nietzsche: A Critical Life* (London: Weidenfeld and Nicolson, 1980), 245.

212   *'of a reawakened'*: Nietzsche, *The Gay Science*, 32.

212n   *'My convalescence'*: Larkin, *Selected Letters*, 746–47.

213   *'Beethoven's thanking'*: Adorno, *Beethoven*, 175.

213   *'recorded what happens'*: Rebecca West, *The Essential Rebecca West* (Harmondsworth: Penguin, 1983), 378

214   *'the strength is'*: Edward Dusinberre, *Beethoven for a Later Age* (London: Faber, 2016), 190.

214   *'the serenity of the convalescent'*: Aldous Huxley, quoted in Dusinberre, *Later Age*, 195.

215   *'we conceive the stars'*: D. H. Lawrence, *Twilight in Italy and Other Essays*, edited by Paul Eggert (Harmondsworth: Penguin, 1997), 107.

215   *'treated God'*; *'Strength is the'*: *Beethoven: Letters, Journals and Conversations*, edited by Michael Hamburger (New York: Anchor, 1960), xiii, 10.

216 'the mortal insult': quoted in Martin Gregor-Dellin, *Richard Wagner: His Life, His Work, His Century* (London: HarperCollins, 1983), 455.

216 'To turn my back'; 'To overcome': Friedrich Nietzsche, *The Birth of Tragedy and The Case of Wagner* (New York: Vintage, 1967), 155.

216n 'almost fatal': Zweig, *Nietzsche*, 50.

217 'If only you': Cosima Wagner, quoted in Gregor-Dellin, *Richard Wagner*, 394.

218 'For years at': Nietzsche, *Ecce Homo*, 92.

218 'a more penetrating knowledge': Ernest Jones, *The Life and Work of Sigmund Freud*, vol. 2 (London: Hogarth Press, 1955), 385.

218 'people read Nietzsche': quoted in Richard Hollinrake, *Nietzsche, Wagner, and the Philosophy of Pessimism* (London: George Allen & Unwin, 1982), 255.

218 'a panegyric in reverse': Thomas Mann, *Pro and Contra Wagner* (London: Faber, 1985), 100.

218 'given mankind the': Nietzsche, *Ecce Homo*, 35.

218 'a devastating experience': Nietzsche, quoted in Hollinrake, *Nietzsche, Wagner*, 1.

218 'This book': Friedrich Nietzsche, *The Antichrist*, in *Complete Works*, vol. 9, 134.

219 'Oh, they are': quoted in Lewis Lockwood, *Beethoven: The Music and the Life* (New York: Norton, 2005), 312.

219 'that one of': Nietzsche, quoted in Chamberlain, *Nietzsche in Turin*, 127.

219 'walk[ed] among': Nietzsche (quoting himself from *Zarathustra*), in *Ecco Homo*, 161.

220 'All that is': Beethoven, in Hamburger, *Beethoven*, 128.

220 'And so he': Moyle, *Extraordinary Life*, 118.

220 'Prince! What you': Beethoven, quoted in Jan Swafford, *Beethoven: Anguish and Triumph* (London: Faber, 2014), 428.

220 'a mean-looking little man': quoted in Ian Warrell, 'J.M.W. Turner and the Pursuit of Fame,' in *J.M.W. Turner*, edited by Ian Warrell (London: Tate Publishing, 2007), 13.

220 'odd little mortal': quoted in Ackroyd, *Turner*, 25.

220 'miserly and miserable': Thomas Cole, quoted in Franklin Kelly, 'Turner and America,' in *J.M.W. Turner*, 233.

220 'an English farmer:' Eugène Delacroix, *The Journal of Eugene Delacroix* (London: Phaidon, 1995), 292.

220 'marked by negligence': quoted in *J.M.W. Turner*, 49.

220 'uncouth ambition': Updike, *Higher Gossip*, 259.

221 'there was something': quoted in Laura Tunbridge, *Beethoven: A Life in Nine Pieces* (London: Viking, 2020), 204.

221 'He is uncouth': John Constable, *Memoirs of the Life of John Constable*, edited by C. R. Leslie (London: Phaidon, 1995), 38.

221 'more concentrated, more energetic': Goethe, quoted in a footnote in *The Gay Science*, 159. (This is my favourite version of a much-translated letter.)

221 'made the acquaintance': quoted in Swafford, *Beethoven: Anguish and Triumph*, 572

221 *'the man who beyond'*: John Ruskin, in *Ruskin Today*, edited by Kenneth Clark (Harmondsworth: Penguin, 1988), 26.

221 *'do nothing without'*: Walter Scott, quoted in Ackroyd, *Turner*, 93.

221n *'almost without education'*: quoted by Alvarez, *Risky Business*, 341.

222 *'was by nature suspicious'*: quoted in Moyle, *Extraordinary Life*, 116.

222 *'avaricious and always mistrustful'*: quoted in Swafford, *Beethoven: Anguish and Triumph*, 707.

222 *'coarse, stout person'*: quoted by Hamilton, *Turner: A Life*, 274.

222 *'a very ugly'*: quoted in Swafford, *Beethoven: Anguish and Triumph*, 525.

222 *'My shit is'*: quoted in Tunbridge, *Beethoven: A Life*, 143.

222 *'a Cockney visionary'*: Ackroyd, *Turner*, 26.

222 *'uncouth'*; *'was particularly averse'*: quoted in Swafford, *Beethoven: Anguish and Triumph*, 649.

222n *'what we know'*: Adorno, *Beethoven*, 30.

223 *'an aristocracy of mind'*: Swafford, *Beethoven: Anguish and Triumph*, 366.

223 *'Germanic deed'*: Wagner, quoted in Tunbridge, *Beethoven: A Life*, 238.

223 *'semi-barbarism'*: Nietzsche, *The Gay Science*, 159.

223n *'Hugo von Hofmannsthal'*: Adam Zagajewski, *A Defense of Ardor* (New York: Farrar, Straus and Giroux, 2004), 66.

224 *'the man in need'*: Nietzsche, *The Gay Science*, 159.

224 *'throw all caution'*; *'embark upon'*: Moyle, *Extraordinary Life*, 356, 357.

224 *'sensuous charm under'*: Adorno, *Beethoven*, 123.

224 *'begins to give'*: Stevens and Swan, *De Kooning*, 607.

224n *'the apostle of the rough'*: W. D. Howells, *Literary Friends and Acquaintances* (Bloomington: University of Indiana Press, 1968), 67.

225 *'a work (or its performance)'*: Roland Barthes, *Image-Music-Text* (Glasgow: Fontana, 1977), 179.

225n *'absurd terms'*: Beethoven, in Hamburger, *Beethoven*, 157.

226 *'In what does'*: Adorno, *Beethoven*, 164.

227 *'questioningly, longingly'*: Karl Holz, quoted in Maynard Solomon, *Late Beethoven* (Berkeley: University of California Press, 2003), 54.

227 *'He is hovering'*: Nietzsche, *Human, All Too Human*, 82.

228 *'the happiest days'*: Nietzsche, quoted in Hollinrake, *Nietzsche, Wagner*, 227.

228 *'the great benefactor'*: Nietzsche, *Ecce Homo*, 61.

228 *'the Nietzsche affair'*: Gregor-Dellin, *Richard Wagner*, 393.

228 *'what is smallest'*: Nietzsche, *Birth of Tragedy and Case of Wagner*, 171.

228 *'despite this Cosima's diary'*: Hollinrake, *Nietzsche, Wagner*, 253.

228 *'by far the fullest'*; *'It was hard to'*: Nietzsche, *Selected Letters*, 209, 208.

229 *'We—Wagner and I'*: Nietzsche, *Complete Works*, vol. 9, 635.

229 *'everything about the man'*; *'Finally R said'*: Wagner, quoted in Hollinrake, *Nietzsche, Wagner*, 267.

229 *'with the recollection'*: Nietzsche, *Ecce Homo*, 126.

229 *'a bonfire of'*: Olivia Manning, *The Balkan Trilogy* (Harmondsworth: Penguin, 1981), 848.

230 *'I had one or two'*: Keith Douglas, *Alamein to Zem Zem* (Harmondsworth: Penguin, 1969), 103.

230 *'audacious insults'*: Thomas Mann, *Last Essays* (London: Secker and Warburg, 1959), 149.

231 *'translated into 7 languages'*: Nietzsche, quoted in Andreas Urs Sommer, afterword to *Complete Works*, vol. 9, 685.

231 *'I would like'*: Nietzsche, *Selected Letters*, 197.

231 *'impossible'*: Vila-Matas, *Bartleby*, 16

231 *'The scope of the'*: Howard Eiland and Kevin McLaughlin, foreword to Walter Benjamin, *The Arcades Project* (Cambridge: Belknap Press of Harvard University, 2002), x.

231 *'some fresh follerey'*: Turner, quoted in Moyle, *Extraordinary Life*, 397.

233 *'porch, preparation, preface'*; *'only the gateway'*: Nietzsche, quoted in Hollinrake, *Nietzsche, Wagner*, 2, 3.

233 *'the most impressive foreword'*: Nietzsche, quoted by Mazzino Montinari in *Complete Works*, vol. 9, 440.

233 *'a preparatory work'*: Nietzsche, *Complete Works*, vol. 9, 554.

234 *'prelude to the* Revaluation'*: Nietzsche, *Complete Works*, vol. 9, 684.

234 *'not fixed upon'*; *'the tail-piece'*; *'an appendix to'*: quoted in J. C. Maxwell, introduction to William Wordsworth, *The Prelude: A Parallel Text* (Harmondsworth: Penguin, 1972), 17, 18, 19.

234 *'perhaps he just'*: *The Oxford Anthology of English Literature: Romantic Poetry and Prose*, edited by Harold Bloom and Lionel Trilling (Oxford: Oxford University Press, 1973), 187.

235 *'The days gone by'*: all quotations are from Wordsworth, *The Prelude*, 478–83.

237 *'think on awakening'*: Nietzsche, *Human, All Too Human*, 189.

238 *'Amongst the small'*: Nietzsche, *Human, All Too Human*, 399.

238 *'glorious'*; *'sweetest' grapes*: Nietzsche, *Selected Letters*, 35, 33.

238 *'a quantity of doom'*: Nietzsche, *Selected Letters*, 340.

238 *'cheerful and profound'*; *'southern'*; *'I shall never'*: Nietzsche, *Ecce Homo*, 62.

239 *'any other musicians'*: Nietzsche, *Birth of Tragedy and Case of Wagner*, 186.

240 *'It was an allusion'*; *'the difficult resolution'*: Kundera, *Unbearable Lightness*, 32, 33.

240 *'pre-existent matrix'*: all quotes from Kundera, *Testaments Betrayed*, 172–76.

241 *'cosmic'*: Charles Tolliver, quoted in Ben Ratliff, *Coltrane: The Story of a Sound* (London: Faber, 2007), 149.

245 *'breaks through the'*: Theodor Adorno, 'Late Style in Beethoven,' *Essays on Music*, edited by Richard Leppert (Berkeley: University of California Press, 2002), 564, 565.

248 *'Nothing transcends'*: Adorno, *Beethoven*, 172.

257 *'My neck is incurable'*: Larkin, *Selected Letters*, 450.

260 *'the timid soul'*: Lawrence, 'The Ship of Death,' in *Complete Poems*, 718.

263 *'with all cheerfulness'*: Nietzsche, *Complete Works*, vol. 9, 710.

263 *'Read one after'*: Nietzsche, *Nietzsche contra Wagner*, in *Complete Works*, vol. 9, 387.

264 *'without a grimace'*: Nietzsche, *Birth of Tragedy and Case of Wagner*, 157.

Acknowledgements

Thanks to: Chris Mitchell for reading an early version of the manuscript; Alex Star and Francis Bickmore for suggesting ways to improve it; Logan Hill for copyediting it scrupulously and sensitively; Ian Van Wye and Hannah Goodwin for skillfully and patiently overseeing its transformation into a book (and keeping track of the shifting maths of the maddening word count); Andrew Wylie, Sarah Chalfant, Luke Ingram, Alba Ziegler-Bailey, Katie Cacouris, and Hannah Townsend at the Wylie Agency for taking care of everything to do with publishing; David St. John, the wonderful chair of English at USC, who saw the Doors when he was eighteen and remains forever young; Rebecca Wilson for life.

Illustration Credits